Collective Bargaining in Professional Sports

Collective Bargaining in Professional Sports provides a timely and practical overview of the impact and importance of the collective bargaining process in the business of professional sports in the United States.

Focusing on the contemporary history of collective bargaining in the National Basketball Association (NBA) and the National Football League (NFL), but drawing out important lessons for all professional sports, the book sheds light on some of the key issues within modern sport business and sport governance. It offers an inside look into topics such as revenue sharing, competitive balance, circumvention of league rules, player free agency, player social activism, player discipline, and the ethical and legal issues around the use of wearable biometric tracking systems to collect player data.

An essential read for sports business industry practitioners and students alike, this is fascinating reading for anybody with an interest in sport business, sport law or labor relations. It is also a valuable resource for anyone who wants to increase their understanding of the business and financial operations of professional sports leagues and teams, player contracts and salaries, and the role and authority of professional sports league commissioners.

Scott Bukstein is Program Director of the Undergraduate Sport Business Management Program and Associate Director of the DeVos Graduate Sport Business Management Program in the College of Business at the University of Central Florida, USA.

Routledge Research in Sport Business and Management

Collective Bargaining in Professional Sports

Player Salaries, Free Agency, Team Ownership, League Organizational Structures and the Power of Commissioners

Scott Bukstein

LONDON AND NEW YORK

First published 2020
by Routledge
2 Park Square, Milton Park, Abingdon, Oxon OX14 4RN

and by Routledge
52 Vanderbilt Avenue, New York, NY 10017

Routledge is an imprint of the Taylor & Francis Group, an informa business

British Library Cataloguing-in-Publication Data
A catalogue record for this book is available from the British Library

Library of Congress Cataloging-in-Publication Data
A catalog record has been requested for this book

ISBN: 978-1-138-70803-7 (hbk)
ISBN: 978-1-315-20126-9 (ebk)

Typeset in Times New Roman
by Wearset Ltd, Boldon, Tyne and Wear

Mom, you have taught me the importance of humility, authenticity, positivity and kindness. You inspire me daily. Dad, thank you for teaching me how to play tennis and dish out assists on the basketball court. You introduced me to sports. Trevor, you are an incredible human being. Pure genius with an unparalleled work ethic. You see the ocean beyond the horizon. The best twin brother, ever. Shine up, smile thru. Ryan, your guidance and perpetual support mean everything. Thank you for always believing in your little brothers. Kevin, you continue to amaze me with the selfless work you do as a firefighter and paramedic. I love each of you.

Contents

1 Introduction to collective bargaining in professional sports

Overview of chapter contents

The primary purpose of this book is to provide an overview of the business of professional sports in the United States while also detailing the impact and importance of collective bargaining. This initial book chapter explains how the overall legal framework and business operations of major professional sports leagues in the United States are direct byproducts of the collective bargaining process.[1] Team owners and league players negotiate comprehensive contracts called collective bargaining agreements, which contain provisions related to player salaries, free agency (player mobility), the distribution of revenue between team owners and players as well as the authority of league commissioners. Imperfect or unclear collective bargaining agreement provisions can create tension and lead to disputes between players, team owners and league commissioners. These labor disputes often result in formal legal proceedings, as both players and team owners attempt to gain negotiation leverage during the collective bargaining process.

This chapter contains an overview of the historical evolution of collective bargaining within professional sports. This chapter also provides an outline of the primary categories and terms generally covered by current collective bargaining agreements within professional sports. In addition, this chapter spotlights the primary legal areas and laws that inform and influence the collective bargaining process. This chapter also discusses the main groups of people usually involved in the collective bargaining process. This chapter then summarizes the typical tactics and strategies utilized by players and team owners in order to develop or shift negotiation leverage during the collective bargaining process. Finally, this chapter previews some of the content that will appear in the remaining chapters within this book on collective bargaining in professional sports.

The evolution of collective bargaining in professional sports

As explained by legal scholars Paul Weiler and Gary Roberts, "Whether through work stoppages or peaceful collective bargaining, sports unionism has transformed all the rules of the game for dealings between individual teams and players."[2] Employee unions within professional sports leagues in the United States began to surface during the 1950s and 1960s. For instance, the National

Basketball Players Association (NBPA) was originally formed in 1954. Two years later, in 1956, the National Football League Players Association (NFLPA) formed. The Major League Baseball Players Association (MLBPA) was founded in 1966.[3] Each of these player advocacy groups "were deliberately named *associations* rather than *unions*, because the latter term was considered appropriate only for the teams' concession vendors or maintenance crews, not for elite athletes."[4]

The primary purpose of a players association is to protect and advocate for the mutual interests of all athletes within a particular professional sports league. A players association also functions as the exclusive collective bargaining representative for all athletes within the league.[5] Collective bargaining describes the process by which a players association negotiates with league management (team owners) to establish the working conditions, salaries, benefits and other important terms of employment for all players within the league. The terms and provisions contained within the resultant collective bargaining agreement (CBA) prevail over a league's enunciated rules or the individual contracts reached between a player and a league.[6] As explained by Professor Gabe Feldman, the fundamental policy underlying collective bargaining in professional sports is to encourage players (labor) and team owners (management) to "enter voluntarily into collective bargaining agreements without government interference."[7]

Early efforts and initial priorities of players associations (1950s to 1970s)

Players associations have fought many "hard battles" since the 1950s in order to bring team owners to the bargaining table to negotiate meaningfully on issues vitally important to players.[8] During the 1950s, 1960s and 1970s, players associations generally raised concerns related to improving player rights, creating heightened player job security, developing athlete pension (retirement) plans, increasing minimum salaries for players, allowing additional player mobility (free agency) and addressing other fringe benefit areas such as health insurance coverage and life insurance policies.[9]

Major League Baseball Players Association (MLBPA)

Before the Major League Baseball Players Association (MLBPA) was formed in 1966, team owners set the rules without consultation from the players, and those rules were subject to change without notice. Players were not even provided with copies of the rules ("the laws of baseball") that applied to them. Instead, players were expected to rely on the good faith of the team owners and the league commissioner (who was hired by the team owners).[10]

Shortly after being named the first executive director of the MLBPA in 1966, Marvin Miller's preliminary priorities were to "shore up the union's finances by beginning a group licensing program and educating the players about the fundamentals of organizing and solidarity."[11] In December 1966, the MLBPA and team owners reached an initial agreement for a player benefit plan, which primarily covered pensions and insurance. More than a year passed before the MLBPA and league management would reach consensus on a comprehensive collective bargaining agreement in February 1968, which covered areas such as minimum thresholds for player salaries along with many other terms and conditions of a major league baseball player's employment.[12] The 1968 Major League Baseball (MLB) collective bargaining agreement, which was the first-ever CBA in professional sports, "raised the minimum salary in baseball from $6,000—the level at which it had been stuck for two decades—to $10,000, and set the tone for future advances."[13]

One of the primary reasons for unionization among professional athletes in the 1960s and 1970s was to generate opposition to the reserve system and to advance an aspiration for free agency. A reserve system prevented a player from negotiating with any team other than the team he played on during the prior season—this elimination in negotiation competition among teams in the league resulted in a reduction in overall wages for players.[14] The "reserve clause" functioned as a provision in the standard MLB player contract, which provided that so long as the player's current team extended a new contract offer to the player by some specified date prior to the next season, the current contract would consequently be extended for one more playing season. MLB teams were permitted to perpetually extend the contract of each player by one season after every season. As a result, players had no ability to sign a contract with another team unless the current team decided not to renew that player's contract.[15] According to the MLBPA official website, MLB team owners "had ruled baseball with an iron fist for nearly a century prior to Marvin Miller's appointment as the MLBPA's executive director. Players had no ability to choose their employer because they were tied to their original club by a 'reserve clause' in every player contract that provided for automatic renewal. Salaries and benefits were low [and] working conditions abysmal."[16] During the 1976 MLB season, the MLBPA and MLB team owners agreed to a modified player reserve clause that would only apply to players who were in their first six years in the major leagues. After six years of service, an MLB player would become a free agent upon expiration of his then-current contract. As explained by legal scholar Stuart Banner, "Football, basketball and hockey lacked an antitrust exemption, but through collective bargaining they reached virtually the same outcome as baseball regarding free agency."[17]

Although the remaining chapters within this book focus primarily on collective bargaining within the National Basketball Association (NBA) and National Football League (NFL), it is important to understand the meaningful role that the MLBPA has played in expanding player rights through the collective bargaining process.[18] The players associations within the NBA and NFL have historically monitored and subsequently borrowed/implemented best practices from the MLBPA with respect to collective bargaining negotiation tactics and player advocacy.

National Basketball Players Association (NBPA)

Before the NBPA was established in 1954, NBA players did not receive any retirement pension or health benefits. In addition, players were not entitled to a minimum wage per season—prior to the formation of the NBPA, the average NBA player salary was approximately $8,000.[19] Some of the top players in the NBA during the 1950s and 1960s, including Bob Cousy and Oscar Robertson, played a pivotal role in the creation and evolution of the NBPA. For example, during the week of the 1955 NBA All-Star Game in New York City, Bob Cousy (star point guard for the Boston Celtics from 1950–1963) voiced the following collective concerns and requests of NBA players to then-current NBA president Maurice Podoloff:

- Payment of back salaries to individuals who played on the defunct Baltimore Bullets club before the team folded;
- Creation of a 20-game limit on exhibition games, after which the players should share in the profits from such games;
- Elimination of the $15 "whispering fine" that referees could impose on a player during a game if a player protested calls/decisions made by a referee;
- Payment of a $25 stipend for public appearances by players (excluding radio, television and certain charitable functions);
- Establishment of an impartial board of arbitration to settle disputes between players and team owners; and
- Reimbursement of moving expenses for players who were traded during the NBA season.[20]

The NBA initially refused to recognize the NBPA as the exclusive collective bargaining representative of league players. However, by the end of the 1957 NBA season (and in part due to the threat of an impending player strike), former NBA president Maurice Podoloff and team owners agreed to recognize the NBPA, and subsequently (yet perhaps reluctantly) decided to accept compromises on several of the items of collective concern initially voiced by the NBPA during the 1955 NBA season.

The NBPA continued to advocate for players throughout the 1960s. Led by Oscar Robertson (then-current NBA player and acting president of the players association), the NBPA negotiated the following improved player rights and benefits during the 1967 NBA season:

- A $600 per month pension plan for all NBA players with at least ten years of service and who were also at least 65 years of age;
- New medical and health insurance benefits;
- An 82-game limit on the regular season;
- The elimination of games played immediately prior to the NBA All-Star Game; and

- A new committee to review the terms of the existing standard NBA player contract.[21]

The NBPA and NBA team owners formally agreed to the league's first comprehensive CBA in 1970. This initial NBA collective bargaining agreement increased pension benefits for retired players and also provided additional medical and dental coverage as well as term life insurance coverage for current players. The 1970 NBA collective bargaining agreement also increased the minimum player salary from $20,000 to $30,000 and provided select players with additional stipends for participating in the NBA All-Star Game.

National Football League Players Association (NFLPA)

In January 1957—only a few months after the NFLPA was formed in November 1956 as the exclusive collective bargaining representative of NFL players—the NFLPA made the following requests via an official proposal to then-current league commissioner Bert Bell:

- Minimum $5,000 per year player salary;
- Standard per diem (allowance for meals and related expenses) for players;
- A rule requiring teams to pay for player equipment; and
- A provision for the continued payment of salary to an injured player.[22]

Bert Bell and team owners were not very receptive to these player requests. The following month, in February 1957, the United States Supreme Court clarified that the business of professional football was subject to the coverage of federal antitrust laws.[23] This meant that the NFL could potentially be exposed to significant financial liability if a court determined that certain league business practices (for example, limitations on player salaries and restrictions on player mobility) constituted anticompetitive conduct in violation of federal antitrust laws. As a direct result of this Supreme Court decision, NFL team owners "quietly granted many of the demands from the players association ... owners knew the players would file another antitrust suit if they continued to deny players' rights."[24]

Minimal negotiation progress was made at the bargaining table between NFL players and team owners throughout the ensuing several years.[25] As explained by the NFLPA, "by mid-1958, players again were frustrated. The injury protection clause the owners had agreed to still was not in place. Owners had agreed to pay $50 above their regular contract for each pre-season game, but some players had not been paid. Proposals for a pension plan, hospitalization and other benefits had been presented to the owners—and ignored."[26] As a result of this lack of traction and progress negotiating for increased player rights, the NFLPA once again threatened to sue NFL team owners for violating federal antitrust laws. Sure enough, the team owners responded immediately, creating a benefit plan that included hospitalization, medical and life insurance with a plan for retirement benefits at age 65.[27]

The NFLPA and NFL team owners eventually agreed to the league's first CBA in 1968. The NFLPA in part initially requested/demanded the following terms from league management:

- Minimum salary of $15,000 for rookies and $20,000 for veteran players;
- Exhibition game pay of $500 per game per player;
- Lowering the retirement age from 65 to 45 years of age; and
- Impartial grievance arbitration process and neutral arbitrator(s) when players were penalized by the league or individual teams.

However, the NFL team owners pushed back on all these requests during negotiation sessions. Final terms of the 1968 NFL collective bargaining agreement included the following management-friendly provisions:

- Minimum salary remained at $9,000 for rookies and $10,000 for veteran players;
- Exhibition game pay for players stayed at $50 per game;
- Retirement age remained at 65 years of age; and
- The NFL league commissioner persisted as the sole grievance arbitrator.[28]

In 1971, the NFLPA hired its first executive director—an attorney named Ed Garvey.[29] Garvey helped reorganize and reenergize the players association as he led collective bargaining negotiations that resulted in a new CBA in 1977. The 1977 NFL collective bargaining agreement included substantial increases with respect to player benefits, an impartial arbitration process for non-injury grievances, as well as the NFL's first (albeit somewhat ineffective) free agency system.[30]

Examples of collectively bargained terms and conditions of employment in professional sports league collective bargaining agreements

Collective bargaining agreements typically contain many pages of legalistic language spelling out the formal relationship between players and the league.[31] Collective bargaining within professional sports commonly centers on two primary areas: (1) Determining how to divide revenue between team owners and players; and (2) Maintaining competitive balance along with assuring the general health of the league and its economic market opportunity.[32] The central focus of bargaining between players and team owners has significantly shifted since the first collective bargaining agreements were entered into during the late 1960s and early 1970s, primarily as a result of the gradual (and more recently, somewhat exponential) increase in overall team and league revenues.[33] Most collective bargaining processes since the 1990s involving players and team owners have tended to focus broadly on the following issues and areas related to player rights, compensation and other benefits:

1. Allocation of player rights to a particular team through a rookie draft along with consequent compensation and contract protections for drafted rookies;
2. Free agency restrictions (that is, limitations on a player's ability to play for another team after his contract expires with his current team);
3. Restrictions on aggregate player salaries through constraints such as team salary caps, luxury taxes and other mechanisms designed to create competitive balance and discourage excessive spending by teams on player salaries; and
4. The overall split/distribution of revenue between team owners and players.[34]

The following list provides a general overview of some of the primary negotiated deal points and topics covered within current professional sports league collective bargaining agreements:[35]

- Uniform/Standard Player Contract:
    - *Minimum required annual player salary*
    - *Maximum allowable annual player salary*
    - *Signing bonus and other player compensation incentives*
    - *Compensation protection if a team terminates a player due to lack of skill, sport-related injury or due to other causes of injury (and for other reasons)*
    - *Promotional appearances required during the season for all players on a team*

- Player Compensation, Eligibility and Mobility:
    - *Player eligibility for league rookie draft*
    - *Rookie salary wage scale and length of rookie contracts*
    - *Maximum term/length of veteran player contracts*
    - *Free agency: restricted and unrestricted free agency*
    - *Contract renewal: team and player contract options*

- Other Player Financial and Health/Wellness Benefits:
    - *Player pension, 401(k) savings plan and other retirement-related benefits*
    - *Player healthcare and other wellness-related benefits*
    - *Moving expense reimbursement and meal expense allowance*
    - *First class travel accommodations and hotel arrangements*
    - *Complimentary tickets for home and away games (for example, up to four tickets per NBA player for home games and two tickets for road games)*
    - *Other ancillary financial perks (for example, academic tuition assistance for NFL players and free subscription for each NBA player to NBA League Pass)*

- Player Conduct:
    - *Expectations for player conduct on the court (or on the field)*
    - *Participation in league and players association programs (for example, player attendance at media training, anti-gambling training, business*

of basketball training and educational life skills programs designated
as "mandatory programs" by the NBA and the NBPA)
- *Player criminal convictions involving alcohol or controlled substances*
- *Unlawful violence and player arrests, and counseling for violent
misconduct*
- *League policies on domestic violence, sexual assault and child abuse*
- *Player obligations to cooperate with league investigations of alleged
player misconduct*
- *Scope of disciplinary authority of league commissioner and all league
teams*
- *Grievance arbitration procedure for players who are disciplined by
commissioner and/or a team*

Team and League Revenue, and Team Payroll (Player Salaries):
- *Formula for determining total league-wide revenue (for example,
"Basketball Related Income" in the NBA collective bargaining agree-
ment and "All Revenues" in the NFL collective bargaining agreement)*
- *Formula for calculating salary cap for all teams in league as well as
minimum required total team salary (also, in the NBA, exceptions to the
salary cap and financial penalties for exceeding the luxury tax threshold)*
- *Trade rules, and rules for re-signing or extending contracts of current
players*
- *Financial audit rights and other rights of players associations*

Additional Common (and Emerging) CBA Provisions:
- *League regulation and certification of player agents*
- *Restriction on the ability of a league and teams to lock out players, and
corresponding restriction on players and players association to engage
in any labor strikes during the term of the CBA*
- *Requirement that all players in a league pay annual membership dues
to the players association*
- *Prevention of current players from acquiring an ownership interest in
teams within the league*
- *Collection and utilization of athlete biometric and health-related data.*[36]

The collective bargaining influencers: team owners (league), professional athletes, players associations, league commissioners and sports agents

The collaborative (and sometimes unavoidably adversarial) collective bargaining process within the professional sports context typically involves many stakeholders and varied priorities. The United States Supreme Court once declared
that "collective bargaining is a brute contest of economic power somewhat
masked by polite manners and voluminous statistics."[37] In general, the priorities
and perspectives of professional athletes, player agents and players associations
tend to align, whereas the concerns and perceptions of team owners and league

commissioners tend to find common ground. Professors Robert Berry and William B. Gould IV echoed this viewpoint when they wrote: "Two of the interests (leagues and teams) are aligned on the side of management while three of the interests (players associations, individual players, and the agents/attorneys for the players) are aligned opposite management."[38]

Management: league/team owners

The combined interests of team owners within a professional sports league are commonly represented by a management council (for example, the NFL Management Council) or a board of governors (for example, the NBA Board of Governors). Typically, one representative from each team (usually the majority team owner/investor) represents a particular team within the broader league management council or board of governors, which functions as the sole and exclusive bargaining representative of all member clubs within that league.[39] Teams that make up a professional sports league are not completely independent economic competitors because all teams depend upon a degree of cooperation and collaboration for economic survival.[40] Despite significant differences in team revenues and athlete salary payrolls, during collective bargaining sessions all teams "must agree on their negotiation positions and strategies."[41] Nonetheless, team owners have not always been on precisely the same page and have not always shared identical priorities and interests during the collective bargaining process.[42]

For example, former MLB commissioner Bud Selig acknowledged that, during an August 1993 team owner summit meeting, internal issues surfaced among team owners. Selig explained that he and team owners "were demonstrating to the union that we were taking steps within our ranks to solve our problems, showing them that we had been listening when they said through the years that we should solve our own problems before coming to them for economic changes. But now we needed to convince the teams with the greatest revenue to share some of it with the teams that were hurting.... We had to make changes so that fans in every city could have faith in their team and hope that it could make the postseason."[43]

Another example of previous internal group contention among team owners in professional sports concerned the revamped NBA revenue sharing model/formula that was developed by team owners in conjunction with the implementation of the 2011 NBA collective bargaining agreement.[44] In the words of one NBA team executive, "Whenever you have 30 teams in 30 different markets, you have 30 different goals and needs." Los Angeles Lakers team executive Jeanie Buss commented: "Any business operator wants to keep their revenue. That's the nature of the business, but we also understand the bigger picture and we want a league with teams that are economically viable so that every team has the opportunity to compete. It makes for a healthier league." According to Joel Litvin, the NBA president of league operations who helped spearhead the creation of the new revenue sharing plan, the complex revenue sharing system "generated a significant amount of spirited debate among the teams. But the planning committee [consisting of team owners] ... was ultimately able to forge a consensus that didn't leave everybody happy, but struck as fair a balance as you can strike on a difficult subject."[45]

League constitution and bylaws

Member teams within professional sports leagues often collectively enter into an additional contract—the league constitution and bylaws—which supplements, but does not supersede, the CBA.[46] For example, several sections of the current 2017 NBA collective bargaining agreement explicitly provide that, other than as expressly agreed to by league players and team owners within the CBA, "nothing contained in [the CBA] shall be deemed to be an agreement of the players association to any provision of the NBA constitution and bylaws."[47] However, it is possible for terms within a league constitution and bylaws to be binding on individual players within a league. For instance, the NBA uniform player contract requires all league players to agree to be bound by Article 35 of the NBA Constitution.[48] Article 35 of the NBA Constitution relates to player conduct expectations and the authority of the league commissioner to penalize players for misconduct.

The NBA constitution and bylaws document, which functions as a binding contract entered into between team owners, covers items and areas such as:

- Team relocation
- Annual required capital contributions to league by each team
- Transfer of ownership (sale of team)
- Eligibility of players
- Team player rosters
- NBA draft logistics
- Authority and duties of league commissioner
- Player conduct
- Media rights contracts

Labor: players (professional athletes) and players association (union)

Marvin Miller, who served as the first executive director of the MLBPA from 1966 through 1982, imparted the following insight onto MLB players during a meeting in 1966 prior to his official election as MLBPA executive director: "I want you to understand that this is going to be an adversarial relationship. A union is not a social club. A union is a restraint on what an employer can otherwise do. If you expect the owners to like me, to praise me, to compliment me, you'll be disappointed. In fact, if I'm elected and you find the owners telling you what a great guy I am, fire me!"[49]

While a player within a professional sports league is not required to become a member of the players association, the player is nonetheless bound by the actions of the players association along with the resultant terms of any collective bargaining agreement that the players association negotiates with the league and its member clubs.[50] Professors Robert Berry and William B. Gould IV elucidated that "to suggest ... that all players' interests are equal and the solutions to their problems are the same, or even compatible, ignores reality."[51] A natural dilemma for players associations relates to the requirement that a union must fairly represent all players within a league, even though the playing abilities, priorities and economic values of players differ (often considerably).[52] For example, veteran players within a league might not have a personal interest in pushing hard to negotiate a sizeable increase in the rookie wage scale, and players who usually start the game on the bench might not have a personal interest in fiercely advocating to negotiate elements related to the maximum number of years and money allowed for "maximum salary" player contracts. As explained by Professor Jason Winfree, "There is a stronger incentive for player unions to fight for policies that help more experienced players ... players unions are more likely to fight for free agency and against salary caps, instead of trying to eliminate player drafts."[53] In addition, friction and tension could also surface between players serving in leadership roles within the players association and a non-player executive director of the players association.[54]

The leadership structure of players associations

Current players within each league usually serve in central leadership roles with the players association for that league. For example, nine current NBA players were elected to comprise the NBPA executive committee. These players are responsible for directing NBPA affairs and the policy-making decisions necessary to carrying out the mission of the players association. In addition, each NBA team selects one current player to represent that team on the NBPA board of player representatives, and serve as the team's delegate during all player representative meetings. This combined group of NBA player leaders (executive committee and board of representatives) is subsequently responsible for appointing a non-player executive director. The responsibilities and duties of the NBPA executive director include the following:

*   Directing all the affairs of the NBPA on a day-to-day basis;
*   Executing all policies of the NBPA;
*   Conducting the collective bargaining relationship between the NBPA and the NBA; and
*   Supervising the administration and enforcement of the Player Agent Regulations program.[55]

The primary mission and objectives of players associations in professional sports

The current NBPA mission is "to ensure that the rights of NBA players are protected and that every conceivable measure is taken to assist players in maximizing their opportunities and achieving their goals, both on and off the court. Whether it is negotiating a collective bargaining agreement, prosecuting a grievance on a player's behalf or counseling a player on benefits and educational opportunities, the NBPA advocates on behalf of the best interest of all NBA players."[56] The NBPA Foundation provides strategic funding for player involvement with charitable initiatives, social entrepreneurship and other community engagement projects.[57]

The NFLPA lists the following items as the primary objectives of the players association:

- Represent all players in matters concerning wages, hours and working conditions, and protect player rights as professional football players;
- Assure that the terms of the collective bargaining agreement are met;
- Negotiate and monitor retirement and insurance benefits;
- Provide other member services and activities;
- Provide assistance to charitable and other community organizations; and
- Enhance and defend the image of players on and off the field.[58]

League commissioner

The commissioner of a professional sports league serves as the principal executive officer of the league and assumes primary responsibility for supervising the general business affairs of that specific league. One of the primary responsibilities of professional sports league commissioners relates to acting in the "best interests of the league" in order to ensure the integrity of the game. As explained by Professor Andrew Zimbalist, "The commissionership was really designed to deal with integrity, not economic, issues."[59] League commissioners commonly serve as "the face of, if not the actual force behind, negotiations over collective bargaining agreements that determine the relationship between players and owners and help shape the future of the game."[60]

Professor Paul Staudohar wrote that, "Theoretically, the commissioner is supposed to serve both management and labor, as well as to be a public spokesperson. As a practical matter, commissioners tend to line up more on the side of management on contentious issues."[61] As explained by Professor Michael McCann, "League commissioners and team owners are aligned in many ways. Most crucially, commissioners work for team owners." Team owners hire league commissioners. Team owners also have the ability to fire commissioners. The general public perception of commissioners and owners is that "they are seated at the same side of the table." However, according to Professor McCann, "the interests of commissioners and owners are not designed for perfect harmony. Commissioners are entrusted with pursuing the best interests of the league—rather than the best interests of owners. This is a distinction with meaning."[62] In the view of Professor Peter Carfagna, "Arguably, the most critical part of a commissioner's duties is to ensure labor peace so that the league can continue to operate."[63] Professional sports league commissioners regularly serve as the "voice" of team owners during collective bargaining sessions with players associations.

Sports agents (athlete representatives)

Collective bargaining is a "bifurcated process whereby the players association establishes minimum contract terms through collective bargaining and the agent negotiates the individual player's contract" directly with team representatives.[64] As explained by Professors Kenneth Shropshire and Timothy Davis, "Unlike other unions ... sports unions have delegated their exclusive authority to negotiate individual player salaries. Thus, players are free to select representatives to negotiate the individual terms of their contract compensation packages within the framework established by the collective bargaining agreement."[65] Players associations such as the NFLPA have developed extensive regulations concerning the certification and conduct of sports agents in order to minimize conflicts of interest, promote competent representation and reiterate that the players association functions as the exclusive representative of all players within the league for collective bargaining purposes.[66] Sports agents possess the ability to influence and impact collective bargaining negotiations by sending emails and other correspondence to player clients (along with influential non-client players within the league) in order to supplement information provided to players by the players association as well as counter/discredit information provided to the players by team owners and league executives.[67]

Sports agents are responsible for zealously protecting the best interests of athlete clients; however, conflicts may arise as a result of the "divided loyalty of agents who represent multiple athletes in the same sport" given that "it is nearly impossible to be an agent for a very long time with only one client, yet it is equally difficult to have a stable of clients without compromising the interests of any one of them."[68] Another inherent potential conflict of interest exists between sports agents and players associations. As explained by Professors Robert Berry and William B. Gould IV, "The agents and the union are in natural conflict since, in many respects, they are doing the same job—representing the athlete. Moreover, it is possible that either the agents or the union could totally supplant the other. The two entities are vying for the same economic unit—the player—and the more they vie, the more likely it is that conflicts will ensue."[69]

Relevant legal areas and laws: the intersection of labor law and antitrust law

The collective bargaining process usually involves an inherent conflict between federal antitrust law and federal labor law with respect to encouraging or prohibiting cooperation and collaboration among competitors. Professor Gabe Feldman astutely describes this natural tension between antitrust and labor laws: "Antitrust law promotes competition and prohibits cooperation among competitors. On the other hand, federal labor law encourages cooperation among competitors. In fact, a foundational principle of federal labor law is that employees may form unions to gain leverage at the bargaining table by eliminating competition among themselves."[70]

Federal labor laws

According to Professor Feldman, federal labor law seeks to promote the follow-ing two primary public policy goals by permitting and encouraging collective bargaining in professional sports: (1) Facilitating good faith bargaining between players and owners; and (2) Creating the opportunity for both players and team owners to gain concessions from each other at the bargaining table. Stated differently, federal labor law provides professional athletes and team/league management with roughly equal bargaining power and creates a process that facilitates the ability of these two groups to agree to terms of a comprehensive collective bargaining agreement.[71]

The National Labor Relations Act of 1935 (NLRA) established certain employee rights, which included the right to negotiate with an employer over hours, wages, and terms and conditions of employment.[72] The overarching objective and primary intent of the NLRA was to encourage "workplace harmony between private employers and employees through collective bargain-ing."[73] A fundamental premise of the NLRA is that individual employees do not have the bargaining power to negotiate a fair deal with their employers.[74] Con-gress passed the complementary Taft-Hartley Act in 1947 (also known as the Labor Management Relations Act (LMRA)), which in part amended the NLRA and also granted further rights to employees such as professional athletes within the collective bargaining context. The following list provides a summary of the primary player rights created and/or strengthened by the NLRA and LMRA:

- Right to form/organize, join and assist labor organizations (for example, unions such as a players association);
- Right to decide not to join or assist labor organizations (for example, unions such as a players association);
- Right to collectively bargain through representatives selected by players;
- Right to engage in concerted activities such as strikes for the purpose of col-lective bargaining; and
- Right to be free from unfair labor practices of an employer (for example, a professional sports team)—examples of unfair labor practices include man-agement refusing to collectively bargain in good faith, management attempting to interfere with the formation and operation of labor organiza-tions or management discriminating against an employee based on union membership status.[75]

Federal antitrust laws

Section 1 of the Sherman Antitrust Act provides in relevant part: "Every con-tract, combination in the form of trust or otherwise, or conspiracy, in restraint of trade or commerce among the several states, or with foreign nations, is declared to be illegal." Congress passed the Sherman Antitrust Act in 1890 in order to prevent monopolies utilized by large corporate trusts from raising prices and reducing competition.[76] As applied to the professional sports industry, the Sherman Antitrust Act requires employers in an industry (league teams) to compete independently for employee (player) services. Similarly, employees are required to individually compete for employment. According to Professor Michael LeRoy, in court decisions that involved professional athletes during the 1890s and early 1900s following the passage of the Sherman Antitrust Act, courts generally determined that certain terms within player contracts (for example, restrictions on player mobility and limitations on player salaries) constituted illegal oppressive monopolies (that is, unlawful anticompetitive combinations that violated federal antitrust law).[77] As explained by Professor Walter Champion, "Player restraints have historically taken many different forms, but [the] objective is to either restrict a player's mobility or to restrict the player's ability to negotiate increases in salary."[78]

As discussed previously in this chapter, one of the fundamental principles of federal labor law is that employees such as professional athletes are permitted to eliminate competition among themselves through the formation of a players association that serves as the exclusive bargaining representative of all players within the professional sports league.[79] This fundamental labor policy of encouraging cooperation in order to minimize/eliminate competition directly conflicts with the pro-competition public policy focus of the Sherman Antitrust Act. In order to reduce this inherent tension and conflict between federal antitrust law and federal labor law, the United States Congress enacted a series of laws that cumulatively formed the statutory labor exemption to antitrust laws. In addition, a series of court decisions (including a decision by the U.S. Supreme Court in 1996) led to the application of a complementary non-statutory labor exemption to antitrust laws within the professional sports context in order to protect the results of collective bargaining from antitrust exposure—even if specific terms in the CBA (for example, caps on salaries for rookies and restrictions on free agency) were innately restrictive and anticompetitive provisions.

The statutory and non-statutory labor exemptions to antitrust law

In October 1914, Congress passed the Clayton Antitrust Act, which contained specific exemptions from antitrust laws related to the existence and operation of labor organizations.[80] Congress also passed the complementary Norris-LaGuardia Act in 1932, which similarly provided broad protections related to allowing employees to organize and bargain collectively. The Norris-LaGuardia Act also restricted the ability of federal courts to make certain procedural decisions in cases that evolved from a labor dispute.[81] This cumulative statutory labor exemption created by the Clayton Act and the Norris-LaGuardia Act for employee unions "was designed to provide employees with sufficient leverage to bargain at arm's length with management ... the statutory exemption protects employee unions, including players associations, from the scrutiny of antitrust laws."[82] Professor Peter Carfagna noted that, "Before Congress added provisions establishing the statutory exemption, courts viewed unions as groups of competitors pursuing common goals. Therefore, union activity constituted a combination in restraint of trade under the Sherman Act."[83]

Nonetheless, the statutory labor exemption to antitrust laws proved to be of somewhat limited value from a practical perspective, as the statutory exemption applied only to the rights of unions to exist and operate. In other words, the statutory exemption did not provide any legal protection for terms of the agreements that would ultimately result from the collective bargaining process. In 1996, the United States Supreme Court applied the non-statutory (court created) labor exemption to the professional sports industry in order to provide protection for terms agreed to by team owners and players through the collective bargaining process. As explained by Supreme Court Justice Steven Breyer in *Brown* v. *Pro Football, Inc.*:

> As a matter of logic, it would be difficult, if not impossible, to require groups of employers and employees to bargain together, but at the same time to forbid them to make among themselves or with each other any of the competition-restricting agreements potentially necessary to make the process work or its results mutually acceptable. Thus, the implicit exemption recognizes that, to give effect to federal labor laws and policies and to allow meaningful collective bargaining to take place, some restraints on competition imposed through the bargaining process must be shielded from antitrust sanctions.[84]

According to Professor William B. Gould IV, preeminent labor law scholar and former Chairman of the National Labor Relations Board, "The owners could be shielded against the formidable treble damage liability provided by antitrust law and could avail themselves of a more employer-friendly labor law so long as they entered into a collective bargaining agreement."[85] To summarize, the statutory exemption protects the formation and activity of players associations whereas the non-statutory exemption protects the collective bargaining agreements reached between players and team owners.[86]

The classic collective bargaining process: unreasonable demands, negotiation impasses, league lockouts, player strikes, union decertifications, antitrust lawsuits and eventual agreement/resolution

In his classic book on collective bargaining in sports, Professor Paul Staudohar explained the typical negotiation process and tactical procedural posturing that occurs:

> Tactically, both sides usually adopt extreme positions. The union has its "shopping list," in which it asks for gains on many issues far beyond what it thinks realistically possible. Management typically offers very little at the outset. Both parties recognize the need to bluff and make dire threats with no real intention of carrying them out. Although the union is ordinarily the

moving party in making demands at the outset of negotiations, an effective position for management is making high, hard demands of its own at the outset. Underlying this tactic is the adage that the best defense is a good offense.[87]

The ultimate result of the collective bargaining process ("labor battle") "will not only impact the leverage in that particular negotiation but will also help dictate the strength of each side's bargaining position for years to come."[88] From 1981 to 2011, eight different labor disputes interrupted a regular season in the NBA, the NFL, MLB and the National Hockey League (NHL).[89] Labor disputes often result from the inability of a players association and team owners (representing the professional sports league) to reach an agreement through the collective bargaining process. Temporary stalemates/deadlocks in the negotiation process are common. As explained by the United States Supreme Court, an impasse in ongoing negotiations "may differ from bargaining only in degree" and "may be manipulated by the parties for bargaining purposes."[90] Impasse frequently occurs "several times during the course of a single labor dispute, since the bargaining process is not over when the first impasse is reached."[91] Stated differently, impasse is "inherently part of the collective bargaining process under labor law … it occurs within the process of negotiating between a labor union and management."[92] If management (for example, team owners within a professional sports league) believes that the negotiation process has reached a bargaining impasse and continued bargaining sessions would be futile, the league will then usually present its "last, best and final offer" to the players association.[93]

Unreasonable requests and an unwillingness to compromise during the negotiation process by both players and team owners—combined with strategic procedural posturing to gain negotiation leverage—regularly results in a players association and/or league representatives claiming that the other group refused to bargain in good faith. For example, in May 2011, the NBPA filed a formal complaint with the National Labor Relations Board in which the players association accused the NBA (and member teams within the league) of the following: (1) Engaging in surface level bargaining intended to provoke a lockout and coerce players into accepting the league's collective bargaining proposals; (2) Refusing to provide relevant financial information related to team and league revenues; (3) Repeatedly threatening to lock out the players; and (4) Making demands and threats that were inherently destructive to the collective bargaining process.[94] A few months later, in August 2011, the NBA and its member teams retaliated by filing a similar formal charge against the NBPA with the National Labor Relations Board. The league claimed that the NBPA had "failed to bargain in good faith with the NBA regarding wages, hours and other terms and conditions of employment for NBA players as required by Section 8(d) of the National Labor Relations Act."[95]

If the players association and team owners are unable to agree to terms of a new CBA before expiration of an existing CBA, both players and league management could then resort to another set of tactical approaches in order to increase negotiation leverage as well as economic control. For example, professional sports leagues have historically decided to "lock out" players immediately following expiration of a league CBA. When a league decides to lock out its players, the players no longer receive paychecks, can no longer train at team facilities and no longer have many other rights that existed when the CBA was in effect.[96] Conversely, upon expiration of a CBA, players can decide to "strike." When players strike, they no longer participate in practices, games or any other team/league events. Similar to league lockouts shifting negotiation leverage in favor of teams, player strikes are designed to shift negotiation leverage in favor of the athletes—given that a professional sports league cannot effectively and efficiently function without its players.[97]

Historically, when going on strike has not swiftly created consensus concerning a new CBA, players have often decided to concede certain rights under federal labor law in order to gain rights under federal antitrust law. In this situation, either the players association renounces and relinquishes it status as the exclusive collective bargaining representative of players ("disclaimer of interest") or players initiate a formal process with the NLRB in which at least 30% of all players in a league choose to no longer be represented by the players association during the collective bargaining process ("decertification").[98] In *Brown* v. *Pro Football, Inc.*, Supreme Court Justice Steven Breyer noted that the non-statutory labor exemption lasts only until the collapse of the collective bargaining relationship, as evidenced by decertification of a union (or, similarly, a union disclaiming interest in functioning as the collective bargaining representative of employees).[99]

Because a players association would no longer exist as the formal representative of players for collective bargaining purposes after the decertification or disclaimer of interest process, a united group of players could then legally file an antitrust lawsuit against team owners.[100] Player threats of filing group class action antitrust claims usually function as one of the primary negotiation devices in collective bargaining—but somewhat illogically and unproductively, the collective bargaining process itself must end before antitrust lawsuits are allowed to be filed in federal court. When players associations adopt the strategy of union decertification (or disclaimer of interest) and subsequent filing of an antitrust lawsuit, the players associations always seem to "miraculously revive and bargain a collective agreement as part of the antitrust settlement."[101] In other words, almost invariably, collective bargaining disputes have ultimately been resolved at the bargaining table instead of inside the courtroom. Nonetheless, players associations and team owners alike have historically resorted to the legal system in order to create negotiation leverage during the collective bargaining process.

Rationale for book focusing on collective bargaining in the NBA and NFL

Players associations throughout the world continue to independently advocate for athlete rights. For instance, in April 2012, the Union of European Football Associations (UEFA)—which functions as the governing body of European football/soccer—and the social partners represented by FIFPro (trade union), the European Professional Football Leagues and the European Club Association negotiated the first agreement establishing minimum contract requirements for football/soccer players in Europe. Based on the terms of this landmark collaborative agreement, player contracts must be in writing, define the rights and duties of a team and player, and address matters such as salary, health insurance, social security and paid leave. Contracts also must refer to the responsibility of players to participate in training, to maintain a healthy lifestyle and to comply with disciplinary procedures.[102] In general, the impact of players associations in Europe "has not been remotely comparable" to that of players associations in the United States.[103]

Another timely example of collective bargaining outside of the United States occurred in Canada in May 2019 when the Canadian Football League (CFL) and the Canadian Football League Players Association (CFLPA) agreed to terms on a new three-year CBA. In announcing the new CBA, Randy Ambrosie (CFL commissioner) commented, "Our new agreement speaks to positive growth for our league and a renewed investment in our players. We have an exciting future ahead of us and people around the world will see us build it together. I want to thank our players, teams and fans for their patience." Jeff Keeping (CFLPA president) similarly remarked, "I would like to thank all CFL players for their commitment and diligence as we worked together toward a fair agreement. I would also like to thank the fans for their support and understanding throughout this process. This new agreement moves us forward as partners in the future of the game."[104]

Players associations have also united and collaborated in order to share best practices, develop a collective set of core values and advance the rights of professional athletes at the global level. For instance, in December 2014, leaders from numerous players associations throughout the world established the World Players Association as the exclusive global association of organized players and athletes across professional sports. The World Players Association aspires to function as the leading voice of organized players in the governance of world sports. The World Players Association is a global collective of approximately 85,000 elite professional athletes, organized primarily through major players associations including FIFPro (the world football/soccer players association), the Federation of International Cricketers Associations (FICA), the International Rugby Players Association (IRPA), the European Elite Athletes Association (EU Athletes), the Japanese Professional Baseball Players Association (JPBPA), the Australian Athletes' Alliance (AAA), the National Hockey League Players Association (NHLPA), the MLBPA, the NBPA and the NFLPA. The development of the World Players Association was the commonsense result of the sustained effort of athletes to organize at the national, regional and global levels. Brendan Schwab, executive director of the World Players Association, provided the following overview of this global athlete collective:

> The World Players Association exists to ensure that, at the global level, the challenges to the wellbeing of professional sport are addressed through

collective bargaining underpinned by the application of internationally recognized labor standards. Whilst history shows that sporting bodies are reluctant to embrace those standards, the long contribution made by organized athletes and the application of the rule of law have been fundamental to ensuring the sustainable growth and good governance of the world's leading professional sports.... The organization of the world's athletes shapes as the most important force through which the governance of sport can be held accountable, its responsible economic growth maximized, its standards advanced, the interests of its stakeholders fairly balanced and the essence of sport restored.... The profound nature of the challenges now facing sport calls for a strong, independent, professional and well-resourced response on behalf of sport's most significant stakeholder—the athletes.[105]

The remaining content within this book intentionally focuses on collective bargaining within the NBA and NFL in order to provide readers with as much depth and detail as possible about timely and relevant topics without being unnecessarily redundant by attempting to cover collective bargaining in every professional sports league within the United States as well as globally. The NFL and the NBA are the two professional sports leagues within the United States that routinely generate the highest total cumulative team and league revenues each year. For example, in 2019, the NFL generated more than $15 billion in total revenue and the NBA generated more than $7.5 billion in total revenue. In addition, the recent collective bargaining processes and outcomes within the NBA and NFL provide the most comprehensive overall foundational framework for scholarly discussion and analysis. An examination of collective bargaining within these two specific professional sports leagues should provide the reader with the most extensive—and hopefully enlightening—set of examples, stories and insight into the underlying dynamics and areas of contention involving professional sports leagues and athletes.

In addition, this book is not intended to serve as a comprehensive resource on all of the historical and present issues, challenges and opportunities involving collective bargaining within professional sports leagues both within the United States and globally. Instead, this book aims to serve as a fact-driven, concise and informative resource for college students and individuals working within the sports business industry that complements and supplements existing work previously published within this space (and referenced within this book).

Chapter 2 and *Chapter 3* of this book provide a detailed discussion and analysis of collective bargaining within the National Basketball Association (NBA) from 2009 through 2019. *Chapter 4* and *Chapter 5* provide a detailed discussion and analysis of collective bargaining within the National Football League (NFL) from 2009 through 2019.

Notes

1 *See* Ohanesian, N.M. (2018). Collective Bargaining and Workforce Protections in Sports, in *The Oxford Handbook of American Sports Law* (Edited by McCann,

M.A.), at page 195. Oxford University Press (explaining the "importance of collective bargaining in U.S. sports cannot be overstated ... it shapes the legal relationship between athletes, teams and leagues").

2 Weiler, P.C. and Roberts, G.R. (2004). *Sports and the Law (Third Edition)*, at page 276. Thomson West.

3 *See* Major League Baseball Players Association (www.mlbplayers.com) (noting that, in 1885, John Montgomery Ward and eight other players formed the first players union in baseball—the Brotherhood of Professional Base Ball Players).

4 Weiler, P.C. and Roberts, G.R. (2004). *Sports and the Law*, at page 277. *See also* Jessop, A. (2016). Labor Law, in *Introduction to Sport Law (Second Edition)* (Edited by Spengler, J.O., Anderson, P.M., Connaughton, D.P., and Baker, T.A., III), at page 249. Human Kinetics (defining unions as "an organized group of employees that uses their collective strength to protect the rights and interests of the group's members"). Professional sports leagues and players association representatives nonetheless tend to utilize the terms "union" and "players association" interchangeably. This book likewise uses the terms "players association" and "union" interchangeably.

5 *See* Champion, W.T., Jr. (2005). *Sports Law*, at page 123. Aspen Publishers (explaining that unions in professional sports protect the interests of the athletes in their struggles against management, and also indicating that professional sports unions initially faced a particularly difficult struggle in organizing).

6 *See* Mitten, M.J., Davis, T., Smith, R.K., and Berry, R.C. (2009). *Sports Law and Regulation (Second Edition)*, at page 514. Wolters Kluwer. *See also* Thornton, P.K. (2011). *Sports Law*, at pages 209–210. Jones and Bartlett Publishers (clarifying that individual players still have the ability to negotiate certain aspects of their employment contract even though the players association is considered the sole representative for players during the collective bargaining process).

7 Feldman, G. (2018). Collective Bargaining in Professional Sports, in *The Oxford Handbook of American Sports Law*, at page 210.

8 *See* Mitten, M.J., Davis, T., Smith, R.K., and Berry, R.C. (2009). *Sports Law and Regulation*, at pages 515, 517.

9 *See* Feldman, G. (2018). Collective Bargaining in Professional Sports, in *The Oxford Handbook of American Sports Law*, at page 213 (explaining that players associations fought for basic economic rights including pensions, health benefits, minimum salaries and greater ease of movement between teams). *See also* Goplerud, C.P., III (1997). Collective Bargaining in the National Football League: A Historical and Comparative Analysis, *Villanova Sports & Entertainment Law Journal*, at page 14 (explaining that, despite the technical existence and recognition of players associations during the 1950s and 1960s, "none were particularly strong nor well accepted by management"). In addition, *see* Staudohar, P.D. (2012). The Basketball Lockout of 2011, *Monthly Labor Review*, at page 28 (noting that, players associations were initially considered "weak and ineffective" but eventually "emerged under new leadership to seek a greater share of the expanding wealth [in professional sports] through collective bargaining").

10 *See* Quirk, J. and Fort, R. (1999). *Hard Ball: The Abuse of Power in Pro Team Sports*, at page 51. Princeton University Press.

11 Major League Baseball Players Association (www.mlbplayers.com).

12 *See* Miller, M. (1991). *A Whole Different Ball Game: The Inside Story of the Baseball Revolution*. Ivan R. Dee Publishing Co.

13 Major League Baseball Players Association (www.mlbplayers.com).

14 *See* Ohanesian, N.M. (2018). Collective Bargaining and Workforce Protections in Sports, in *The Oxford Handbook of American Sports Law*, at pages 202–203.

15 *See* Quirk, J. and Fort, R. (1999). *Hard Ball: The Abuse of Power in Pro Team Sports*, at page 54 (writing that the original reserve clause was invented in 1879 by Arthur Soden, one of the owners of the Boston Braves).

16 Major League Baseball Players Association (www.mlbplayers.com). *See also* Kahn, L.M. (2009). Sports, Antitrust Enforcement and Collective Bargaining, *The Antitrust Bulletin*, at page 864 (explaining that during the early pre-free agency period in professional sports, "a major goal in collective bargaining for players associations was the attainment of free agency for players").

17 Banner, S. (2013). *The Baseball Trust: A History of Baseball's Antitrust Exemption*, at page 238. Oxford University Press.

18 Upon the passing of Marvin Miller in November 2012, the NFLPA issued the following statement: "Marvin exemplified guts, tenacity and an undying love for the players he represented.... His most powerful message was that players would remain unified during labor strife if they remembered the sacrifices made by previous generations to make the game better. His passion for the players never faltered, and men and women across all sports are in a better place thanks to his tireless work.... By challenging team owners and league commissioners and successfully protecting and enhancing the rights of players, he proved that labor unions were necessary in sports." Official Release—NFLPA Statement on the Passing of Marvin Miller (2012), *available at* www.nflpa.com.

19 *See* National Basketball Players Association (www.nbpa.com).

20 *See* National Basketball Players Association (www.nbpa.com).

21 *See* National Basketball Players Association (www.nbpa.com).

22 *See* National Football League Players Association (www.nflpa.com) (noting that the player representatives "never did get a chance to meet with the owners" and "never got a response from any of the proposals at the time").

23 *See Radovich* v. *National Football League* (1957), 352 U.S. 445. Federal antitrust laws "prohibit agreements or practices that restrict business competition to the detriment of consumers." Weisman, S.J.J. (2018). *Sports Law: The Essentials*, at page 5. West Academic Publishing.

24 National Football League Players Association (www.nflpa.com).

25 *See* Abrams, R.I. (2010). *Sports Justice: The Law & Business of Sports*, at page 163. Northeastern University Press (articulating that, in the early years, the NFLPA proved to be "woefully ineffective in its efforts to better the work life of players. Involvement in union activity was risky for players. A club's union representatives were almost certain to be traded, benched or waived—a clear violation of [labor] law that went unaddressed").

26 National Football League Players Association (www.nflpa.com).

27 *See* National Football League Players Association (www.nflpa.com).

28 *See* National Football League Players Association (www.nflpa.com).

29 *See* Abrams, R.I. (2010). *Sports Justice: The Law & Business of Sports*, at page 166 (explaining that, with respect to the NFL throughout the early 1970s, "management's lack of respect for the union was apparent, and bargaining did not bring about the fundamental improvements in the labor relations system which the players had sought").

30 *See* National Football League Players Association (www.nflpa.com) (noting that "the first refusal/compensation system governing free agents in the 1977 CBA saw

very little player movement because a first-round draft choice (or more) was too high a price to pay for signing another team's free agent").

31 *See* Staudohar, P.D. (1986). *The Sports Industry and Collective Bargaining*. ILR Press. The collective bargaining agreement between the NBPA and the NBA sets out the terms and conditions of employment for all professional basketball players playing in the National Basketball Association, as well as the respective rights and obligations of the NBA teams, the NBA and the NBPA. *See* National Basketball Players Association (www.nbpa.com).

32 *See* Yasser, R., McCurdy, J.R., Goplerud, C.P., and Weston, M.A. (2011). *Sports Law Cases and Materials (Seventh Edition)*, at page 377. LexisNexis. *See also* Abrams, R.I. (2010). *Sports Justice: The Law & Business of Sports*, at page 149 (explaining that, "in order to achieve the competition that consumers seek, sports clubs must cooperate in setting the rules of the game ... each club must have worthy opponents in order to produce sports entertainment. There is a need, therefore, to strive to equalize talent and ensure that the outcome of each game is uncertain"). In addition, *see* Lee, T. (2010), Competitive Balance in the National Football League After the 1993 Collective Bargaining Agreement, *Journal of Sports Economics*, at page 78 (reiterating that "competitive balance is thought to be an important part of demand for sports entertainment").

33 *See* Kaplan, R.A. (2004). The NBA Luxury Tax Model: A Misguided Regulatory Regime. *Columbia Law Review*, at page 1616 (noting that "revenue distribution was substantially less complicated during the early days of American professional team sports, as team owners essentially possessed unilateral power over the terms and conditions of the players' employment").

34 *See* Mitten, M.J., Davis, T., Shropshire, K., Osborne, B., and Smith, R.K. (2013). *Sports Law: Governance and Regulation*, at page 316. Wolters Kluwer. *See also* Mitten, M.J., Davis, T., Smith, R.K., and Berry, R.C. (2009). *Sports Law and Regulation*, at page 514 (explaining that as the economics of sports have changed, so has much of the emphasis of collective bargaining). In addition, *see* Weiler, P.C., and Roberts, G.R. (2004). *Sports and the Law*, at page 277 (explaining that tension related to how to divide available revenue is more likely "when the size of the pie is changing dramatically rather than remaining constant or growing incrementally"). In the words of Professor Paul Staudohar, "labor-management relations in sports have been characterized by conflict over money and power." Staudohar, P.D. (2012). The Basketball Lockout of 2011, *Monthly Labor Review*, at page 28.

35 This list of sample CBA provisions is not meant to be exhaustive or all-inclusive; rather, the goal of this list is to provide readers of this book with a general understanding of basic topics covered by current collective bargaining agreements in professional sports leagues such as the NBA and NFL.

36 *See* Osborne, B. and Cunningham, J.L. (2017). Legal and Ethical Implications of Athletes' Biometric Data Collection in Professional Sport, *Marquette Sports Law Review*, at page 59 (noting that current CBAs and standard player contracts within professional sports leagues "generally allow for broad collection, use, and disclosure of athlete health-related data ... CBAs should be viewed as a strong potential future means to protect player rights and privacy toward biodata").

37 *National Labor Relations Board* v. *Insurance Agents' International Union* (1960), 361 U.S. 477.

38 Berry, R.C., and Gould, W.B., IV (1981). A Long Deep Drive to Collective Bargaining: Of Players, Owners, Brawls, and Strikes, *Case Western Law Review*, at page 694.

39 *See* National Football League Collective Bargaining Agreement [hereinafter NFL CBA] (2011), Preamble, at page xv. Adam Silver, commissioner of the NBA, prefers to utilize the term "governor" instead of "owner" when describing those with a controlling financial interest in teams within the NBA. In September 2019, NBPA executive director Michele Roberts voiced her perception that team owners "continue to view players as property." Spears, M.J. (2019). Michele Roberts Wants to Stop Chatter About Player Power Being a Problem, *available at* www.the undefeated.com.

40 In particular, *see* the analysis by the United States Supreme Court in *Brown* v. *Pro Football, Inc.* (1996), 518 U.S. 231, at page 237. *See also* Rosner, S. and Shropshire, K. (2010). *The Business of Sports (Second Edition)*, at page xi. Jones & Bartlett Publishers (explaining that, "In almost every sports venture, the competitors must cooperate for the venture to be profitable"). *See also* Vrooman, J. (2012). The Economic Structure of the NFL, in *The Economics of the National Football League* (Edited by Quinn, K.G.), at page 7. Springer Publishing (reiterating that, "Sports leagues are unique in that individual clubs are mutually interdependent in their cooperative production of competitive games").

41 Masteralexis, L.P. (2014). Labor Relations & Collective Bargaining, in *Sport Law: A Managerial Approach (Third Edition)* (Edited by Sharp, L., Moorman, A.M., and Claussen, C.L.), at page 206. Routledge.

42 *See* How the NBA Lockout Came to Be, *Northwestern Business Review* (2011) (providing the following example related to the potential lack of complete alignment among team owners: "While a stricter salary cap may be in the best interests of the majority of the owners, it is not in the best interests of the wealthiest owners and the owners who would be willing to spend large sums of money to sign the NBA's most elite talent. In this situation, some owners (including [Mark] Cuban) have views more in line with the players union than they do with their fellow owners").

43 Selig, B. (2018). *For the Good of the Game: The Inside Story of the Surprising and Dramatic Transformation of Major League Baseball*, at pages 142–145. HarperCollins Publishers. *See also* Goplerud, C.P., III (1997). Collective Bargaining in the National Football League: A Historical and Comparative Analysis, *Villanova Sports & Entertainment Law Journal*, at page 15 (writing that typically "management consists of extremely wealthy individuals or groups of individuals with a minimal knowledge of the game or its history and culture").

44 In December 2011, the NBA Board of Governors approved a revenue sharing plan that quadrupled the funds previously shared among NBA teams. Then-current NBA commissioner David Stern remarked that team owners "realized that it was imperative that our revenue sharing program be improved. We have found a solution that should provide our league with better competitive balance." Official Release—NBA Board of Governors Ratifies 10-Year CBA (2011), *available at* www.nba.com.

45 Lombardo, J. (2012). Inside NBA's Revenue Sharing, *Sports Business Journal*. In 2006, the owners of eight NBA teams sent a letter to then-current NBA commissioner David Stern in which the owners demanded that David Stern address the growing financial disparity between small market teams like the Minnesota Timberwolves and big market teams such as the Chicago Bulls. The letter from team owners in part read: "We are asking you to embrace this issue because the hard truth is that our current economic system works only for larger-market teams and a few teams that have extraordinary success on the court and for the latter group of teams, only when they experience extraordinary success. The rest of us are looking at significant

and unacceptable annual financial losses." *See* Windhorst, B. (2011). How 'Small Market' Owners Took Control, *available at* www.espn.com.

46 *See* Mitten, M.J., Davis, T., Smith, R.K., and Berry, R.C. (2009). *Sports Law and Regulation*, at page 610 (explaining "if professional athletes form a labor union and engage in collective bargaining with the owners, the resulting labor agreement takes precedence over the league's internal rules as to most labor-management issues and relations").

47 National Basketball Association Collective Bargaining Agreement [hereinafter NBA CBA] (2017), Article X, Section 3(b); and NBA CBA (2017), Article X, Section 8.

48 NBA Uniform Player Contract, Section 5(d).

49 Miller, M. (1991). *A Whole Different Ball Game: The Inside Story of the Baseball Revolution*, at page 47.

50 *See* Mitten, M.J., Davis, T., Shropshire, K., Osborne, B., and Smith, R.K. (2013). *Sports Law: Governance and Regulation*.

51 Berry, R.C. and Gould, W.B., IV (1981). A Long Deep Drive to Collective Bargaining: Of Players, Owners, Brawls, and Strikes, *Case Western Law Review*, at page 708. *See also* Lowell, C.H. (1973). Collective Bargaining and the Professional Team Sport Industry, *Law and Contemporary Problems*, at page 5 (reiterating that "individual players may not complain about the terms and conditions negotiated" by the players association because all players are equally bound by the actions of the players association; also similarly writing that the "basic labor policy of submitting the will of the minority to that of the majority may bear most heavily upon the so-called superstars, for once the majority of average ballplayers realize the power in their hands, they may use the interests of the stars for the furtherance of their own self-interest"). In addition, *see* Dworkin, J.B. (2016). The Evolution of Collective Bargaining in Sports, in *Research Handbook of Employment Relations in Sport* (Edited by Barry, M., Skinner, J., and Engelberg, T.), at page 143. Edward Elgar Publishing, Inc. (indicating that "part of the reason for the success of collective bargaining in sports is due to its flexibility and adaptability ... a key factor has been the ability to negotiate master contracts which both set minimum salary levels for players early in their careers ... and allow for individual salary negotiation between more senior players and clubs").

52 *See* Mitten, M.J., Davis, T., Smith, R.K., and Berry, R.C. (2009). *Sports Law and Regulation*, at page 405.

53 Winfree, J.A. (2017). No Seat at the Table: Representation in Collective Bargaining in Professional Sports. *Managerial and Decision Economics*, at pages 697–698 (noting that "less experienced players are not the only ones to be impacted from a lack of representation ... former players do not have a say as well"). During negotiations related to the 2011 CBA, nine players served on the NBPA executive committee, averaging 9.56 years in prior NBA playing experience; the average playing experience for all NBA players at that time equaled 4.79 years. Typically, players with less NBA playing experience have made less prior income, on average, than experienced players and therefore may be more sensitive to the timing of future paychecks. As a result, the more experienced players within a professional sports league may be more willing to engage in a lockout than some of the inexperienced players the NBPA executive committee represents during the bargaining process, which can create a principal-agency problem. Stated differently, players associations could potentially tend to disproportionately benefit more experienced players as compared

with less experienced players. *See* Sadler, T.R. and Sanders, S. (2016). The 2011–2021 NBA Collective Bargaining Agreement: Asymmetric Information, Bargaining Power and the Principal Agency Problem, *Managerial Finance*, at pages 896–897. *See also* Black, D.A. and Parker, D.F. (1985). The Division of Union Rents, *Journal of Labor Research* (concluding that older workers reap more of the rents of unionization than do younger workers). *See also* Vrooman, J. (2012). The Economic Structure of the NFL, in *The Economics of the National Football League*, at page 8 (reiterating that, "Sports unions are also divisive in that the internal politics of current players are often incongruent with interests of unrepresented future and former players").

54 For instance, the current executive directors of the NBPA and NFLPA both have a background in litigation (former careers as trial lawyers). In 2018, NFLPA executive director DeMaurice Smith commented that the players association must "prepare for war" with respect to upcoming negotiations with team owners. Jones, M. (2018). NFLPA's DeMaurice Smith: 'We Prepare for War' on Negotiations with NFL, *USA Today*. Smith also acknowledged that he is "kind of wired to be combative." Babb, K. (2019). DeMaurice Smith is Ready to Battle the NFL Again: Not Everyone Wants to Join Him, the *Washington Post* (explaining that DeMaurice Smith had become so polarizing by 2015 that eight finalists—among them a retired Navy admiral, two lawyers and a pair of former NFLPA employees during Smith's early years as executive director—were on the ballot to unseat him).

55 National Basketball Players Association (www.nbpa.com).

56 National Basketball Players Association (www.nbpa.com). Although collective bargaining often limits the rights of individual professional athletes, the collective bargaining process increases the overall bargaining power of all athletes within a professional sports league through bargaining as a collective unit. *See* Weisman, S.J.J. (2018). *Sports Law: The Essentials*, at page 5.

57 National Basketball Players Association (www.nbpa.com). The NBPA Foundation highlights the collaborative work that league players do worldwide to build their communities and create meaningful change.

58 National Football League Players Association (www.nflpa.com). The NFLPA in-house communications department is responsible for educating the media on the benefits of the collective bargaining agreement and the free agency system for all professional football players.

59 Zimbalist, A. (2006). *In the Best Interests of Baseball? Governing the National Pastime*, at page 210. University of Nebraska Press. In 1921, Judge Kenesaw Mountain Landis became the first commissioner of a professional sports league. Major League Baseball decided to create this new commissioner position as a direct result of the infamous "Black Sox" match fixing scandal that took place during the 1919 MLB World Series. In granting Commissioner Landis extensive administrative, investigative and disciplinary powers, MLB team owners established a pattern of executive authority that other major professional sports leagues eventually embraced. *See* Jones, M.E. (2016). *Sports Law: Rules of the Game*, at pages 78–79. Rowman & Littlefield (explaining that, in some situations, the power and authority of a professional sports league commissioner is subject to review by team owners, arbitrators and/or judges).

60 Golen, J. and Zola, W.K. (2018). The Evolution of the Power of the Commissioner in Professional Sports, in *The Oxford Handbook of American Sports Law*, at page 19.

61 Staudohar, P.D. (1986). *The Sports Industry and Collective Bargaining*, at page 9.

62 McCann, M.A. (2018). Leagues and Owners: The Donald Sterling Story, in *The Oxford Handbook of American Sports Law*, at page 45. *See also* Jones, M.E. (1999). *Sports Law*, at page 116. Prentice Hall (reiterating that "the legal relationship between leagues, teams, and owners is a complex one").

63 Carfagna, P.A. (2011). *Sports and the Law: Examining the Legal Evolution of America's Three 'Major Leagues' (2nd Edition)*, at page 38. Thomson Reuters.

64 Berry, R.C. and Gould, W.B., IV (1981). A Long Deep Drive to Collective Bargaining: Of Players, Owners, Brawls, and Strikes, *Case Western Law Review*, at page 705.

65 Shropshire, K.L. and Davis, T. (2008). *The Business of Sports Agents (Second Edition)*, at page 135. University of Pennsylvania Press.

66 *See* NFLPA Regulations Governing Contract Advisors (2011), at page 6 (explaining that the objective of the NFLPA in implementing the regulations was "to enable players to make an informed selection of a contract advisor and to help assure that the contract advisor will provide effective representation at fair, reasonable, and uniformly applicable rates to those individual players the contract advisor represents, and to avoid any conflict of interest which could potentially compromise the best interests of NFL players"). For a historical perspective on the ethical and legal responsibilities of athlete agents, *see* Dee, P.T. (1992). Ethical Aspects of Representing Professional Athletes, *Marquette Sports Law Journal*. Although no federal or state laws require any specific qualifications for sports agents, "the various professional sports unions have enacted requirements that must be met in order to represent" a player within the league. Weisman, S.J.J. (2018). *Sports Law: The Essentials*, at page 143. *See also* Shropshire, K.L. and Davis, T. (2008). *The Business of Sports Agents (Second Edition)*, at page 96 (clarifying that "all agents are governed by regulations promulgated by players associations. Whether agents are subject to additional proscriptions often depends on the existence of state-enacted agent regulations or whether the agent is also an attorney").

67 *Chapter 2* of this book provides several examples of how sports agents representing NBA players attempted to involve themselves in the overall collective bargaining process for a new CBA in 2010 and 2011.

68 Rosner, S. (2004). Conflicts of Interest and the Shifting Paradigm of Athlete Representation, *UCLA Entertainment Law Review*, at page 210.

69 Berry, R.C. and Gould, W.B., IV (1981). A Long Deep Drive to Collective Bargaining: Of Players, Owners, Brawls, and Strikes, *Case Western Law Review*, at page 710.

70 Feldman, G. (2018). Collective Bargaining in Professional Sports, in *The Oxford Handbook of American Sports Law*, at page 216. While antitrust law establishes a mechanism by which to attack illegal collusion, labor law seeks to protect and regulate collective action by employees, particularly in the form of labor unions. *See* Grow, N. (2006). There's No 'I' in 'League'—Professional Sports Leagues and the Single Entity Defense, *Michigan Law Review*, at page 201.

71 *See* Feldman, G. (2018). Collective Bargaining in Professional Sports, in *The Oxford Handbook of American Sports Law*, at page 210.

72 *See* Basic Guide to the National Labor Relations Act: General Principles of Law Under Statute and Procedures of the National Labor Relations Board, *available at* www.nlrb.gov, at page 24 (explaining that "the duty to bargain covers all matters concerning rates of pay, wages, hours of employment, or other conditions of employment. These are called 'mandatory' subjects of bargaining about which the

employer, as well as the employees' representative must bargain in good faith, although the law does not require 'either party to agree to a proposal or require the making of a concession' ... mandatory subjects of bargaining [also] include but are not limited to such matters as pensions for present employees, bonuses, group insurance, [and] grievance procedures").

73 Masteralexis, L.P. (2014). Labor Relations & Collective Bargaining, in *Sport Law: A Managerial Approach*, at page 203. As explained by Dr. Edwin Elliott, then-current Regional Director of the National Labor Relations Board, "The nearest to a cure-all in labor-management relations that we know is the practice of honest, fair, good-faith collective bargaining." Elliott, E.A. (1948). The Labor Management Relations Act of 1947. *The Southwestern Social Science Quarterly*, at page 108.

74 Feldman, G. (2012). *Brady* v. *NFL* and *Anthony* v. *NBA*: The Shifting Dynamics in Labor-Management Relations in Professionals Sports, *Tulane Law Review*, at page 834 (explaining that the NLRA and the LMRA established collective bargaining as the framework to govern the relationship between employers and unionized employees).

75 National Labor Relations Act (1935), Sections 7–9; Labor Management Relations Act (1947), Sections 7–9. Congress also perceived that some union conduct needed correction; as a result, the LMRA also "imposed on unions the same obligation to bargain in good faith that the NLRA placed on employers." National Labor Relations Board, 1947 Taft-Hartley Act Substantive Provisions, *available at* www.nlrb.gov.

76 *See* Mitten, M.J., Davis, T., Shropshire, K., Osborne, B., and Smith, R.K. (2013). *Sports Law: Governance and Regulation*, at page 334 (noting that "one of the more perplexing aspects of labor relations in professional team sports is the inherent tension between, and intersection of, federal antitrust and labor law").

77 *See* LeRoy, M.H. (2014). *Collective Bargaining in Sports and Entertainment*, at pages 12–13. Wolters Kluwer (examining whether uniform player contracts in professional sports violate federal antitrust law). It is important to note that, in 1922, the United States Supreme Court determined that Major League Baseball was exempt from federal antitrust law scrutiny because professional baseball did not involve interstate commerce. The scope of the antitrust exemption for professional baseball remains a controversial topic for scholars and practitioners alike, especially given that the economic realities of professional baseball today drastically differ from the business of baseball in 1922. In addition, the Sports Broadcasting Act of 1961 provided additional antitrust immunity for select professional sports leagues with respect to league regulation and monetization of television broadcasting rights.

78 Champion, W.T., Jr. (2005). *Sports Law*, at page 178.

79 *See* Feldman, G. (2012). Antitrust Versus Labor Law in Professional Sports: Balancing the Scales after *Brady* v. *NFL* and *Anthony* v. *NBA*, *UC Davis Law Review*, at page 1227 (reiterating that "antitrust law promotes competition and condemns cooperation among competitors ... federal labor law, by contrast, encourages cooperation among competitors in employment").

80 *See* Clayton Antitrust Act (1914), Section 6 (exempting labor unions from being considered illegal monopolies).

81 *See* Norris-LaGuardia Act (1932), Section 2. *See also* Masteralexis, L.P. (2014). Labor Relations & Collective Bargaining, in *Sport Law: A Managerial Approach*, at page 203 (writing that the Norris-LaGuardia Act "strengthened the Clayton Act's exemption of union activities from antitrust laws").

82 Carfagna, P.A. (2011). *Sports and the Law: Examining the Legal Evolution of America's Three 'Major Leagues,'* at page 75.

83 Carfagna, P.A. (2011). *Sports and the Law: Examining the Legal Evolution of America's Three 'Major Leagues,'* at page 74.

84 *Brown* v. *Pro Football, Inc.* (1996), 518 U.S. 231, at page 237. *See also Mackey* v. *National Football League* (Eighth Circuit, 1976) 543 F.2d. 606, at page 614 (applying the following three-factor test for determining whether labor policy favoring collective bargaining may potentially be given preeminence over federal antitrust laws: (1) The restraint on trade primarily affects only the parties to the collective bargaining relationship (that is, players and teams); (2) The agreement sought to be exempted concerns a mandatory subject of collective bargaining (player salaries, work hours and other terms/conditions of employment); and (3) The agreement sought to be exempted is the product of bona fide arms-length bargaining).

85 Gould, W.B., IV (2011). *Bargaining with Baseball: Labor Relations in an Age of Prosperous Turmoil*, at page 119. McFarland & Company, Inc. *See also* Goplerud, C.P., III (1997). Collective Bargaining in the National Football League: A Historical and Comparative Analysis, *Villanova Sports & Entertainment Law Journal*, at page 32 (explaining that the Supreme Court "placed heavy emphasis on the importance of labor harmony and the national policy favoring free and private collective bargaining … [and] indicated it was simply carrying out what it saw as the preference of Congress to curtail judicial use of the antitrust laws to resolve labor disputes").

86 *See* Carfagna, P.A. (2011). *Sports and the Law: Examining the Legal Evolution of America's Three 'Major Leagues.'*

87 Staudohar, P.D. (1986). *The Sports Industry and Collective Bargaining*, at page 13. *See also* Feldman, G. (2012). *Brady* v. *NFL* and *Anthony* v. *NBA*: The Shifting Dynamics in Labor-Management Relations in Professionals Sports, *Tulane Law Review*, at page 832 (writing that "the last two decades have seen a shift from aggressive union bargaining to aggressive management bargaining").

88 Feldman, G. (2018). Collective Bargaining in Professional Sports, in *The Oxford Handbook of American Sports Law*, at page 222. *See also* Weisman, S.J.J. (2018). *Sports Law: The Essentials*, at page 21 (explaining that the result of both league lockouts and player strikes within professional sports produces an identical reality/result—the "games do not go on and it becomes a matter of which side is better able to weather the loss of income that comes about as a result of a work stoppage"). *See also* Feldman, G. (2012). *Brady* v. *NFL* and *Anthony* v. *NBA*: The Shifting Dynamics in Labor-Management Relations in Professionals Sports, *Tulane Law Review*, at page 847 (explaining that the 2011 "NBA and NFL labor disputes signify more than a battle over player salaries and salary cap issues. Rather, these negotiations represent a fight over the balance of power in labor-management relations, and the battleground is now at the intersection of federal labor law and antitrust law").

89 *See* Berri, D. (2012). Did the Players Give Up Money to Make the NBA Better? Exploring the 2011 Collective Bargaining Agreement in the National Basketball Association, *International Journal of Sport Finance*, at page 158 (reiterating that "strikes and lockouts have become commonplace" in professional sports). According to Professor William B. Gould IV, "From 1912 to 1972, no strike occurred in baseball or any other sport except for a threatened walkout at the NBA All-Star Game in the mid-1960s when the basketball players were first starting to put together a union … but the problems were there"). Gould, W.B., IV (2010). The State of Sports Law and Policy: Views from a Labor Law Professor, in *Reversing Field: Examining Commercialization, Labor, Gender, and Race in 21st Century*

Sports Law (Edited by andré douglas pond cummings and Lofaso, A.M.), at page 117. West Virginia University Press.

90 *Charles D. Bonanno Linen Service* v. *NLRB* (1982), 454 U.S. 404, at page 12.

91 *Brown* v. *Pro Football, Inc.* (1996), 518 U.S. 231, at page 246.

92 *Brady* v. *National Football League* (Minnesota District Court, 2011), 779 F. Supp. 2d 992.

93 *See* Walsh, D.P. (2010). 1994 Baseball Player's Strike: A Case Study in Labor's Use of its Most Effective Economic Weapon, in *Reversing Field: Examining Commercialization, Labor, Gender, and Race in 21st Century Sports Law*, at page 107 (explaining that, based on provisions within the National Labor Relations Act, "when negotiations for a collective bargaining agreement reach the point where further bargaining would be fruitless, the employer is permitted to declare an 'impasse' and unilaterally implement the last offer it placed on the bargaining table for a new collective bargaining agreement").

94 NBPA Unfair Labor Practice Charge Against NBA (May 2011), filed with National Labor Relations Board.

95 NBA Unfair Labor Practice Charge Against NBPA (August 2011), filed with National Labor Relations Board.

96 *See* Conrad, M. (2011). *The Business of Sports: A Primer for Journalists*, at page 137. Routledge (explaining that during a lockout, team owners save money by not paying any players salaries while simultaneously putting pressure on the players association to settle the bargaining dispute).

97 *See* Quirk, J. and Fort, R. (1999). *Hard Ball: The Abuse of Power in Pro Team Sports*, at page 53 (noting that players associations "wield more bargaining power in negotiations than do more conventional unions because of the unique skills possessed by their members").

98 The remaining chapters within in this book provide additional information on how professional sports leagues routinely challenge the merit and legality of decertifications or disclaimers of interest by players associations.

99 *See Brown* v. *Pro Football, Inc.* (1996), 518 U.S. 231.

100 *See* Staudohar, P. (2012). The Basketball Lockout of 2011, *Monthly Labor Review*.

101 *See* Gould, W.B., IV (2011). *Bargaining with Baseball: Labor Relations in an Age of Prosperous Turmoil*, at page 119.

102 *See* Agreement Regarding the Minimum Requirements for Standard Player Contracts in the Professional Football Sector in the European Union and in the Rest of the UEFA Territory (2012), *available at* www.fifpro.org.

103 *See* McArdle, D. (2015). *Dispute Resolution in Sport: Athletes, Law and Arbitration*. Routledge.

104 Media Release—CFL and CFLPA Ratify New Collective Agreement (2019), *available at* www.cflpa.com. Since 1965, the CFLPA has worked to establish fair and reasonable working conditions while protecting the rights of all CFL players. In addition to negotiating and enforcing the terms of the CFL collective bargaining agreement, the CFLPA provides a variety of member services, builds corporate and community partnerships and works diligently for the betterment of its player membership.

105 Schwab, B. (2015). UNI World Athletes: The New Global Players' Association for Professional Sport, *available at* www.uniglobalunion.org. UNI Global Union is a Switzerland based labor organization that represents more than 20 million workers from more than 900 trade unions in the fastest growing sectors in the world, including media and sports.

2 Collective bargaining in the NBA
Part 1

Overview of chapter contents

The primary objective of this chapter is to provide a comprehensive overview of collective bargaining within the National Basketball Association (NBA).[1] The first section of this chapter summarizes the current NBA business model and overall economic climate at the team and league levels. This initial chapter section also explains how the NBA's current lucrative national media rights agreements along with recent team profitability and increased franchise valuations impact the probability of both players and team owners seeking negotiation leverage during future collective bargaining discussions. The next section of this chapter examines the somewhat contentious collective bargaining process between NBA team owners and players in 2010 and 2011, and also highlights some of the key business ("system") issues negotiated in the 2011 NBA collective bargaining agreement. This section includes a detailed analysis of how both the National Basketball Players Association (NBPA) and NBA team owners utilized the United States legal system in order to boost overall negotiation leverage during the collective bargaining process in 2010 and 2011. The next part of this chapter details the more collaborative and far less adversarial collective bargaining process between NBA owners and players in 2016 and 2017, which resulted in the current league CBA that is scheduled to expire on June 30, 2024.[2] The final chapter section contains a discussion of select key provisions within the current NBA collective bargaining agreement.

The NBA business model and economic climate: how league media rights, team profitability and franchise valuations impact collective bargaining

Similar to other professional sports leagues in the United States, the NBA attempts to create competitive balance among the 30 teams within the league.[3] For instance, one of the reasons why the NBA claimed the league needed a new collective bargaining agreement in 2011 was "to address the league's competitive balance problems."[4] Competitive balance essentially means overall team parity that produces unpredictable game outcomes. This unpredictable nature of game results is what in part generates consumer interest in attending and otherwise watching NBA games.[5]

The NBA utilizes several mechanisms to create and sustain competitive balance among teams within the league. For example, the NBA utilizes a reverse-order draft in which teams with the worst records during the previous season are generally provided with the opportunity to select higher in the annual NBA draft as compared with teams with much higher winning percentages. Revenue sharing and salary caps are two additional mechanisms that attempt to produce competitive balance among all teams within the NBA.[6] The NBA's current revenue sharing plan aims to redistribute money from teams that generate significant local revenue (for example, big market teams such as the Chicago Bulls, Los Angeles Lakers and New York Knicks) to teams that generate less local revenue (for example, small market teams such as the Minnesota Timberwolves, Charlotte Hornets and Orlando Magic). The NBA's salary cap limits the amount of money each team is allowed to spend on player salaries. Salary caps strive to facilitate competitive balance on the basketball court by creating competitive financial balance with respect to limiting the amount of money teams are permitted to spend on player compensation each NBA season.[7] From a league management point of view, salary control routinely functions as the paramount goal of professional sports leagues in the United States.[8]

The NBA salary cap directly impacts player salaries. In 1983, the NBA became the first professional sports league to establish a salary cap through collective bargaining, which was initially created as a mechanism to stabilize the finances of the league and its member teams.[9] The salary cap amount each year is now calculated based on a percentage of "basketball related income" (BRI).[10] The NBA collective bargaining agreement contains a detailed formula for determining BRI, which includes most revenue earned at the league and team levels. Sources of league and team revenue include league licensing income, leaguewide media rights deals and league corporate partnership agreements as well as team revenue streams such as gate receipts (ticket sales), local regional sports network media rights contracts and team sponsorship agreements. The overall financial health of the NBA can be inferred from the total BRI metric each NBA season. Player salaries correlate with aggregate team and league revenue totals.

For example, total BRI equaled approximately $3.6 billion for the 2009–2010 NBA season.[11] Based on the terms of the CBA in effect from 2005–2011, NBA players received 57% of the aggregate BRI amount in player salaries and related benefits each season (subject to a few limited exceptions that would increase players' share to 58%).[12] The resultant player share of revenues amounted to approximately $2.1 billion in 2009–2010.[13] The salary cap for each NBA team during the 2009–2010 season was $57.7 million.[14]

For comparison purposes, total BRI exceeded $7.5 billion during the 2019–2020 NBA season. Based on the terms of the current 2017 CBA, NBA players receive a minimum of 49% of the total BRI amount in player salaries and related benefits each season.[15] Therefore, the player share of revenues likely amounted to more than $3.6 billion during the 2019–2020 season; keep in mind that total league BRI equaled approximately $3.6 billion just ten years prior during the 2009–2010 NBA season.[16] Based on the terms of the current 2017 CBA, the NBA salary cap for each season is equal to 44.74% of projected BRI for that season minus projected expenses for player benefits.[17] The NBA salary cap for each team in the league during the 2019–2020 season was approximately $109.1 million.[18]

The 2017 CBA contains an extensive list of revenue sources that are classified as BRI elements and therefore count toward calculating operating revenues for each NBA season. BRI includes any source of league and team revenue "derived from, relating to, or arising directly or indirectly out of, the performance of players in NBA basketball games or in NBA-related activities."[19] The following list provides a snapshot of some of the key sources of revenue included within the definition of BRI in the 2017 CBA:

- Regular season gate receipts (ticket sales) for each team, including proceeds from playoff games as well as preseason and other exhibition games (after subtracting taxes and expenses such as facility fees and charges associated with arena financing);
- Luxury suite and arena club revenues (including revenue from personal seat licenses);
- Team sponsorship deals (including the sale of jersey patch rights as well as the sale of naming rights to arena and/or team practice facility along with any resultant arena signage);
- Food and beverage (concessions) sales as well as apparel and other merchandise sales at NBA arenas (or at a team-owned store within the immediate perimeter of the arena);
- Media rights (television and streaming) for any NBA-related content (both domestically and internationally);
- NBA All-Star Game, non-NBA basketball tournaments and other NBA special events;
- Revenue generated from gambling on NBA games (excluding revenues generated by team-owned casinos or other gambling businesses whose total revenues are not predominately derived from gambling on NBA games); and
- Other categories such as revenue generated from mascot and dance team appearances, arena tours, team-sponsored summer camps, team championship parades and arena automated teller machine (ATM) fees.[20]

NBA league and team finances

The NBA is a private company, so the league's financial statements are not publicly available. As a result, the true profitability of the league and its 30 individual teams is somewhat uncertain and difficult to definitively determine.[21] For example, according to the NBA, the league lost money during every year of the now-expired CBA that was in effect from 2005 to 2011—including estimated losses of $340 million during the 2009–2010 NBA season.[22] Media outlets such as *Forbes* and the *New York Times* have attempted to estimate the profits/losses of NBA teams without access to complete league and team-audited financials. During the same 2005–2011 time period for which the NBA claimed the league lost money each year, statistician Nate Silver concluded the NBA was a "fundamentally healthy and profitable business" that made $183 million in 2009–2010 before interest and taxes.[23] In addition, while *Forbes* claimed 17 out of the 30 NBA teams lost money during the 2009–2010 NBA season, the NBA countered with its claim that 23 NBA teams had net income losses during that same season.[24] The NBPA also questioned the NBA's exact financial figures in 2011, stating that a large portion of the "losses" reported by the NBA were actually accounting "book losses" rather than actual cash losses.[25] One key take-away is that players and owners have consistently disagreed on how to define and calculate league and team revenues and expenses.

In October 2014, Commissioner Silver mentioned that "roughly a third" of all NBA teams (approximately ten teams) were still not profitable under the then-current 2011 CBA and corresponding NBA financial system; this team profit/loss metric represented a noteworthy improvement from the 23 teams the NBA claimed lost money less than five years earlier.[26] In addition, according to internal NBA league financial records, 14 of the NBA's 30 teams lost money during the 2016–2017 season before distributing or collecting revenue sharing payouts, and nine teams reported negative net income even after accounting for revenue sharing related payments.[27] According to the NBA league office, during the 2018–2019 NBA season, fewer than ten NBA teams reported negative net income after accounting for revenue sharing related payments. Despite the lack of completely reliable detailed data on league and team profitability, the league and its member teams are unquestionably in better financial shape today as compared with ten years ago during the 2009–2010 NBA season.

Recent sales of NBA teams combined with two new leaguewide media rights deals also impact the perceived (and actual) financial viability of the league and its member teams. In October 2014, the NBA announced a nine-year, $24 billion combined media rights agreement with Turner Broadcasting and Disney/ESPN.[28] Beginning with the 2016–2017 NBA season, NBA teams received a significant boost in annual revenue distributions based on these two specific new leaguewide media rights deals—from approximately $30 million per team each year under the previous leaguewide media rights deals to more than $80 million per team each year under the new media rights agreements with Turner Broadcasting and ESPN. Upon learning about the new league media rights deals, Michele Roberts, executive director of the NBPA, commented: "The new television and media deals are good news for all of the stakeholders in the NBA.... Although we have seen strong revenue growth and significant increases in franchise values over the past three years, it is clear that the league is now entering a period of unprecedented revenue growth. Our job will be to ensure that the players receive their fair share of the results of their efforts."[29]

Recent transfers of controlling interests in NBA franchises also highlight the financial health of the NBA. For example, in August 2019, the Brooklyn Nets were sold for a cumulative total sales price of $2.35 billion.[30] In September 2017 the Houston Rockets were sold for approximately $2.2 billion.[31] Two seasons prior, in

April 2015, the Atlanta Hawks were sold for approximately $730 million.[32] Also, in August 2014, Steve Ballmer purchased the Los Angeles Clippers for $2 billion, which equaled more than 12 times the expected team revenue of the Clippers for the 2014–2015 NBA season.[33] Before Steve Ballmer purchased the Clippers, the record amount paid for an NBA team was $550 million for the Milwaukee Bucks earlier in 2014; this sales price reflected a "5× multiple" of the Bucks' annual revenue.[34] While some NBA teams might incur expenses that exceed revenue in particular years, NBA owners invest in teams with the expectation that the team will appreciate in value so that the owner will experience substantial capital gains upon selling the team.[35] For example, the Sacramento Kings were sold for $534 million in 2013, less than 15 years after the Maloof brothers purchased the franchise in 1999 for $185 million.[36] According to estimates by *Forbes*, the average franchise value of an NBA team equaled $1.9 billion as of February 2019.[37] Differing views related to franchise values along with the actual profits and losses of the NBA and its member teams have historically played a momentous role in the collective bargaining process between players and team owners.[38]

Untapped revenue from international media rights deals, ticket sales, sponsorship agreements and licensing royalties from merchandise sales resemble another source of future potential increased revenue for the NBA. According to a former NBA league executive, "The value of live sports content, both locally and nationally, is growing and the league has the potential to significantly increase media rights revenues in markets like China, India and Africa. There is a big delta between what the league currently draws in international views and the number of prospective fans abroad."[39] In July 2019, the NBA announced a five-year expansion of the league's existing partnership with Tencent—the deal will now run through the 2024–2025 NBA season. Tencent is the "exclusive official digital partner" of the NBA in China. Tencent provides extensive NBA coverage on its platforms, including live NBA game broadcasting, interactive fan experiences, NBA-themed mobile games, innovative advertising products and social media content.[40] Similarly, in October 2019, NBA teams hosted a series of pre-season games in India for the first time in the history of the league. In the words of Commissioner Silver, "Our inaugural NBA India Games will help further untap the enormous basketball potential in a country with a thriving sports culture and a growing, young and engaged population."[41] Likewise, in February 2019, the NBA announced plans to develop a new 12-team professional basketball league in Africa. Commissioner Silver emphatically stated, "Africa has a huge economic engine."[42] The NBA and FIBA (the global governing body of professional basketball) plan to dedicate financial support and resources toward the continued development of Africa's basketball ecosystem, including training for players, coaches and referees, and infrastructure investment.[43]

The NBA collective bargaining process in 2010 and 2011

The 2005 NBA collective bargaining agreement was scheduled to expire on June 30, 2011.

Team owners had the option to extend the 2005 CBA for one year (through June 30, 2012) but declined to exercise that option. The NBA owners jointly determined that the revenue allocation required under the 2005 CBA was not financially sustainable.[44] Negotiations for a successor CBA—along with strategic planning and attempts to control the narrative—informally started in February 2009 at the NBA All-Star Game in Phoenix. During a press conference, then-current NBA commissioner David Stern made the following comments directed at then-current NBPA executive director Billy Hunter: "The beauty of the NBA is that we have this perpetual flow of extraordinary talent that flows into Billy's union, for whom he gets 57% of every dollar that we generate. We spend 43% on other expenses and the owners wind up with nothing.... We meet with the union regularly. We turn over everything we possibly can."[45] Also during February 2009, prominent sports agent David Falk commented that, "The owners have the economic wherewithal to shut the [league] down for two years, whatever it takes, to get a system that will work long term. The players do not have the economic wherewithal to sit out one year."[46]

The vast majority of substantive CBA related negotiations took place in 2010 and 2011. In January 2010, NBA team owners sent an initial official CBA proposal to the NBPA. This owner-drafted proposal sought to implement a hard salary cap, drastically decrease the players' share of BRI (for example, reduce and roll back player salaries) as well as reduce contract length and salary guarantees. The NBPA quickly rejected the NBA proposal; then-current NBPA executive director Billy Hunter stated, "Our position was it was a non-starter."[47] In general, the NBPA was content with many of the core provisions in the 2005 CBA. Conversely, the owners were pushing for some significant system changes to the 2005 CBA.

The NBPA eventually responded with a counter-proposal in July 2010. Little bargaining progress was made between players and team owners from July 2010 through December 2010. The owners and players fundamentally disagreed over league revenue figures as well as overall league financial viability. For example, before the start of the 2010–2011 NBA season, then-current NBA commissioner David Stern indicated that a reduction of at least $750 million in salaries was needed under a new CBA in order to ensure the continued financial health of all teams in the league. In December 2010, NBA spokesperson Mike Bass issued the following statement: "Our goal remains the same—a sustainable business model that encourages teams to make necessary investments and provides the opportunity for all 30 teams to compete for a championship."[48] In February 2011, Billy Hunter issued a statement on behalf of the NBPA, which in part claimed that, "There has been ongoing debate and disagreement regarding the numbers and we do not agree that the stated loss figures reflect an accurate portrayal of the financial health of the league."[49] Also, between November 2010 and February 2011, the NBPA systematically and strategically distributed a 56-page "Lockout Handbook" to all NBA players in which Billy Hunter wrote: "Prepare yourself financially. A lockout is very likely and you must be financially prepared to manage it. The revenue increases and unprecedented growth the league is experiencing has done nothing to assuage ownership's demand that we drastically reduce player salaries and benefits."[50]

With little progression evident at the negotiation table, the NBPA turned to the legal system in May 2011 by filing a complaint with the National Labor Relations Board (NLRB), alleging that the NBA was failing to negotiate in good faith. The NBPA accused the league of making "harsh, inflexible and grossly regressive takeaway demands," failing to "provide relevant financial information," "repeatedly threatening" to lock out the players, and "making demands and threats that are inherently destructive of the collective bargaining process."[51] In other words, the players felt as though the owners were "rigid and sought to unilaterally dictate their preferred terms rather than earnestly engage in collective bargaining negotiations."[52]

The NBA and the NBPA failed to reach agreement on a new CBA before the June 30, 2011 deadline. On June 30, 2011, Adam Silver (who, at that time, was deputy commissioner of the NBA), stated: "The expiring collective bargaining agreement created a broken system that produced huge financial losses for our teams ... We will continue to make every effort to reach a new agreement that is fair and in the best interests of our teams, our players, our fans, and our game."[53] The NBA announced that it was commencing a lockout of its players effective as of 12:01 a.m. on July 1, 2011. As explained in *Chapter 1*, locking out athletes is a strategy of exerting economic pressure on the players so that the league would have increased leverage in obtaining concessions from the NBPA during the negotiation process.[54] In the words of Professor Paul Staudohar, "A lockout can motivate the players to make concessions and often leads to a better deal for the owners."[55]

A little over a month later, on August 2, 2011, the NBA decided to file its own complaint with the National Labor Relations Board, claiming that the NBPA has failed to collectively bargain in good faith. The NBA also alleged that the NBPA had engaged in the "impermissible negotiating tactic" of threatening to decertify (or disclaim interest in) representing players and subsequently filing an antitrust lawsuit as a means to create leverage in the collective bargaining process.[56] Also on August 2, 2011, the NBA filed a lawsuit asking a federal court to rule that the league's lockout was protected by the non-statutory labor exemption and therefore did not violate antitrust laws.[57] More specifically, the NBA alleged the following in its class action complaint against the NBPA:

> In the course of the negotiations over a new collective bargaining agreement, the Union has threatened on more than two dozen occasions to abandon or renounce (to "disclaim interest" in) its role as the exclusive bargaining representative of NBA players. The Union has threatened to pursue this course not because it is defunct or otherwise incapable of representing NBA players for purposes of collective bargaining, and not because NBA players are dissatisfied with the representation they have been provided by the NBPA or no longer wish to engage in concerted activities in negotiating the terms and conditions of their employment. To the contrary, the NBPA's threatened "disclaimer" is nothing more than an impermissible

negotiating tactic, which the Union in turn believes would strengthen its position in negotiations over a renewed labor agreement.... The NBA also requests a declaration that the lockout is lawful and protected from antitrust attack by virtue of the non-statutory labor exemption. Because the NBPA's threatened disclaimer would not be a good faith, permanent relinquishment of the right to bargain with the NBA concerning the terms and conditions of the employment of NBA players and would not be effective as a matter of federal labor law, it has no effect on the continuing application and validity of the non-statutory labor exemption.... In virtually every collective bargaining negotiation since 1970, the players have commenced or have threatened to commence antitrust litigation as a tactic to pressure the NBA to accede to the Union's bargaining demands. Not one of these litigations proceeded to a final adjudication, or even to trial. Indeed, despite the NBPA's repeated invocation of the antitrust laws in an effort to gain leverage in bargaining, the ultimate resolution on each such occasion (i.e., in 1976, 1983, 1988, 1994, and 1999) has always been the same: a collectively bargained agreement between the NBA and the NBPA negotiated pursuant to federal labor law containing the very practices the NBPA had challenged as antitrust violations).[58]

Despite the ongoing litigation, the NBA and the NBPA continued to engage in collective bargaining sessions, including a meeting on October 4, 2011. A letter from then-current NBPA executive director Billy Hunter and then-current NBPA president Derek Fisher to all NBA players summarized the October 4, 2011 collective bargaining session, and in part provided the following updates on negotiations with the league:

> As you know, we have two main issues in this negotiation: the system and the split. On the system, we have fought to preserve our soft cap structure. After two years of hard cap proposals, the owners recently agreed to consider retaining a soft cap system. They have asked us to address their concerns that we (1) help to better match pay for performance and (2) improve competitive balance among the teams. We have discussed different ways to accomplish these objectives, and while we still maintain significant differences on these points, we believe that with some hard work and fresh thinking, our differences can be bridged.... Recognizing all the owners' arguments about the state of the business and the condition of the economy, in our view, the owners can and should share more of the record revenues our players generate. Reducing our share of BRI by 7 points to 50%—a level we have not received since the early 1990s—is simply not a fair split. We refused to back down. As we have done since the beginning, we again indicated a willingness to compromise, and asked the owners to do the same. They refused.... We will continue to review the numbers and assess the various proposals, but we will hold firm until we can get a fair deal. While this negotiation is far from over, we cannot now say when it will

resume again in earnest. For today, the players made a stand. It was the right stand to make for ourselves and for the generations of players to follow.[59]

Also, in early October 2011, a group of NBA agents wrote a letter to all players in the league. The letter included the following observations, guidance, suggestions and advice:

- The owners demand a long-term deal with the players but do not want to share in the tremendous growth and success of the league over the past six seasons;
- The NBA demands deep cuts and major "givebacks" that would negatively impact players' earning potential (players would compete against each other for shorter and smaller contracts);
- A reduction of the players' share of BRI to 52% would result in severe restrictions on free agency and the ability of players to obtain their true market value; and
- Players must demand that the NBPA submit any proposed agreement to a vote by all NBA players, and provide every player with a reasonable amount of time to review and consider the proposed deal.[60]

On October 10, 2011 the NBA canceled the first two weeks of the regular season.[61] Then-current NBA commissioner David Stern proclaimed, "It's not practical, possible or prudent to have a full season now. Billy Hunter said that he was not willing to go a penny below 52% [of BRI], that he had been getting many calls from agents. And he closed up his book and walked out of the room." When asked to predict what the league's next offer might entail, Stern responded that the league would need to "recalculate how bad the damage is" and that the next offer would "reflect the extraordinary losses that are starting to pile up." On the other hand, Billy Hunter asserted the owners had essentially issued an ultimatum: "It was '50–50, take it or leave it.' And we just said, 'Well, today we're leaving it, like we left it last week.' "[62]

On November 13, 2011 the NBA sent a memo to all players that included an overview of the NBA's revised proposal that purportedly contained several improvements for the players as compared with the team owner's previous proposal. The memo encouraged the players "to focus on the numerous compromises that were made to the NBA's initial bargaining positions in these negotiations, including our move away from a 'hard' salary cap, the withdrawal of our proposal to 'roll back' salaries in existing player contracts, our agreement to continue to allow players to negotiate fully guaranteed contracts, and our agreement to a 50/50 split of BRI."[63] The NBA memo also expressed the following general perspective and collective mindset of team owners: "While we understand fully that our proposal does not contain everything that the Players Association wanted in this negotiation, the same is true for the NBA. It is now time to conclude our bargaining and make an agreement that can stop the ongoing damage to both sides and the countless others that rely on our game for their livelihoods and enjoyment. We urge you to study our proposal carefully, and to accept it as a fair compromise of the issues between us."[64]

The following day, all players on the NBPA Executive Committee (along with Billy Hunter and Derek Fisher) distributed another letter to every NBA player that read in relevant part:

> For two and a half years and through more than 50 collective bargaining sessions, we sat at the table and attempted to negotiate a fair labor agreement with the owners ... with the issuance of yet another ultimatum—a take it or leave it final offer of a long-term agreement with unacceptable terms—Commissioner Stern and the owners left us with no other option. It has become clear to us that we have exhausted our rights under the labor laws and continuing in that forum (collective bargaining) would not be in the best interests of the players.[65]

The letter also indicated that the NBPA officially disclaimed its status as the NBA players' collective bargaining representative. The letter explained to players that, "With no labor union in place, it is our sincere hope that the NBA will immediately end its now illegal boycott and finally open the 2011–12 season. Individual teams are free to negotiate with free agents for your services. If the owners choose to continue their present course of action, it is our view that they subject themselves to significant antitrust liability."[66] In addition, the letter made clear that the players association: (1) would no longer be permitted to engage in collective bargaining with team owners; (2) could no longer assert labor law rights on behalf of players; (3) would be withdrawing the unfair labor practice charge with the National Labor Relations Board; (4) would no longer be able to file individual grievances on behalf of NBA players; and (5) would no longer be able to regulate sports agents who represent NBA players.

One day later, on November 15, 2011, a group of NBA players filed two separate yet similar class action lawsuits in federal courts in Minnesota and California, alleging that the NBA was in violation of antitrust laws because the league refused to allow players to work.[67] The complaints included the following major legal claims, allegations and assertions:

> On November 10, 2011, the NBA presented its final bargaining ultimatum, which, among other things, would have reduced the players' share of BRI from 57% to 50% and imposed a new set of restrictions on player competition that would have wiped out the competitive market for most NBA players. The NBA informed the NBPA that it was making this final "revised" offer for just a few days and that if the NBPA did not accept this offer by the following Monday or Tuesday, the offer would be withdrawn and replaced with an even more onerous offer that would reduce the players' share of BRI to 47% and impose what amounted to a hard salary cap. The NBA also indicated that its offers would continue to get worse as time went on. The NBA unequivocally stated that it would not entertain any counter-offer from the

NBPA to its final "take it or leave it" proposal. Instead, the NBA declared that further bargaining over these terms was at an end.... The NBA Defendants' anticompetitive agreements include a boycott that has eliminated competition in the free agent marketplace for players no longer under contract, as well as a boycott of rookie players seeking an NBA contract for the first time. The NBA Defendants have also conspired to refuse to deal with or to honor the contracts of players who have NBA contracts. The anticompetitive purpose of this group boycott is to coerce [NBA players] to succumb to a new anticompetitive system of player restraints which will, among other things, drastically reduce player compensation levels below those that would exist in a competitive market.... The NBA Defendants cannot defend their violations of the federal antitrust laws by hiding behind the non-statutory labor exemption to the antitrust laws. Under Supreme Court precedent and settled law in [the Eighth] Circuit, that exemption only conceivably applies as long as a collective bargaining relationship exists between the NBA Defendants and the players. Here, however, the collective bargaining process and relationship have completely broken down, and the NBA players have exercised their labor law right not to be in a union. Specifically, after more than two years of futile bargaining, and the refusal of the NBA to negotiate any further, the NBA players ended the role of the National Basketball Players Association as their collective bargaining representative and no longer have a collective bargaining relationship with the NBA Defendants. The consequence is that any labor exemption to the antitrust laws no longer applies.[68]

Commissioner Stern subsequently warned that, as a result of these antitrust lawsuits, "We're about to go into the nuclear winter of the NBA."[69] Commissioner Stern expressed additional thoughts on the NBPA antitrust lawsuits: "It's just a big charade. To do it now, the union is ratcheting up I guess to see if they can scare the NBA owners or something. That's not happening."[70]

Within two weeks of the players filing antitrust lawsuits, the NBA and its players had a tentative agreement in place on November 26, 2011. The NBA issued a "Summary of Principal Deal Terms" document, which detailed the key negotiated provisions (for example, BRI split, salary cap and luxury tax system, contract length, and salary and free agency rules).[71] On December 8, 2011— after a 161-day lockout that resulted in 16 lost games for each team during the 2011–2012 NBA regular season—the NBA announced that a new CBA had been officially approved and the NBA would begin the 2011–2012 regular season on Christmas Day (December 25, 2011).[72] Commissioner Stern explained, "I am pleased to announce that we have concluded the collective bargaining process and have reached an agreement that addresses many significant issues that were challenges to our league.... This collective bargaining agreement will help us move toward a better business model, a more competitive league and better alignment between compensation and performance."[73]

In the words of Professor William B. Gould IV, the NBPA lawsuits "seem to have moved the parties together ... [the lawsuits] most certainly called the

NBA's bluff, in that the league's regressive or inferior option was quickly forgotten."[74] Professor David Berri reiterated that the importance of filing the antitrust lawsuits "was not so much the likelihood the courts would side with the players. The key issue was that this move posed a serious threat to the owners' revenues" because any monetary damages awarded by a court based on federal antitrust violations are automatically tripled based on a federal statute called the Clayton Act of 1914—this financial reality is what functioned as a genuine revenue threat to the owners.[75] Professor Gabe Feldman shared a similar perspective on the strategy and impact of the NBPA antitrust lawsuits when he commented that, by resorting to litigation, the NBPA "suddenly had the threat of inflicting some (economic) pain on the owners. And that was enough to make the owners move off of some of their demands. The players weren't able to use the disclaimer as a sword to gain anything new from the owners, but they were able to use it as a shield to limit the damage—something they were struggling to do through continued collective bargaining."[76] The NBA and NBPA reached agreement on a new CBA before any of the ongoing lawsuits and NLRB disputes were resolved. As a result, numerous legal questions regarding the overall collective bargaining process were not decided by the NLRB or the courts.

The general term of the 2011 CBA was ten NBA seasons, from December 8, 2011 through June 30, 2021.[77] However, the NBA and the NBPA each had options to terminate the agreement effective as of June 30, 2017 following the sixth season of the 2011 CBA. The NBA and the NBPA would need to exercise the termination option on or before December 15, 2016.[78] A few years into the 2011 CBA, indications already began to surface that NBA players were expected to opt out of the 2011 CBA prior to the December 15, 2016 deadline. NBA owners also possessed the ability to opt out of the 2011 CBA regardless of any decision made by NBA players.[79]

As explained in more detail later in this chapter, team owners and NBA players actually reached a tentative agreement on a new 2017 CBA on December 14, 2016—one day prior to the deadline for the league or players to opt out of the 2011 CBA. On December 14, 2016, the NBA issued a press release that read as follows: "The NBA and NBPA have reached a tentative agreement on a new collective bargaining agreement, pending ratification by players and team owners. In order to give both sides enough time to review the terms of the agreement and vote to ratify, the parties have agreed to extend the mutual deadline to opt out of the existing CBA from December 15, 2016, to January 13, 2017."[80]

Key business and system issues during the 2010–2011 collective bargaining process

The following examples provide a representative overview of some of the principal deal terms that were negotiated and incorporated into the 2011 NBA collective bargaining agreement, which resulted from the extensive and intensive bargaining and legal processes that eventually led to the league and players agreeing on a new 2011 CBA.[81]

Basketball Related Income (BRI)

The split of revenue between team owners and players may have been the most significant (and contentious) issue during the negotiation process to finalize the 2011 CBA.[82] NBA players were guaranteed 57% of BRI in salaries and benefits under the 2005 CBA.[83] NBA team owners wanted to substantially reduce players' share of BRI in the 2011 CBA. In June 2011, the NBPA countered the NBA owners' offer by proposing to reduce players' share of BRI to 52.4% during the first year of the CBA and then gradually increasing that percentage over the course of a six-year deal to 54%—resulting in an average of 53%.[84] The NBPA alleged that NBA owners insisted on reducing the players' share of BRI to an average of 46–47%. For instance, in October 2011, NBPA leaders sent a letter to all NBA players that claimed NBA owners "had stood on an offer averaging 46% of BRI, rolling back this year's salaries and benefits to $2 billion flat and growing very slowly over ten years ... [the owners eventually offered] an increase of just over one point—to an average of 47%. They characterized the proposal as a 50–50 split, but with a new $350 million expense deduction, their offer would actually result in the players receiving only 47% of current BRI."[85]

In November 2011, Commissioner Stern sent a memo to NBA players explaining that under the NBA's proposal the players would be guaranteed to receive 50% of BRI.[86] The players and owners eventually agreed that, for the 2011–2012 NBA season, players would receive 51.15% of BRI.[87] For all subsequent seasons under the 2011 CBA, players would receive salaries and benefits equal to 50% of BRI (subject to a few exceptions and adjustments that could either increase players' split of BRI to a maximum of 51% or decrease players' share of BRI to a minimum of 49%).[88] The decrease in players' share of BRI from 57% under the 2005 CBA to approximately 50% under the 2011 CBA resulted in an estimated annual revenue shift of between $225 million to $300 million from players to team owners.[89]

Salary cap and luxury tax

The salary cap for the 2011–2012 NBA season was set at $58.044 million, which was equal to the salary cap for the prior NBA season (2010–2011) based on the terms of the 2005 CBA.[90] Under the 2005 CBA, teams were only required to spend at least 75% of the salary cap on player salaries.[91] The 2011 CBA required teams to spend at least 85% of the salary cap during the first two years of the CBA and a minimum of 90% of the salary cap amount for all future seasons during which the 2011 CBA was in effect.[92]

NBA owners initially proposed a hard salary cap, which would not allow teams to exceed a specific payroll (i.e., salary cap) threshold. The owners eventually backed off from this stance and agreed to maintain the existent soft cap system. As explained by NBPA representatives, "After two years of hard cap proposals, the owners recently agreed to consider retaining a soft cap system.

They have asked us to address their concerns that we help to better match pay for performance and improve competitive balance among the teams."[93]

Owners nonetheless insisted on a "harder cap" that would modify existing salary cap exceptions while also eliminating other exceptions.[94] For example, owners and players agreed to revise the Mid-Level Salary Exception, which resulted in modifications to contract length and allowable salaries. Under the 2005 CBA, the Mid-Level Salary Exception allowed teams to sign players to five-year contracts starting at 108% of the average NBA player salary with 8% annual increases permitted.[95] The 2011 CBA contains different Mid-Level Salary Exceptions based on a team's payroll. For instance, under the 2011 CBA, for non-taxpaying teams (i.e., teams that do not exceed a specified team payroll of $4 million more than the luxury tax threshold), the Non-Taxpayer Mid-Level Salary Exception allows teams to sign a player for a contract of up to four years in length, with a starting salary of $5 million in 2011–2012 and with 3% annual raises permitted after the 2012–2013 NBA season.[96] For tax-paying teams (i.e., teams that exceed the specified luxury tax threshold for an NBA season), the Taxpayer Mid-Level Salary Exception in the 2011 CBA allows teams to sign a player for a contract of up to three years, with a starting salary of $3 million and with 3% annual increases permitted.[97] The 2011 CBA also contains a third exception, the Mid-Level Exception for Room Teams. This exception allows teams that have not exceeded the salary cap to sign a player to a contract of up to two years in length with a starting salary of $2.5 million and 3% annual increases.[98]

To increase competitive balance, NBA owners also proposed modifications to the luxury tax system.[99] NBA players conceded on this issue. The 2005 CBA required teams who exceeded the luxury tax threshold to pay $1 to the league for every dollar the team's payroll exceeded the luxury tax threshold; this money was the primary source of funding for the league's revenue sharing system.[100] The 2011 CBA provided that this dollar-for-dollar luxury tax penalty would remain consistent for the first two seasons of the 2011 CBA. However, beginning in the third season (2013–2014), a progressive luxury tax system would apply in which the tax rate increases for every $5 million that a team exceeds the tax level. For instance, the tax rate is $1.50-for-$1 if a team exceeds the tax level but is less than $5 million above the level. The tax rate is $2.50-for-$1 for teams that exceed the tax level by at least $10 million but by less than $15 million. And, the tax rate is $3.75-for-$1 if a team exceeds the tax level by at least $20 million but by less than $25 million.[101] In addition, the 2011 CBA provides for even more punitive financial penalties if teams exceed the luxury tax threshold in at least four out of any five seasons.[102] The overall goal of this new luxury tax system is to deter teams from spending significantly above the luxury tax threshold in order to decrease the financial disparity between big market and small market teams.[103] The NBA is permitted to dis-tribute up to 50% of the proceeds from the luxury tax system to teams that do not exceed the luxury tax threshold as one component of the league's current revenue sharing plan.[104]

Player contracts: guaranteed contracts, contract length, annual salary increases and qualifying offers

The NBA owners initially proposed eliminating guaranteed contracts.[105] NBA players understandably pushed back on this issue. Team owners and players eventually agreed that salary guarantees would remain the same as under the 2005 CBA (i.e., the industry standard is that all player salaries are 100% guaranteed unless otherwise agreed to by a team and player). While owners conceded on the contract guarantee issue, players conceded on several other items related to maximum contract lengths and annual increases for rookie contract extensions as well as veteran contract extensions.

For example, based on the 2005 CBA, teams were allowed to offer six-year contracts with 10.5% annual increases in order to retain a free agent who played at least the prior three seasons with that team (i.e., a "Bird player"); the Larry Bird Exception is also known as the "Veteran Free Agent Exception," which allows the incumbent team to offer a higher salary amount and a longer salary length as compared with a new team.[106] In addition, based on the 2005 CBA, teams could offer five-year contracts with 8% annual increases to free agents who played for a different team the preceding season.[107] The 2011 CBA reduced allowed contract lengths and decreased permitted annual percentage raises. For instance, the maximum contract length allowed for Bird players under the 2011 CBA got reduced to five years (as compared with six years in the 2005 CBA) and maximum allowable annual increases decreased to 7.5% under the 2011 CBA (as compared with 10.5% in the 2005 CBA). In addition, for other free agents the maximum contract length allowed was lessened to four years (as compared with five years in the 2005 CBA) and maximum annual increases were likewise reduced to 4.5% (as compared with 8% in the 2005 CBA).[108]

Players and team owners also negotiated and agreed to several additional provisions related to player contracts and player mobility (i.e., free agency). For example, the 2011 CBA contains an "amnesty provision" that allows each team to waive one player that was under contract when the CBA was entered into in December 2011. The team would still be required to pay the player but that player's salary would not count for salary cap purposes.[109] In addition, the 2011 CBA included a new provision indicating that qualifying offers would be based in part on past player performance. This was a notable change from the qualifying offer model in the 2005 CBA. For example, based on the new qualifying offer formula in the 2011 CBA, if a player originally picked 10th to 30th in the first round of the NBA draft meets one of the following two "starter criteria," then the player's qualifying offer amount would be equal to the qualifying offer for the 9th overall draft pick in that same draft year: (1) the player started an average of 41 regular season games or played an average of 2,000 regular season minutes during third and fourth seasons of his rookie scale contract combined; or (2) the player started at least 41 regular season games or played at least 2,000 minutes during the fourth season of his rookie scale contract. In addition, if a player picked 1st to 14th in the first round failed to meet the starter criteria, then the player's qualifying offer amount would be equal to the qualifying offer for the 15th overall draft pick in the player's original draft year.[110] This new qualifying offer model in the 2011 CBA attempted to address the issue that a player's market value (and corresponding salary) during his fifth year in the league should not be determined solely by when that player was drafted four years prior.

Similarly, players and team owners also agreed to shorten the period that a player's team has to match an offer sheet extended to a restricted free agent from a period of seven days under the 2005 CBA to three days under the 2011 CBA.[111] This change was intended to address the issue of teams demonstrating reluctance to extend offer sheets to restricted free agents because the amount of that offer was "on the books" for salary cap purposes for seven days under the 2005 CBA.[112]

Reviewing and summarizing the principal deal terms in the 2011 CBA

The NBA and NBPA agreed to the following principal deal terms as part of the 2011 CBA:

- *Basketball Related Income (BRI)*: NBA players and team owners agreed to a 50/50 split of BRI each season (subject to various exceptions and adjustments)
  - Players receive a greater share of BRI to the extent BRI exceeds projections, and a smaller share of BRI to the extent BRI falls short of projections
  - Resultant overall share of BRI for players each season must equal no less than 49% and no greater than 51% (if for any season aggregate player salaries and benefits fall short of the agreed-upon share of BRI, the difference would be paid by the NBA to the NBPA for distribution to all players who were on a team roster in that season on a proportional basis as reasonably determined by the NBPA)

- *Salary Cap and Tax System*: Continued existence of a soft salary cap combined with a revamped and more punitive luxury tax model
  - Salary cap for first season of CBA (2011–2012) equal to approximately $58 million
  - Continuation of salary cap exceptions from 2005 CBA with creation of three different mid-level exceptions to replace the single mid-level exception contained within the 2005 CBA—each team's payroll determines which mid-level exception is applicable (salary cap room, non-taxpayer or taxpayer exceptions)
  - Minimum team salary floor requirement equal to 85% of salary cap for first two years of CBA with eventual increase to 90% of salary cap starting with year three (2013–2014 season)[113]
  - Luxury tax rate of $1 for every $1 in salary over the tax level during first two seasons under 2011 CBA; beginning with the third season

(2013–2014), luxury tax rates for incremental spending above the tax level scheduled to increase as follows:
- ○ $0–5 million over luxury tax level: $1.50 for $1
- ○ $5–10 million over luxury tax level: $1.75 for $1
- ○ $10–15 million over luxury tax level: $2.50 for $1
- ○ $15–20 million over luxury tax level: $3.25 for $1
- ○ Rates increase by $0.50 for each additional $5 million above luxury tax level
- • For the first five years of the 2011 CBA (2011–2012 through 2015–2016), each team was permitted to waive one of its player contracts that was in effect prior to the 2011–2012 season and have 100% of the player's salary removed from the team's salary for salary cap and luxury tax calculation purposes (each team could only utilize this amnesty provision one time on a player already on the team's roster as of July 1, 2011)

- • *Player contracts and compensation*:
  - • Reduction by one year in maximum length of a player contract in specific situations; for example, maximum contract length of five years (instead of six years under the 2005 CBA) for a team's own players who become free agents, and maximum contract length of four years (instead of five years under the 2005 CBA) for free agents who played on another team during the prior season
  - • Salaries in new player contracts permitted to increase by up to 7.5% per year for a team's own players (as compared with 10.5% under the 2005 CBA) and 4.5% per year for free agents who played on another team during the prior season (as compared with 8% under the 2005 CBA)
  - • Maximum of four new years for rookie extensions (except maximum of five years for "designated player rookie extension" with salary ranging from 25–30% of salary cap—dependent upon certain performance criteria being met—with 8% annual salary increases); for example, any player in his fifth season (e.g., following his rookie scale contract) would be eligible to receive from his own team a maximum salary contract that provides for a starting salary of up to 30% of the salary cap if one of the following occur: (1) named to the All-NBA first, second, or third team two times; (2) voted in as an All-Star starter two times; or (3) named NBA MVP one time
  - • Escrow withholding of 10% from each player paycheck to account for potential situation in which BRI metrics fall far short of projections and therefore player share of BRI would exceed the 51% threshold (if players earned more than they were guaranteed based on CBA terms related to the BRI split between team owners and players, then the amount of the overage would be disbursed from the escrow account to NBA teams; conversely, in the event of a shortfall in which BRI is much higher than projected, some or all of the money

held in escrow—potentially also including additional disbursements from the league—would be distributed back to the players in order to ensure that the player share of BRI would be at least 49%)[114]

The above examples are intended to provide a general overview of some of the key business issues that were negotiated and ultimately resolved in 2010–2011.[115] Agreeing on the above deal terms took immense amounts of time and energy, and reaching a finalized agreement was not without numerous business, legal and logistical challenges. According to Professor Gabe Feldman, the collective bargaining process in 2010 and 2011 "was never a question of who would win. We knew it would be the owners—the only question was by how much."[116] Professor Feldman also expressed the viewpoint that, after the team owners sent the NBPA a very aggressive initial proposal, the "players were really just fighting to stop the owners from getting everything [the owners] asked for."[117] Another sports business scholar who evaluated the results of the 2011 collective bargaining process wrote, "If you were an owner and you were interested in capturing more revenue, than this agreement clearly works. In other words, the players clearly lost."[118] Professor Matthew Parlow similarly noted that "emotions, rather than economics, propelled players to make financially irrational decisions during negotiations … when one considers the four major deal points, the players made key concessions, the magnitude of which can be aptly described as ranging from significant (for the salary cap modifications), to substantial (for the changes in contract terms), to massive (for the reduction in BRI for the players)."[119]

Collective bargaining should focus on "win/win" (and "assist/assist") solutions instead of creating an apparent winner and loser. The collective bargaining process outside of professional sports typically has been far less adversarial.[120] Nevertheless, there is certainly no easy or simple solution "when it comes to managing the shared and competing concerns affected by the economic regulatory mechanisms employed in professional team sports leagues."[121]

Preparing for another round of collective bargaining after expiration of the 2011 CBA: examining the strategic actions of players, the NBPA, sports agents, team owners and the NBA league commissioner in 2014 and 2015

In early 2014, league players as well as NBA team owners and the league commissioner started the strategic planning process related to the possibility of either the players or the owners exercising the right to opt out of the 2011 CBA prior to the December 15, 2016 deadline. However, in early 2014, neither the players nor the league wanted to conclusively state whether the NBPA or team owners definitively planned to opt out of the 2011 CBA. For example, in April 2014, Ron Klempner—then-acting executive director of the NBPA—explained that the players association "negotiated for the right to opt out of the CBA, and just as the owners will do, the players will consider [all] options at the appropriate time.

It's way too early to commit to any decision one way or the other."[122] NBA commissioner Adam Silver responded that league owners will "always be prepared, but I have no expectation that [the players are] going to opt out. I mean, we haven't had any discussions whatsoever about that possibility."[123]

Nonetheless, both the NBPA and league owners made business decisions throughout 2014 and 2015 knowing it was possible that games might eventually be canceled during the 2017–2018 NBA season due to a labor dispute that would result in a lockout (work stoppage). During a lockout, NBA players would not receive salary compensation (including team-funded healthcare benefits) and would not be allowed to use team facilities for training or any other purpose; in addition, teams would not be allowed to negotiate player contracts or conduct any practices or similar basketball-related training sessions with players.[124] In mid-2014, the NBPA advised players to accept paychecks over an 18-month period for the 2016–2017 NBA season instead of the standard 12-month period as one mechanism to help players prepare financially for a potential work stoppage during the 2017–2018 NBA season.[125] Also, team owners entered into agreements with media rights partners in which rights fee payments from the networks to the NBA would still be made in the event of a work stoppage. Ron Klempner claimed: "As we have learned in the past, the owners have made provisions with the TV networks to continue to receive rights fees throughout a work stoppage, and there is no reason the players should not make every effort to take the same precaution.... Every chance the owners have had they've opted out of an agreement. We can't control what they're going to do. All we are going to do is prepare ourselves."[126]

NBA owners and NBPA leaders were also carefully scrutinizing the existing 2011 CBA and beginning to identify specific terms and provisions each group thought should perhaps be added, eliminated and/or revised in a new CBA as part of the overall negotiation preparation process. For example, in April 2014, league owners met to discuss the effectiveness of the 2011 CBA. NBA commissioner Adam Silver said, "We presented sort of the facts as we know them so far under this agreement. Is [the CBA] working in ways we predicted, here are things that we would not have predicted under the agreement, here is the amount of free agency movement we're seeing, here is how it's working economically for the league. And I would assume the union at some point will do those same things."[127] In July 2014, newly elected NBPA executive director Michele Roberts commented, "As far as I'm concerned, preparations for CBA negotiations started yesterday. It's at the top of my list of things that I've been instructed to begin the process of preparing for, and sure it is a lot to do, but I've never been shy about hard work and long hours, so we'll get it done. We'll be ready."[128]

Commissioner Silver served as the principal negotiator for the NBA during the collective bargaining process with the NBPA throughout 2010 and 2011.[129] On the other hand, Michele Roberts, a former public defender, trial lawyer and corporate attorney with little prior sports business or collective bargaining experience, immediately became responsible for "controlling the narrative"[130] as well as building consensus and creating common objectives among all NBA players as soon as she was elected as the executive director of the NBPA in July 2014.[131] Roberts' initial focus was to "rally the troops, restore their confidence in collective bargaining, [and] instill some credibility in terms of her own leadership."[132] Roberts would play a central role in the negotiation process as well as in the potential litigation process should the NBA and NBPA reach another actual (or alleged) impasse in collective bargaining.[133]

One NBA player agent was of the view that Roberts was "itching for a fight," and another prominent player agent commented that the NBPA needed "a skilled, innovative, experienced businessperson at the top of the chain ... [Otherwise] there will be a lockout and the players will suffer."[134] Based on Roberts' legal background as a trial lawyer, her preferred initial forum for reaching consensus could have plausibly been in the courtroom instead of at the negotiating table. A separate NBA player agent commented, "If there's a lockout, I would bet you she would decertify the next day and get it into a courtroom. She's a trial lawyer, that's her strength ... Hunter occasionally offered [the decertification] threat, but was never really on board with decertification. Roberts, though, comes to the NBPA with a reputation as one of the nation's strongest trial lawyers."[135]

During an October 2014 press conference that followed an NBA Board of Governors meeting in New York, Commissioner Silver downplayed any possible level of concern about a potential work stoppage in the NBA during the 2017–2018 NBA season: "I've said previously, we didn't get everything we wanted in the last collective bargaining cycle.... It's premature even for me to be concerned. We negotiated a 10-year collective bargaining agreement, there is a six-year out for either side. We are going into year four. We have, in my mind, something that is incredibly positive and that is two new great media deals. Fifty-one percent of that money goes to the players."[136] In November 2014, NBPA executive director Michele Roberts responded: "I'll give the league credit. They have done a great job controlling the narrative."[137] Roger Mason Jr., then-current NBPA director of player relations, similarly commented that, "No player, no fan, and even the union, we don't want a lockout, we don't want a strike. But, at the same time, sometimes the cost of doing business is standing firm on what you believe in. And I think us, as players, we believe in the fact that we work really hard. We're all very fortunate to even be in a position to make this kind of money."[138]

In an interview on *ESPN Outside the Lines* in December 2014, ESPN reporter and journalist Andy Katz asked Commissioner Silver to comment on the threat of the NBPA opting out of the 2011 CBA. Commissioner Silver responded:

> I take everything that Michele Roberts says very seriously.... It's something our owners and teams will study as we get closer to the six-year mark, how the agreement works for us—and obviously they are studying it from their standpoint. But, my sense is the league is going really well right now and I think we have a very fair system. But, they are our partners. And to the extent they think it is unfair and we need to then get together and reexamine it, we will. They have the right to do that and we have the obligation to respond.[139]

Commissioner Silver also made comments during this same interview that indicated NBA owners were perhaps less likely than NBA players to opt out of the 2011 CBA. When asked to identify the right BRI percentage split between owners and players, Commissioner Silver said, "I think the right split is the split that we negotiated with our players in the last collective bargaining agreement, and that's a split that is a sliding scale between 49–51%.... At the time the new television money comes in in the 2016–2017 season the players will be receiving 51% of something that looks very much like the gross revenue that comes into the league. So, that strikes me as very fair."[140] Commissioner Silver also explained that, "It's too early to talk about collective bargaining. When the time comes to negotiate a new collective bargaining agreement, the facts regarding our finances will speak for themselves ... obviously, we don't agree on every issue, but we have a strong relationship based on mutual respect and our joint interest in the success of the league and game."[141]

Commissioner Silver was being both honest and strategic. As discussed earlier in this chapter, the owners were able to convince players to compromise on a number of significant system issues during the collective bargaining process in 2010 and 2011, including a significant reduction in players' share of BRI (from 57% to between 49–51%). Overall, the BRI formula/system seemed to be working well for NBA owners throughout the 2014–2015 NBA season. Therefore, owners might not have seen much upside to opting out of an agreement that contained many owner-friendly provisions. In addition, even if the owners viewed opting out of the 2011 CBA by December 2016 as the best approach, from a media coverage and public perception perspective the owners likely preferred that it be the players who would decide to opt out.[142] This strategy would have allowed the owners to frame any potential work stoppage as the result of unreasonable player demands instead of owner decisions. During a November 2014 interview, Michele Roberts commented, "To the extent that there's going to be any pressure on the players to accept some proposal from the owners, that pressure will come from fans, and it will come from fans if they have an image of the players as greedy and unappreciative."[143]

One specific proposal made by league management in late 2014 related to "smoothing" salary cap increases. The new combined nine-year, $24 billion leaguewide media rights deals with Turner Broadcasting and ESPN were scheduled to start during the 2016–2017 NBA season. As a result, the NBA salary cap was projected to exponentially increase from $70 million during the 2015–2016 season to more than $94 million during the 2016–2017 season. The NBA proposed a gradual increase in the salary cap over a period of several years in order to avoid such a massive jump in the salary cap for the 2016–2017 season. The NBA proposed artificially reducing the salary cap figure for the 2016–2017 season to around $78 million. Instead of a sudden rise in the salary cap, the league offered to provide players with a lump-sum check to split that would account for the proposed artificially depressed salary cap in 2016–2017.[144]

The NBPA refused to agree to this proposal. Michele Roberts indicated that she was "suspicious of any proposal where the model is based upon artificial decreases of the compensation that an individual player can negotiate." Roberts also commented that, "Historically, when salary has gone up for some, it has gone up for all. If you're not a free agent now, you may be one next year when the salary cap remains high. I have significant concerns over this."[145] In March 2015, the NBA issued the following statement regarding the salary cap smoothing concept proposal:

> The National Basketball Players Association has informed the NBA that it will not agree to "smoothing" in the increases in the Salary Cap that will result from the new national media agreements beginning in the 2016–17 season. Smoothing would have avoided a substantial salary cap spike in 2016–17. Under the league's smoothing approach, the salary shortfall resulting from more gradual cap increases would have been paid directly to the Players Association for distribution to all players, and thus the total compensation paid to players in any given season would not have been impacted.[146]

Differences in player perceptions and league management viewpoints related to the overall financial health of the NBA also continued throughout much of 2015. For instance, when Commissioner Silver was asked about team profitability in July 2015, he remarked:

> I don't know the precise number and don't want to get into it, but a significant number of teams are continuing to lose money and they continue to lose money because their expenses exceed their revenue. Teams are spending enormous amounts of money on payroll.... They still have enormous expenses in terms of arena costs. Teams are building new practice facilities. The cost of their infrastructure in terms of their sales people, marketing people, the infrastructure of the teams have gone up, and in some cases their local television is much smaller than in other markets.[147]

Two days later, NBPA executive director Michele Roberts responded with the following statement:

> All of the data we have access to indicates that our business is thriving and will continue to do so in the near future. We agreed not to debate some of the finer points of negotiation in public, and aren't going to change that approach now in response to some remarks from the Commissioner.... We are, however, going to take him up on his offer to share the audited financials with the union. We also want to ensure that everyone understands the facts of this business. Under the CBA, we do not have a gross compensation system. The players' 50% share is calculated net of a substantial amount of expenses and deductions. New and renovated arenas around the league have proven to be revenue drivers, profit centers, and franchise valuation boosters.... Virtually every business metric demonstrates that our business is healthy. Gate receipts, merchandise sales and TV ratings are all at an

all-time high. Franchise values have risen exponentially in recent years, and the NBA has enjoyed high single digit revenue growth since 2010–11.[148]

Nonetheless, in July 2015, during the annual NBA Board of Governors meeting, Commissioner Silver reiterated that, "It's clear that the goal is to avoid any type of work stoppage whatsoever."[149]

Anticipated key business and system issues for a successor CBA— examining the NBA economic and collective bargaining landscape in 2014 and 2015

Similar to the 2010–2011 collective bargaining process, throughout 2014 and 2015 both players and team owners attempted to shape the narrative (i.e., media reports and public perception) and create negotiation leverage related to the collective bargaining process. In addition, the league and its players began to develop priorities and strategic approaches for the impending collective bargaining sessions that were anticipated to commence sometime in late 2015 or early 2016. The league and its players were expected to primarily focus on the following items and areas during bargaining sessions for what ultimately ended up materializing into the 2017 NBA collective bargaining agreement.

Basketball Related Income (BRI)

Similar to collective bargaining related negotiations in 2010–2011, team owners were once again expected to initially push for a reduction in the percentage of BRI that players receive as well as a modification to the formula for determining BRI. Remember that in 2010–2011, the owners' initial proposal set players' share of BRI at 46–47%. Therefore, owners were forecasted to potentially demand that specific revenue streams be excluded from the BRI formula in order to reduce the total amount of money that NBA owners are required to share with players (even if the technical BRI share for players remained the same 49–51% range as in the 2011 CBA). NBA owners were also expected to request a modification to Article VII, Section 12(b)(3) of the 2011 CBA, which provided that the players designated share would increase by 60.5% of the difference between actual BRI and projected BRI in years where actual BRI exceeds forecasted BRI. This provision provided significant upside to players in years where actual BRI greatly exceeds forecasted BRI. The players' designated share of BRI could not exceed 51% of BRI under the 2011 CBA.

On the other side, it seemed probable that the NBPA would seek to increase players' share of BRI—which fluctuated between 49–51% each season under the 2011 CBA. In November 2014, Michele Roberts said the following about the BRI split: "Why don't we have the owners play half the games. There would be no money if not for the players … I know that as a result of the last CBA, at least $1.3 billion in revenue that would have otherwise been on the players' side is now on the owners' side. I see the valuations of these teams going through the roof.... How much more do you need to make money?"[150] Roberts reiterated that it is the responsibility of the NBPA "to ensure that the players receive their fair share of the results of their efforts."[151] NBA superstar LeBron James similarly quipped: "The whole thing that went on with the [2011 CBA] negotiation process was that the owners were telling us that they were losing money. There is no way they can sit in front of us and tell us that right now."[152]

Salary cap

NBA owners were projected to make another push to implement a harder salary cap with fewer exceptions than in the salary cap system embedded within the 2011 CBA. For example, in October 2014, Commissioner Silver opined that his "preference would be to have a harder cap, where teams couldn't elect to spend so much more than other teams.... There are gradations of hardness in terms of the cap as well. I wish our current cap system was harder. It's what we proposed last time around, but we compromised."[153] Michele Roberts did not appear to be a proponent of a salary cap altogether. In November 2014, Roberts stated, "I don't know of any space other than the world of sports where there's this notion that we will artificially deflate what someone's able to make, just because. It's incredibly un-American. My DNA is offended by it."[154] Commissioner Silver immediately responded to Roberts' comments with a statement that in part provided that there is nothing "unusual or 'un-American' in a unionized industry to have a collective system for paying employees—in fact, that is the norm.... The salary cap system, which splits revenues between team owners and players and has been agreed upon by the NBA and the Players Association since 1982, has served as a foundation for the growth of the league and has enabled NBA players to become the highest-paid professional athletes in the world."[155]

Player contracts: contract length, salary amount and guaranteed salaries

It was also foreseeable that team owners could once again push for reductions in contract length and allowable salary amounts. The NBPA was also expected to want to revise rules related to rookie scale salaries and maximum player contracts. In November 2014, Michele Roberts offered her view on maximum contracts: "I can't understand why the [players association] would be interested in suppressing salaries at the top if we know that as salaries at the top have grown, so have salaries at the bottom. If that's the case, I contend that there is no reason in the world why the union should embrace salary caps or any effort to place a barrier on the amount of money that marquee players can make."[156]

Free agency system and qualifying offers

The NBPA could have also potentially decided to advocate for changes to the NBA's restricted free agency system and qualifying offer rules. The 2011 CBA rules pertaining to restricted free agency gave a player's prior team a significant advantage in being able to retain the player's services under a new contract. More specifically, any first round pick completing the fourth season of his rookie scale contract (which is for two guaranteed years with two additional team option years), and any veteran free agent with three or fewer years of service entering the off-season, would be a restricted free agent if his prior team makes a qualifying offer to the player at any time from the day following the season (e.g., in mid-June after the NBA Finals) through June 30. If such a qualifying offer was made, then, on July 1, the player would become a restricted free agent, which would mean the prior team has a right of first refusal to match any offer sheet that the player signs with another team.[157] It was projected that the NBPA might decide to attempt to shift the leverage from team to player during the restricted free agency process.

In addition, it was expected that the NBPA might decide to eventually demand a change to the qualifying offer system—a seldom used and imbalanced one-year contract model that usually does not produce fair and mutually beneficial results for teams and players.[158] Under the 2011 CBA, when a team extended a qualifying offer to a player, that player automatically became a restricted free agent.[159] A player who received a qualifying offer would then be given until at least October 1 (i.e., usually a few days before training camp) to accept the offer. If a qualifying offer was neither withdrawn nor accepted and the deadline for accepting it passes, the team's right of first refusal continued, but the player would no longer have the option of signing the one-year qualifying offer and the current team could either offer a minimum salary contract or wait until the player signs an offer sheet with another team and determine whether to match the offer.[160]

Franchise player designation system (franchise tag)

At one point during the negotiation process for the 2011 CBA, team owners proposed adding a new element to the then-current free agency rules—a "franchise player designation."[161] A franchise tag would have allowed each NBA team to designate one player (who would otherwise have been a free agent) as a "franchise player" each season. That player would only be allowed to sign a contract with his incumbent (prior) team. The primary purposes of a franchise tag system are to reduce the probability of a team losing its best player(s) in free agency as well as increase the likelihood that teams are able to retain their key players for the maximum number of years possible. The ideal outcome is that a player and his prior team agree to a long-term contract extension to avoid application of the franchise player designation altogether.

The NBA owners proposed a variation of the National Football League's (NFL) franchise tag. Unlike the franchise tag system in the NFL, the model proposed by NBA owners would have required a player's consent to being "franchise-tagged." In addition, the "tagged" players would have also received contract sweeteners that "untagged" players would not be eligible to receive (for example, longer contract length, higher overall salary and more guaranteed money). The primary objective of the proposed franchise tag was to improve the ability of teams to keep star players by increasing "the gap between what teams can offer a 'designated player' and what non-designated players can get on the open market." However, by the time the CBA was finalized in December 2011, players and the league failed to agree on the issue of integrating a franchise tag provision into the 2011 CBA. The franchise tag concept/system was also anticipated to be a potential negotiation priority for team owners during the next round of formal collective bargaining from 2015 through 2016.

Minimum age requirement to enter NBA draft

In a December 2014 interview with *GQ Magazine*, Commissioner Silver was asked the following question: "If you could instantly change anything about the NBA, without having to negotiate the terms or compromise your position, what change would you make?" Silver explained that the first thing he would do is create a harder salary cap. The second item he wanted to change was raise the minimum age required to enter the NBA draft from 19 to 20 years of age. Silver explained that the NBA "bargained with the union many years ago in order to move it from 18 to 19. Going to 20 was on the table during the last bargaining cycle [in 2011], but it was an issue we parked, having already lost several weeks of the season [due to the lockout], and we were anxious to get the season going. But it's something I hope to address in the near future."[162] Commissioner Silver also commented that the NBPA's "principal argument is that it's a restriction on players. And as a philosophical argument, I totally understand that. Of course it's a restriction, in the same way a draft is a restriction. But our view is that it would make for a better league. You'd have more skilled players, more mature players. The draft would be better. It would be better for basketball in general. Strong college basketball is great for the NBA."[163]

Understandably, Michele Roberts had a different perspective than Commissioner Silver on the age limit issue. In November 2014, Roberts countered Silver with the following viewpoint: "It doesn't make sense to me that you're suddenly eligible and ready to make money when you're 20, but not when you're 19, not when you're 18. I suspect that the players association will agree that this is not going to be one that they will agree to easily."[164]

Player conduct: league domestic violence policy and commissioner authority

As of late 2014, the NBA planned to "take a fresh look" at its domestic violence policies and procedures (for example, by creating programs to further educate players on domestic violence issues) in wake of widespread criticism of the NFL for the league's handling of recent domestic violence situations. Commissioner Silver explained the NBA learns "from other leagues' experiences. We're studying everything that's been happening in the NFL. We're working with our players association.... We have in place the appropriate mechanisms for discipline, although we'll take a fresh look at those as well. But most importantly, it's education, and it's not just the players, but it's the players' families. That's what we are learning, too."[165]

During the 2014–2015 NBA season, the 2011 CBA stipulated a minimum ten-game suspension for any player convicted of a violent felony.[166] NBA team owners (and Commissioner Silver) appeared to have an interest in revising this CBA provision so that domestic violence that does not rise to a felony conviction is still punishable (e.g., minimum ten-game suspension) and so that Commissioner Silver would also possess more flexibility in general to fine and suspend players for this type of egregious misconduct.

For example, in November 2014, Commissioner Silver suspended Charlotte Hornets' player Jeffery Taylor for 24 games after Taylor plead guilty to misdemeanor domestic violence assault and malicious destruction of hotel property. In issuing the suspension, Commissioner Silver proclaimed:

> Mr. Taylor's conduct violates applicable law and, in my opinion, does not conform to standards of morality and is prejudicial and detrimental to the NBA.... While the suspension is significantly longer than prior suspensions for incidents of domestic violence by NBA players, it is appropriate in light of Mr. Taylor's conduct, the need to deter similar conduct going forward, and the evolving social consensus—with which we fully concur—that professional sports leagues like the NBA must respond to such incidents in a more rigorous way.[167]

Following the announcement of this suspension, Michele Roberts wrote a memo to all players that in part read:

> The CBA contemplates a minimum 10-game suspension in any case involving a conviction for a violent felony, including domestic violence.... In contrast, Jeff Taylor was charged with a misdemeanor that is likely to be dismissed at the end of a probationary period. The 24-game suspension is one of the longest in the history of the league.... We have a scheme of discipline that was the result of collective bargaining between the parties that has been applied consistently over the years. While we appreciate the sensitivity of this societal issue, the commissioner is not entitled to rewrite the rules or otherwise ignore precedent in disciplinary matters.[168]

Michele Roberts clearly indicated that no changes to the league's domestic violence policy should (or would) take place until the next round of formal collective bargaining. In an October 2014 interview with *Sports Illustrated*, Roberts clarified: "There are existing policies in place that were negotiated. That said, we would be open to discussions about increased training and education and, most importantly, developing strategies to prevent domestic violence from happening in the first place."[169]

The NBA collective bargaining process from late 2015 through early 2017: how strategic collaboration, effective communication and mutual respect led to consensus and a new 2017 CBA

In December 2015, the league and its players officially initiated discussions about a successor CBA. The NBA and NBPA issued a joint statement following the initial bargaining session. The joint statement in part provided that the conversation represented a "preliminary meeting that included constructive dialogue, and we agreed to continue our discussions."[170] The league and the NBPA established subcommittees involving core substantive areas such as sponsorships, media rights, licensing and international business. Each subcommittee was comprised of three player representatives from the NBPA along with three league representatives. This approach of creating subcommittees to discuss and negotiate specific collective bargaining issues represented a fundamental change from collective bargaining processes in prior years.[171]

During a March 2016 interview with Rachel Nichols on ESPN, Commissioner Silver seemed hopeful that the league and its players could avoid the collective bargaining landscape in 2010 and 2011 that resulted in a lock out and lawsuits: "The tenor has been very positive. I mean the tenor is ... we have an obligation to the game ... those words have been used in the meetings. I think we are starting very early in our discussions. We are approaching it in a very serious way. I'm extraordinarily optimistic that we are going to work through our issues and get something done."[172]

In June 2016, Commissioner Silver mentioned that, in his view, NBA "players are partners with the [team] owners."[173] During this same interview—when current NBA player CJ McCollum asked Adam Silver about his perspective on the overall dynamic between the league and the NBPA—Silver responded with the following genuine opinions:

> I feel that we have a great relationship. I think that Michele is doing a tremendous job. She's very focused on the well-being of the players. She's doing a terrific job getting out there, hearing directly from the players, talking to the agents, meeting people around the NBA family so that she knows what the issues are.... I think that part of negotiating deals is building relationships and building trust. And I feel we're doing that now.[174]

During an August 2016 interview, Michele Roberts stated she was likewise "optimistic" about getting a new labor deal completed before any chance of a lockout. When commenting on the "civil relationship" between Commissioner Silver and herself, Roberts acknowledged: "I actually like him. I think that he's a pro."[175] Roberts also provided some additional information on the initial collective bargaining progress between the league and its players:

We've had discussions. Our teams have been in discussions for some months now and we have made progress and we're inclined to continue along those lines. We have meetings this summer and we're meeting next week and [consistently] after that. We're trying to get a deal as quickly as we can, ideally before the start of the season. Nothing is certain but I cannot imagine that if we don't have an agreement on December 14th and the opt-out deadline is December 15, 2016 ... I think it's probably a safe bet that we would opt out. I think it's probably a safe bet that the league would. We want a deal. We don't want to play the opt-out game. We want a deal.[176]

In October 2016, during the annual NBA Board of Governors meeting, Commissioner Silver continued to remain encouraged about how collective bargaining conversations/negotiations were progressing:

In terms of our present bargaining discussions with the players, I'd say they are going very well and there has been a great sense and spirit of cooperation across the table and desire to move forward.... There is a sense from both the owners and the union management that there is a lot at stake here and I think everyone is feeling the pressure from all the constituents involved in this league for all the jobs that we provide that it's incumbent upon us to work something out ... I remain optimistic that we are going to get something done relatively soon.... We meet and we seek to solve problems. Both sides have been very engaged and eager to get a deal done.[177]

Commissioner Silver also acknowledged, "the fortunes of the league—the fact that there is more money to distribute among our players and teams—has created an atmosphere that makes it more conducive to continue a deal that looks a lot like the [2011 CBA] deal. I think there is a sense across the table that we have a system that we both fought hard for in the last round of collective bargaining that for the most part is working pretty well."[178] Michele Roberts also emphasized the importance of negotiating CBA elements beyond financial related provisions. For instance, in October 2016, Roberts commented that "a great deal of what we have to negotiate about involves working conditions and health, life after basketball. All of that is important to the player."[179] Despite some small differences in priorities, perceptions and perspectives, Commissioner Silver and Michele Roberts developed a "relationship built on mutual respect and trust," which facilitated consistent honest dialogue and extremely productive bargaining sessions throughout much of 2016.[180]

On December 23, 2016, the NBA issued a statement indicating that, "The new collective bargaining agreement was ratified this week by the NBA players and NBA Board of Governors. The new agreement will take effect on July 1, 2017, and run through the 2023–2024 season. The [NBA players and team owners] voted based on a term sheet that outlined the key deal points. Once the NBA and NBPA finish drafting and execute the complete agreement, specific details will be released."[181] On January 19, 2017, the NBA announced the official signing and completion of the new 2017 CBA.[182] Subject to a few limited exceptions, the 2017 CBA terms took effect on July 1, 2017.

The finalized CBA was the "culmination of months of work between NBA commissioner Adam Silver and NBPA executive director Michele Roberts, whose comity toward each other set the tone for the discussions…. Discussions between the league and union were held in relative quiet over the past several months, with almost none of the rancor between the sides that had impeded progress in previous CBA talks."[183] As explained by NBA salary cap expert Larry Coon, "Many factors were involved in the comparative ease of the 2016 negotiation process, including the improved financial state that resulted from changes made in the 2011 CBA, the influx of new revenue starting in 2016 that came as a result of new national TV contracts, an improving economy, skyrocketing franchise values, and new leadership at both the league and union."[184] In the words of Professor Michael McCann, "Both leaders [Silver and Roberts] deserve credit for striking a deal before a labor dispute—and accompanying antitrust litigation—arose … the new CBA is more about targeted tweaks than fundamental shifts."[185]

Examples of select provisions and overall system concepts in the 2017 CBA

The NBA and NBPA agreed to the following principal deal terms as part of the 2017 CBA:

- *Term of CBA*: The 2017 CBA includes a seven-year term from the 2017–2018 NBA season through the 2023–2024 NBA season (both the NBA and NBPA have the ability to opt out of the CBA after the 2022–2023 season by providing written notice of its intent to opt out by December 15, 2022).
- *Basketball Related Income (BRI)*: Players and owners agreed to maintain the general BRI definition and revenue share/split formula—players' share remains in the 49–51% of BRI range.[186]
  - One example of a minor modification to the BRI definition involved increasing the percentage of certain revenue streams that are included in the aggregate BRI calculation (for example, the percentage of gross proceeds for luxury suites and arena signage increased from 40% in the 2011 CBA to 50% in the 2017 CBA).
  - Similar to the 2011 CBA, players receive a greater share of BRI to the extent BRI exceeds projections, and a smaller share of BRI to the extent BRI falls short of projections.
  - The league and players also agreed to adjust certain BRI inclusion and deduction rules.

- *"Right-Sizing" Player Contract Elements*: Several elements related to player compensation were adjusted upward in order to maintain the relative proportionate position of these elements within the broader player compensation system.

- *Mid-Level Salary Cap Exceptions*: All three mid-level salary cap exceptions increased by 45% from the amounts in the 2011 CBA—as a result, for the 2017–2018 NBA season, the non-taxpayer mid-level exception equaled $8.4 million, the taxpayer mid-level exception equaled $5.2 million and the mid-level exception for teams operating below the salary cap ("room teams") equaled $4.3 million.[187]
- *Rookie Scale Contracts*: The rookie scale also increased by 45%, with a three-year period from 2017–2018 to 2019–2020 for gradually phasing in the 45% salary increase; in addition, existing rookie scale contracts were amended to reflect a 15% salary increase for the 2017–2018 season, a 30% increase for the 2018–2019 season, and a 45% increase for the 2019–2020 season (teams will be reimbursed for these increased payments related to existing rookie scale contracts out of a leaguewide fund created and maintained by the NBA—also, these "rookie scale conforming increase" payments will be excluded from the calculation of each team's total player payroll for salary cap purposes).[188]
- *The Luxury Tax Apron*: If a team utilizes the non-taxpayer mid-level salary exception or the bi-annual exception (which equaled $3.3 million for the 2017–2018 season), or acquires a player in a sign-and-trade transaction, that team would not be allowed to exceed a specific threshold above the luxury tax level known as the "tax apron"—the tax apron amount increased from $4 million in the 2011 CBA to $6 million for the 2017–2018 season; this $6 million tax apron amount adjusts each year beginning with the 2018–2019 NBA season by applying one half the percentage increase (or decrease) in the salary cap (for example, if the salary cap increases by 15% from 2018–2019 to 2019–2020, the apron threshold would correspondingly increase by 7.5%).[189]
- *Annual Salary Increase Percentage in Player Contracts*: The 2017 CBA permits annual increases of 8% (as compared with 7.5% in the 2011 CBA) for players who are classified as either a "Qualifying Veteran Free Agent" or "Early Qualifying Veteran Free Agent"—to be eligible for 8% annual salary increases, at a minimum a player must have previously been under contract with the same team for at least two preceding NBA seasons (subject to a few limited exceptions for players who played on more than one team during the two preceding NBA seasons as a result of being traded, claimed off waivers or signed after a season started).[190] All other players are permitted to receive 5% annual salary increases (as compared with 4.5% annual increases in the 2011 CBA).[191]
- *Maximum Annual Cash Limit in Trades*: The limit on cash paid or received in trades for the 2017–2018 season increased from $3.6 million in the 2011 CBA to $5.1 million; this amount increases or decreases annually beginning with the 2018–2019 season at the same percentage rate as the salary cap.[192]

- *Contract Extensions (Player Retention Rules)*: The 2017 CBA includes multiple changes to the rules involving contract extensions for veteran players as well as players on a rookie scale contract.
  - *Veteran Player Contract Extensions*: Veteran extensions are generally permitted to cover five total NBA seasons (four additional seasons if one year remains on the current contract, or three additional seasons if two years remain on the current contract). The maximum allowable salary in the first year of a veteran extension increased from 107.5% of the player's salary in the last year of the original term of the contract under the 2011 CBA to 120% of the greater of: (a) the player's salary in the last year of the original term of the contract, or (b) the estimated average player salary for the year in which the extension is signed. In addition, the 2017 CBA allows teams to have up to two players on a roster signed to a "designated veteran player extension." To qualify for a designated veteran player extension, a player must:

    1   Have seven or eight seasons of prior service in the NBA with his current team (with an exception for players who were traded within their first four seasons in the NBA);
    2   Have one or two years left on his current contract; and
    3   Meet at least one of the following performance criteria at the time of signing the contract extension:

       A   The player was NBA MVP during one of the preceding three seasons, or
       B   The player was named to the All-NBA first, second, or third team, or was named Defensive Player of the Year, in the immediately preceding season or in two of the immediately preceding three seasons.

    Designated veteran player extensions cover six seasons from the date the extension is signed, and are required to provide for a first-year salary of at least 30% and no more than 35% of the salary cap (under the 2011 CBA, such players' applicable maximum first-year salary was 30% of the salary cap). These designated veteran player extension contracts can only be negotiated and signed during the off-season, and players signed to designated veteran player extensions cannot be traded for one year from the date of signing the extension.[193]

  - *Rookie Scale Contract Extensions*: The rule allowing a team and a player who meets certain performance criteria to negotiate a maximum salary of up to 30% of the salary cap in rookie scale extensions remained in effect, but the performance criteria changed in order to be the same as the performance-based criteria for designated veteran player extensions. In addition, for rookie scale extensions where, at the time the extension is signed, the player has not already met the performance-based criteria, a team and player can agree to a five-year extension with a starting salary at different percentages of the salary cap (between 25% and 30%) based upon how and whether the player satisfies the performance-based criteria. For example, a team and player might agree that the player's salary in the first season of the extended term will be 30% if the player wins the MVP award, or 27% if the player is named to the All-NBA second team, during his fourth season in the league (final season of rookie scale contract). A team will continue to be limited at any point in time to a total of two designated rookie scale player extensions (one of which could be acquired by trade).[194]

- *The NBA G League—Two-Way Contracts*: Each NBA team is permitted to have on its roster up to two players under "two-way contracts." A "two-way player" provides services primarily to the NBA team's G League affiliate (development league team), and can be on the NBA team's active or inactive roster for up to 45 days during the NBA regular season, as well as on the NBA team's roster prior to the start of G League training camp (including during NBA training camp) and after the conclusion of the G League regular season. Two-way players earn a tiered salary based on whether the player is performing services on a particular day for an NBA team or its G League affiliate. During the term of a two-way contract, a two-way player is only eligible to sign a standard NBA contract with his current team. A two-way player's team has the right to "convert" the two-way contract during its term to a standard NBA contract at the player's applicable minimum salary and for the same contract term. The annual salary for a two-way player during the 2019–2020 season equaled almost $80,000 (with maximum base compensation protection of $50,000 per season).[195]

- *Additional Notable Provisions*: The 2017 CBA consists of 598 total pages, and certainly contains many other important (and intriguing) elements.
  - *Player Use of Performance-Enhancing Substances*: Penalties increased for positive tests for steroids and performance-enhancing drugs—for example, NBA players who use steroids or performance-enhancing drugs will be suspended for 25 games for a first violation (up from 20 games in the 2011 CBA) and 55 games for a second violation (up from 45 games in the 2011 CBA). Players who test positive for steroids or performance-enhancing drugs will also be required to participate in a leaguewide anti-drug program. A third positive test for steroids or performance-enhancing drugs will result in a player being "immediately dismissed and disqualified from any association with the NBA."[196]
  - *Educational and Life Skills Programs:* All NBA players are required to attend and participate in multiple mandatory educational and life skills programs each season. The programs are collaboratively developed by the league and players association, and include a Rookie Transition Program and Team Awareness Meetings (covering topics such as gambling awareness and substance abuse awareness).[197] In addition, each season all NBA players are required to attend and actively participate in: (1) a media training session; (2) a "business of basketball" program; and (3) an anti-gambling training session.[198]

- *Player Fines and Charitable Organizations:* In general, 50% of all player fine money goes to the NBPA Foundation, which utilizes this funding to host youth basketball camps, develop community education and wellness initiatives, and support other charitable organizations that promote literacy, healthy eating and the game of basketball. The other 50% of player fine money goes to official community partners of the NBA Cares program (for example, Autism Speaks, Beyond Sport, Boys & Girls Clubs of America, the Special Olympics and Hoops 4 Hope).[199]
- *Sports Agents and Player Contracts:* NBA players are permitted to negotiate their own contracts with NBA teams. All player agents/representatives must be certified by the NBPA, otherwise the league will not approve the player contract. In addition, teams could be subject to a $50,000 fine if teams negotiate a player contract with an agent/representative who is not certified by the NBPA.[200]
- *Group Licensing Rights for NBA Players*: THINK450 is the new for-profit licensing and business development entity wholly-owned by the NBPA and its members (NBA players), which "maximizes revenue and restores NBPA members' control over their name, likeness, data, and intellectual property."[201] Historically, the NBPA essentially rented players' marketing and licensing rights to the league, who in turn would sell those rights to corporate sponsors and then share the resultant revenue with the players association. Starting in October 2017, NBA players assigned their collective group marketing and licensing rights to the NBPA instead of to the league. As a result, players are still permitted to control individual endorsement deals, teams still control any use of team names and logos, and the NBPA controls the rights to utilize player names, images and likenesses as a group (as long as players are not wearing NBA uniforms). According to NBA player Chris Paul, "It's a big deal. As the union has become stronger, players have become more educated and better understand their value. There are a fortunate few players who have a business team or agency working on their behalf on a daily basis, but with the union it's about everybody. This gives the union a chance to see what business opportunities are there for the collective group."[202]
- *Player Promotional Appearances:* All NBA players are required to make a minimum of 12 promotional appearances each season—at least seven personal appearances (which must include two or more season ticketholder events) and at least five group appearances with teammates. Two of the 12 minimum appearances can also be on behalf of NBA Properties, which operates as the marketing and licensing division of the NBA. Players receive a minimum $3,500 for each of the required promotional appearances made on behalf of team corporate partners; teams are permitted to provide players with more than $3,500 per promotional appearance if the higher amount is consistent with the team's past practice and is not otherwise unreasonable. Players also get

reimbursed for the actual expenses incurred in connection with these promotional appearances. In addition, players are prohibited from making public appearances, participating in radio or television programs, writing or sponsoring newspaper/magazine articles or sponsoring commercial products without the written consent of their team; however, teams are only allowed to withhold consent if it is "in the reasonable interests" of the team or NBA.[203]

○ *Player Benefits*: The NBA and NBPA agreed to significant enhancements to player pension, health and other benefits, including an agreement to share the cost of a new health insurance plan and increased pension benefits for eligible currently-retired players who helped pave the way for the game's current success; the health and welfare benefit plan also provides up to $101,000 per player for reimbursement of eligible tuition and career transition expenses.[204]

○ *Player Care Survey:* The NBA and the NBPA agreed to jointly conduct a confidential player survey once every two years in order to seek players' input and opinion regarding the adequacy of medical care provided by their respective medical and training staffs, and subsequently commission independent analyses of the results of such surveys.[205]

○ *Limitation on Player Ownership of Teams*: NBA players are not permitted to acquire a direct ownership interest in any NBA team or invest in an entity that holds an ownership interest in any NBA team (with an exception for allowing players to invest in publicly traded companies that directly or indirectly hold ownership interests in an NBA team).[206]

○ *Career Opportunities for Former Players:* The NBA league office established three-month long G League apprenticeship and assistant coach programs to provide immersive business and basketball operations training for former NBA players in areas such as basketball administration, coaching, community relations, sales and marketing.[207]

Notes

1 This book was initially published in 2020, which is why the book focuses on contemporary collective bargaining in the NBA from 2009 through 2019. In addition, this book does not primarily focus on historical collective bargaining in the NBA prior to the 2009 NBA season because a central goal of the book is to focus on current collective bargaining related challenges and opportunities within professional sports. *Chapter 1* provided a concise synopsis of the evolution of collective bargaining in professional sports. Numerous existing books provide exceptional extensive historical overviews of collective bargaining within professional sports.

2 The NBA and NBPA each have the option to terminate the CBA on June 30, 2023, one year before the scheduled June 30, 2024 expiration of the CBA. *See* NBA CBA (2017), Article XXXIX, Sections 1–2. In addition, the NBPA would be able to terminate the CBA if either several or all NBA teams engage in collusion (for example, all league teams agree to only offer two-year contracts to free agents or agree to avoid making an offer to a specific player). Also, the NBA would be able to

terminate the CBA early if its current leaguewide media rights agreements with ESPN and Turner Broadcasting experience a significant decrease in value (for example, more than a 35% reduction in future media rights contracts).

3 *See* Rosner, S. and Shropshire, K. (2010). *The Business of Sports (Second Edition)*, at page 141 (explaining that "all professional sports leagues are deeply concerned about the same two basic issues: competitive balance and revenue sharing").

4 Berri, D.J. (2012). Did the Players Give Up Money to Make the NBA Better? Exploring the 2011 Collective Bargaining Agreement in the National Basketball Association, *International Journal of Sport Finance*, at page 161.

5 *See* Rosner, S. and Shropshire, K. (2010). *The Business of Sports*, at page 146 (explaining that "a predictable league ultimately becomes of little interest to its followers").

6 Revenue sharing can be defined as "the amount of revenues earned by members of a professional sports league that are shared by [some or] all league teams, regardless of the teams' contributions to the generation of these revenues." Rosner, S. and Shropshire, K. (2010). *The Business of Sports*, at page 141.

7 The NBA has a "soft" salary cap, which means there are several exceptions that allow teams to exceed the salary cap in specific situations. *See* NBA CBA (2017), Article VII. Former NBA commissioner David Stern once stated, "Even in a league where one team could pay [$100 million] to its roster, another team could pay [$50 million] and would be economically successful—our owners and our fans don't want it because it wouldn't be competitive." Aschburner, S. (2011). Revenue Sharing a Vital (Yet Secretive) Component to Talks, *available at* www.nba.com. *See also* Dietl, H., Lang, M., and Rathke, A. (2011). The Combined Effect of Salary Restrictions and Revenue Sharing in Sports League, *Economic Inquiry* (concluding that a salary cap produces a more balanced league and decreases the cost per unit of talent).

8 *See* Conrad, M. (2011). *The Business of Sports: A Primer for Journalists*, at page 139. Routledge.

9 *See* Conrad, M. (2011). *The Business of Sports: A Primer for Journalists*, at page 161 (explaining that many NBA teams were experiencing financial difficulties prior to 1983; for example, franchises in Cleveland, Denver, Indiana, Kansas City, Utah and San Diego reported significant financial losses, and some teams even fell behind on deferred payments to former players). During the early 1980s before the players and league agreed to the 1983 CBA, the NBA "was in rough financial shape. The NBA was searching for national television exposure, and the concomitant advertising revenue. Two-thirds of its teams were losing money. The owners convinced the players association that the league could not survive without some sort of curtailment of salaries." Jones, M.E. (1999). *Sports Law*, at page 66. Prentice Hall. The official website for the NBPA notes that by the 1984–1985 season, the average player salary had increased to $275,000 and the stability of the league improved.

10 *See* NBA CBA (2017), Article VII, Section 1 for the definition of "Basketball Related Income." Players negotiate with the owners to receive a percentage share of BRI each season. A "Salary Cap Year" (i.e., NBA season) means July 1 to June 30 each calendar year. *See* NBA CBA (2017), Article I. Before the start of each NBA season, team owners, the league commissioner and the NBPA meet for the purpose of agreeing upon a projected BRI amount. If the league and the players are unable to agree to a BRI number, then the following formula is utilized to calculate projected BRI for that specific NBA season ("salary cap year"): With respect to BRI sources

other than national television contracts, projected BRI includes BRI for the preceding salary cap year, increased by 4.5%. *See* NBA CBA (2017), Article VII, Section 1(b).

11 *See* Official Release—2010–11 NBA Season BRI Audit Finalized (2011), *available at* www.nba.com.

12 *See* NBA CBA (2005), Article VII, Section 2(e)(1). According to the NBA, from 2005–2011 "player compensation increased in each season of the six-year CBA, while the NBA has cited losses in each of the six seasons totaling more than $1.5 billion. While BRI has increased, the owners have said their non-player expenses have risen at a greater rate." Aschburner, S. (2011). NBA, Union Finalize Audit of Revenues, Player Compensation, *available at* www.nba.com.

13 *See* Official Release—2010–11 NBA Season BRI Audit Finalized (2011), *available at* www.nba.com.

14 *See* Official Release—NBA Salary Cap Set for 2009–10 Season (2009), *available at* www.nba.com.

15 NBA CBA (2017), Article VII, Section 12(b)(3) (explaining that players will share between 49% and 51% of BRI). The specific salary cap percentage figure of 44.74% of BRI represents a 10.5% discount from 50% of BRI (which is the midpoint between the 49–51% range to which players are entitled). Historically, many NBA teams have exceeded the soft salary cap because the NBA CBA contains numerous exceptions that allow team payrolls to eclipse the salary cap threshold. For example, the payroll of almost every NBA team exceeded the salary cap during the 2018–2019 season. The presumption is that the 44.74% amount will actually end up yielding player salary payments of closer to 49–51% of total BRI based on actual combined team payroll figures.

16 The substantial increase in total BRI from $3.6 billion during the 2009–2010 season to more than $7.5 billion during the 2019–2020 season is a direct byproduct of sustained innovation and collaboration among players, team owners and the league office. Keep in mind that the NBA salary cap was $3.6 million during the 1984–1985 season.

17 *See* NBA CBA (2017), Article VII, Section 2(a)(1). Programming, health insurance and other costs for NBA player benefits during the 2019–2020 season equaled approximately $400 million.

18 The luxury tax threshold for the 2019–2020 season was $132.6 million. *See* Official Release—NBA Salary Cap Set at $109.14 million for 2019–20 Season (2019), *available at* www.nba.com. In September 2019, the NBA informed all member teams that the projected salary cap for the 2020–2021 season would be approximately $116 million and the projected salary cap for the 2021–2022 season would be approximately $125 million. The NBA generated approximately $7.1 billion in BRI for the 2017–2018 season and approximately $7.7 billion in BRI for the 2018–2019 season. It is worthwhile to note that the 2017 CBA forecasted BRI to equal $5.3 billion during the 2017–2018 season, $5.6 billion for the 2018–2019 season, $5.8 billion during the 2019–2020 season, $6 billion during the 2020–2021 season and $6.3 billion during the 2021–2022 season. In other words, the 2011 CBA forecasts have proven to be much lower than actual total BRI in recent years. *See* NBA CBA (2017), Article VII, Section 12(b).

19 NBA CBA (2017), Article VII, Section 1(a). BRI includes revenues generated by all NBA league subsidiaries (for example, NBA Properties and NBA Media Ventures) along with income from companies that are at least 50% owned by the NBA or an NBA subsidiary.

20 *See* NBA CBA (2017), Article VII, Section 1(a). It is important to note that, for some of these sources of revenue, only a specific percentage of proceeds are included for BRI calculation purposes (for example, 50% of proceeds from arena and practice facility naming rights). The 2017 CBA also contains an extensive list of revenue sources that are expressly excluded from the definition of BRI. For example, BRI does not include revenue generated by NBA G League teams, monies collected from team-related charitable fundraising, proceeds from the sale or rental of real estate or proceeds from businesses outside the arena besides team-operated stores (e.g., restaurants, casinos, hotels and retail businesses). In addition, the NBA and league-related entities are permitted to deduct from BRI expenses related to the development and operation of the league's international business, subject to a deduction limit of 10% of the league's gross BRI international revenues each season.

21 It is plausible that some team owners shift revenue from the basketball franchise into related business ventures. As a result, owners may misrepresent the true/complete financial condition of the team. The potential for financial non-disclosure and related party transactions could lead to the presence of asymmetric information between team owners and players during the collective bargaining process. *See* Sadler, T.R. and Sanders, S. (2016). The 2011–2021 NBA Collective Bargaining Agreement: Asymmetric Information, Bargaining Power and the Principal Agency Problem, *Managerial Finance*. *See also* Zirin, D. (2012). *Bad Sports: How Owners Are Ruining the Games We Love*. Simon & Schuster, Inc.

22 *See* Official Statement—NBA's Response to July 6 Story on League's Financial Losses (2011), *available at* www.nba.com.

23 *See* Silver, N. (2011). Calling Foul on NBA's Claims of Financial Distress, the *New York Times*. *See also* Berri, D.J. (2012). Did the Players Give Up Money to Make the NBA Better? Exploring the 2011 Collective Bargaining Agreement in the National Basketball Association, *International Journal of Sport Finance*, at page 160 (writing that "the NBA officially disputed [Nate] Silver's analysis but failed to release objective numbers that contradicted Silver's analysis").

24 *See* Silver, N. (2011). Calling Foul on NBA's Claims of Financial Distress, the *New York Times*. *See also* Official Statement—NBA's Response to July 6 Story on League's Financial Losses (2011), *available at* www.nba.com. The NBPA "disagreed over the extent of the losses, and maintained that the league's problems could be addressed through better management and revenue sharing." Coon, L. (2017). NBA Salary CAP FAQ: 2017 Collective Bargaining Agreement, *available at* www.cbafaq.com.

25 *See* Sedeh, M. (2013). The NBPA Disclaimer: The End of the Bargaining Relationship or a Sham?, *Willamette Sports Law Journal*, at page 57. *See also* Coon, L. (2011). Is the NBA Really Losing Money?, *available at* www.espn.com. *See also* Parlow, M.J. (2014). Lessons from the NBA Lockout: Union Democracy, Public Support, and the Folly of the National Basketball Players Association, *Oklahoma Law Review*, at page 23 (explaining that the value of a team owner's investment continues to appreciate in value even during seasons in which the team experiences budget (cash-flow) losses).

26 *See* Youngmisuk, O. (2011). Commish: 'Premature' to Worry, *available at* www.espn.com.

27 *See* Windhorst, B. and Lowe, Z. (2017). A Confidential Report Shows Nearly Half the NBA Lost Money Last Season, *available at* www.espn.com (revealing that the nine teams which lost money during the 2016–2017 NBA season, based on the

league's accounting for net income—which includes revenue sharing and luxury tax payments—were the Atlanta Hawks, Brooklyn Nets, Cleveland Cavaliers, Detroit Pistons, Memphis Grizzlies, Milwaukee Bucks, Orlando Magic, San Antonio Spurs and Washington Wizards). For example, for the 2016–2017 NBA season, the Orlando Magic reported negative net income of ($1.9 million), whereas the Los Angeles Lakers reported positive net income of $116.9 million. For this same season (2016–2017), the Lakers contributed $48.2 million into the league revenue sharing pool, whereas the Orlando Magic received $13.7 million via the league revenue sharing plan.

28 *See* Press Release—NBA Extends Partnership with Turner Broadcasting & Disney (2014), *available at* www.nba.com. Commissioner Silver and other leaders at the NBA league office completely understand that some fans might prefer to watch NBA games, highlights and other league and team content via social media and other streaming platforms. For example, in April 2018, Commissioner Silver provided the following insight related to the NBA's approach to content creation and distribution: "Although the social media platforms have been a new revenue stream for the league, it doesn't come anywhere near our conventional media deals. We have built an enormous global social media community. We estimate roughly 1.4 billion people are connecting with the NBA in some way. One of our strategies has been to embrace experimentation with all these different platforms. Whether it is Facebook or Twitter or YouTube, we've told them: We have a lot of content; let's try new things.... As an example, we've experimented in India with streaming games through Facebook. Also, these over-the-top platforms aren't just thinking about taking the conventional productions that you see on cable and satellite and repositioning those streams on the platforms. They're instead thinking about what advantages their technology offers, and how they can find new and better ways to present the games that lead to potentially even more engagement from the fans.... We just announced a new partnership with Magic Leap, which is considered a 'mixed reality' platform. Whether through mixed, virtual, or augmented reality, we think we can greatly enhance the experience of watching NBA games." Vollmer, C. and Gross, D. (2018). NBA Commissioner Adam Silver Has a Game Plan, *available at* www. strategy-business.com. In July 2019, the NBA, NBPA and Dapper Labs (an innovative consumer blockchain company) announced the development of "NBA Top Shot," a digital platform for basketball fans to collect, trade and own some of the greatest moments in league history. NBA Top Shot features a social experience built around digital collectibles as well as an immersive complementary head-to-head game designed to create a fun, authentic and accessible fan engagement on blockchain. Team rosters are built by acquiring live in-game moments from the NBA season. These moments, such as a Devin Booker three-point shot, or Deandre Ayton dunk, which are acquired as digital collectibles or tokens, can then be either owned forever or used to compete against other players in online tournaments and leagues all via a blockchain platform. *See* Official Release—NBA, NBPA and Dapper Labs Bring First-of-its-Kind Blockchain Game to Basketball Fans Around the Globe (2019), *available at* www.nba.com. Simply put, the NBA is definitely a "global sports and media business" focused on continuous innovation in order to optimize fan engagement. *See* National Basketball Association—About the NBA (2019), *available at* www.nba.com.

29 Zillgitt, J. (2014). NBA Will Have More Programming Under New TV Deal, *USA Today*.

30 *See* Official Release—Mikhail Prokhorov to Sell Full Ownership of Barclays Center and Controlling Interest in the Brooklyn Nets to Joe Tsai (2019), *available at* www. nba.com. Mikhail Prokhorov entered into a definitive agreement to sell full ownership of Barclays Center and his 51% controlling interest in the Brooklyn Nets for $1.35 billion to an entity controlled by Joe Tsai (founder of the e-commerce company Alibaba). With the purchase of Prokhorov's remaining shares of the Nets, Tsai became the sole investor in the team. Tsai previously purchased 49% of the Nets in 2018 for $1 billion.

31 *See* Press Release—Houston Rockets Sold to Tilman Fertitta, Reportedly for $2.2 Billion (2017), *available at* www.nba.com.

32 Ozanian, M. (2015). Atlanta Hawks Sales Price is Being Greatly Overstated, *Forbes*.

33 *See* Bank of America Merrill Lynch (2014). Project Claret: Preliminary Indicative Valuation Considerations, *available at* www.espn.com (projecting expected annual revenue of $164.9 million for the Clippers during the 2014–2015 NBA season).

34 *See* Bank of America Merrill Lynch (2014). Project Claret: Preliminary Indicative Valuation Considerations, *available at* www.espn.com (explaining that the Los Angeles home market is "strikingly different" than the Milwaukee Bucks' and Sacramento Kings' home markets and, therefore, the valuation for the Clippers should not be based on the sales valuations for the Bucks and Kings).

35 *See* Rosner, S. and Shropshire, K. (2010). *The Business of Sports*, at page 10 (explaining that the capital gains an owner receives from selling a team can more than offset any losses the team has incurred from its ongoing operations).

36 From 2002 to 2012, 16 NBA teams were sold for amounts between $200 million and $450 million. *See* Bank of America Merrill Lynch (2014). Project Claret: Preliminary Indicative Valuation Considerations, *available at* www.espn.com.

37 *See* Badenhausen, K. and Ozanian, M. (2019). NBA Team Values 2019, *Forbes* (indicating that "NBA teams are more profitable than ever. The average earnings before interest, taxes, depreciation and amortization, or EBITDA, of $61 million per NBA team is double what it was two seasons ago").

38 *See* Robbins, J. (2014). Orlando Magic CEO Says the Franchise Still Doesn't Make a Profit, *Orlando Sentinel* (quoting Orlando Magic executive Alex Martins: "The assertion that the Magic made a profit last year is inaccurate. We did not make a profit last year. We have not made a profit in over a decade").

39 Leff, C. (2019). Brooklyn Heights, *SportsBusiness Journal*, at page 6 (explaining that the NBA recently announced a new $1.5 billion deal with Tencent that keeps the company as its exclusive digital partner in China).

40 *See* Official Release—NBA, Tencent Announce Five-Year Partnership Extension (2019), *available at* www.nba.com. NBA commissioner Adam Silver has consistently expressed support for players and team personnel educating themselves and sharing their views on social justice and other matters important to them. For example, in October 2019, the general manager of the Houston Rockets posted a message on Twitter related to humanitarian protests in Hong Kong. Several international NBA corporate partners in China expressed discontent with the Twitter post. Commissioner Silver was put in a difficult predicament—managing relationships and balancing the perspectives ("voices") of players and team executives with collaborative partners such as Tencent (a company that pays the league approximately $300 million per year). Commissioner Silver released the following statement in response to this complex situation: "Over the last three decades, the NBA has developed a great affinity for the people of China. We have seen how basketball

can be an important form of people-to-people exchange that deepens ties between the United States and China. At the same time, we recognize that our two countries have different political systems and beliefs. And like many global brands, we bring our business to places with different political systems around the world. But for those who question our motivation, this is about far more than growing our business. It is inevitable that people around the world—including from America and China—will have different viewpoints over different issues. It is not the role of the NBA to adjudicate those differences. However, the NBA will not put itself in a position of regulating what players, employees and team owners say or will not say on these issues. We simply could not operate that way. Basketball runs deep in the hearts and minds of our two peoples. At a time when divides between nations grow deeper and wider, we believe sports can be a unifying force that focuses on what we have in common as human beings rather than our differences." Official Release—Adam Silver's Statement on NBA and China (2019), *available at* www.nba.com. In the days that followed the statement from Commissioner Silver, more than ten of NBA China's local corporate partners—including Tencent, Luckin Coffee and Vivo—either suspended or terminated their sponsorship agreements with the NBA. Basketball operations executives at several NBA teams reportedly began to consider a potential decline to the projected salary cap for the 2020–2021 NBA season as a direct result of reduced sponsorship dollars and other revenue from companies and consumers in China. Commissioner Silver acknowledged that the immediate financial losses were substantial; he candidly observed that "the financial consequences have been and may continue to be fairly dramatic." ESPN News Services (2019). NBA Commissioner Adam Silver Says Financial Losses in China 'Substantial,' *available at* www.espn.com. The NBA accepted the fact that the manner in which the China situation ultimately materialized would directly impact the NBA's global brand—not only in China but also in the United States and with the international companies with whom the league does business. As explained by Professor Michael McCann, "The longer the controversy lasts, the less confident Chinese companies might become in the predictability of doing business with the NBA. This is particularly true if conflicting statements expressed by team executives and players are perceived as reflecting an inability on the part of the league to speak with one voice." McCann, M.A. (2019). LeBron's China Comments and the Financial Fallout for the NBA, U.S., *Sports Illustrated.*

41 Yeung, J. (2019). The NBA is Playing in India for the First Time Ever, *available at* www.cnn.com.

42 Reynolds, T. (2019). NBA, FIBA Announce Plans for Pro League in Africa. The NBA is collaborating with FIBA to develop the Basketball Africa League initiative.

43 *See* Official Release—Basketball Africa League Announces Seven Host Cities for Inaugural Season (2019), *available at* www.nba.com. In August 2019, the NBA and Disney opened "The NBA Experience," which is a 44,000 square foot, two-story entertainment venue at Walt Disney World Resort in Orlando, Florida that from the outside is modeled after an NBA arena. The attraction gives visitors a sense of what NBA or WNBA players experience through the interactive immersive elements at the venue. For example, the "combine experience" allows visitors to replicate basketball drills and compare their vertical leap and wingspan to an NBA or WNBA player. And, the "shooting activity" lets visitors step onto a court amid a computer-generated crowd and shoot last-second shots before the clock expires. According to Scott Lazaruk, NBA vice president of global partnerships, "The NBA has hundreds

of millions of fans around the world, many of which will never have the opportunity to come to an NBA game, or who want to experience the league in new ways ... hands-on activities [and] immersive entertainment [represent] a way for us to connect with new audiences, with Disney audiences. Fans coming in from Latin America, Europe and elsewhere. For the league it is about fan engagement." Lombardo, J. (2019). Nothing But Net for NBA, Disney, *SportsBusiness Journal*, at pages 16–17. *See also* Official Release—NBA Experience Tips Off August 12 at Walt Disney World Resort (2019), *available at* www.nba.com.

44 *See* CBA 101: Highlights of the Collective Bargaining Agreement Between the National Basketball Association and the National Basketball Players Association (2010), *available at* www.nba.com.

45 Abrams, J. (2011). The NBA Lockout Timeline, *Grantland. See also* Weiler, P.C. and Roberts, G.R. (2004). *Sports and the* Law, at page 277 (explaining that tension related to how to divide available revenue is more likely "when the size of the pie is changing dramatically rather than remaining constant or growing incrementally").

46 Abrams, J. (2011). The NBA Lockout Timeline, *Grantland.*

47 Associated Press (2010). Hunter: No Lockout Imminent, *available at* www.espn. com. Billy Hunter was terminated from his role of NBPA executive director in February 2013. *See* Zillgitt (2013). Billy Hunter Fired by NBA Players, *USA Today* (quoting former NBPA president Derek Fisher: "Players representatives in the general body of our association have made their voice and their votes heard. Today, the motion was raised, seconded and passed unanimously that we will terminate the employment of Billy Hunter.... Going forward, we will no longer be divided, misled, misinformed. This is our union and we are taking it back").

48 Garcia, A. (2010). Hunter Lays Out Proposal for Players, Shoots Down Hard Cap, *available at* www.nba.com.

49 Abrams, J. (2011). The NBA Lockout Timeline, *Grantland.*

50 NBPA, Lockout Handbook: Hope for the Best, Prepare for the Worst (2011). *See also* Levinson, M. (2011). NBA Union Urges Players 'Prepare for the Worst' in Lockout Handbook, *Bloomberg.*

51 *See* NBPA Unfair Labor Practice Charge Against NBA (May 2011), filed with National Labor Relations Board. *See also* Beck, H. (2011). Turning to Labor Board, NBA Union Fires First, the *New York Times.*

52 Parlow, M.J. (2014). Lessons from the NBA Lockout: Union Democracy, Public Support, and the Folly of the National Basketball Players Association, *Oklahoma Law Review*, at pages 23–24.

53 Official Release—NBA Commences Lockout of Its Players (2011), *available at* www.nba.com.

54 *See* Gould, W.B., IV (2012). The 2011 Basketball Lockout: The Union Lives to Fight Another Day—Just Barely, *Stanford Law Review.*

55 Staudohar, P.D. (2012). The Basketball Lockout of 2011, *Monthly Labor Review*, at page 29. *See also* Coates, D. and Humphreys, B.R. (2001). The Economic Consequences of Professional Sports Strikes and Lockouts, *The Southern Economic Journal* (analyzing whether labor disputes in professional sports leagues result in any statistically significant reductions in taxable sales, and whether cities with NBA teams would experience significant negative economic consequences during a work stoppage because of lost spending in and around the basketball arena).

56 *See* NBA Unfair Labor Practice Charge Against NBPA (August 2011), filed with National Labor Relations Board. As explained in *Chapter 1*, federal labor law

encourages collective bargaining and insulates the results of collective bargaining from antitrust scrutiny, even in situations where agreed upon terms might be anti-competitive. *See Brown* v. *Pro-Football, Inc.* (1996), 518 U.S. 231, at page 237 (noting that "the implicit [non-statutory labor] exemption recognizes that, to give effect to federal labor laws and policies and to allow meaningful collective bargain-ing to take place, some restraints on competition imposed through the bargaining process must be shielded from antitrust sanctions"). Historically, players associ-ations have disclaimed interest in functioning as the exclusive collective bargaining representative of players (i.e., terminate the collective bargaining relationship between a players association and the respective league) to attempt to take advantage of federal antitrust laws. As explained in *Chapter 3*, NFL players resorted to this negotiation tactic in 2011, as the National Football League Players Associ-ation (NFLPA) purportedly disclaimed interest in functioning as the collective bar-gaining representative of players; players subsequently filed an antitrust lawsuit against the NFL. *See Tom Brady et al.* v. *National Football League et al.*, Class Action Complaint, United States District Court, District of Minnesota (March 2011).

57 *See National Basketball Association et al.* v. *National Basketball Players Associ-ation et al.*, Class Action Complaint for Declaratory Relief, United States District Court for the Southern District of New York (August 2011).

58 *National Basketball Association et al.* v. *National Basketball Players Association et al.*, Class Action Complaint, United States District Court, Southern District of New York (August 2011), at pages 2–3, 10–11.

59 Letter from Billy Hunter and Derek Fisher to All NBA Players (October 2011) (explaining that, "The owners have long been pushing for significant economic relief and we have differences about the extent of the owners' losses. There have been numerous proposals to shift more dollars to the owners' side and help cover the increased cost of running this business. In our last formal proposal, we offered to reduce our share of BRI to 52.4%, and then gradually increase that percentage over the course of a six-year deal to 54%, yielding an average of 53%").

60 *See* Letter from NBA Agents to NBA Players (October 2011), at pages 1–2 (encour-aging all NBA players to remember, "it is not about when or how fast a deal is reached, [rather] it is about taking the time to secure the best deal").

61 Official Release—NBA Cancels First Two Weeks of 2011–12 Regular Season (2011), *available at* www.nba.com.

62 Beck, H. (2011). NBA Talks Stall and Games Are Canceled Through November, the *New York Times* (reiterating that, "The economic divide always promised to be the toughest to bridge, even as the parties found agreement on other key issues, including contract lengths and changes to the luxury-tax system").

63 Memorandum from Commissioner David Stern to NBA Players (November 2011).

64 Memorandum from Commissioner David Stern to NBA Players (November 2011). David Stern also remarked that the overall NBA proposals were "not about sup-pressing salaries ... this is about distributing talents and salaries in a different way than we currently do ... that is what our proposals have been about." Abbott, H. (2011). Sticking Point: Competitive Balance, *available at* www.espn.com.

65 Letter from Billy Hunter, Derek Fisher and the NBPA Executive Committee to All Players (November 2011).

66 Letter from Billy Hunter, Derek Fisher and the NBPA Executive Committee to All Players (November 2011). *See also* Parlow, M.J. (2014). Lessons from the NBA Lockout: Union Democracy, Public Support, and the Folly of the National Basketball

Players Association, *Oklahoma Law Review*, at page 32 ("The union also had strategic reasons for the disclaimer of interest; it thought that such a move would satisfy the hardline players and agents. Interestingly, many agents that represented players were actually shocked that the union chose the disclaimer of interest method of decertification. One reason for this surprise was that the disclaimer of interest approach proceeds rather quickly—which would seem to be against the players' interest. If the players had, instead, petitioned for a vote on decertification, there would have been a forty-five day period before the actual vote. This time period could have then been used for further negotiations with the owners—with the leverage of the looming decertification vote. Instead, the union may have purposely avoided the player-initiated method for fear that once the players convened for the vote, they would have rejected decertification and accepted Stern's latest proposal— something that union leadership did not want the players to do").

67 *See Carmelo Anthony et al.* v. *National Basketball Association et al.*, Class Action Complaint, United States District Court of Minnesota (November 2011) (alleging the NBA was engaged in an illegal group boycott and price fixing system to reduce the salaries, terms, benefits, and conditions of employment available in the market for players). The NBA players eventually withdrew the lawsuit that was filed in California court. According to David Boies, the attorney representing the NBA players, "The likelihood was we would get a faster result in Minnesota than California. I think the result would be the same." The general counsel for the NBA offered the following perspective on the dual lawsuits filed by NBA players: "This is consistent with Mr. Boies' inappropriate shopping for a forum that he can only hope will be friendlier to his baseless legal claims." Cohen, R. (2011). NBA Players Move Legal Fight to Minnesota, *Star Tribune*.

68 *See Carmelo Anthony et al.* v. *National Basketball Association et al.*, Class Action Complaint, United States District Court of Minnesota (November 2011), at pages 2, 3, 14.

69 Official Release—NBPA Rejects Owners' Offer, Begins to Disband as Union (2011), *available at* www.nba.com.

70 Official Release—NBPA Rejects Owners' Offer, Begins to Disband as Union (2011), *available at* www.nba.com.

71 *See* Berri, D.J. (2012). Did the Players Give Up Money to Make the NBA Better? Exploring the 2011 Collective Bargaining Agreement in the National Basketball Association, *International Journal of Sport Finance*, at page 169 (opining that "the big winners [with respect to the 2011 NBA CBA] were the owners of small-market teams … [the new agreement] will allow small-market teams to earn more money, regardless of the quality of the product offered on the court").

72 *See* Official Release—NBA Board of Governors Ratify 10-Year CBA (2011), *available at* www.nba.com.

73 Official Release—NBA Board of Governors Ratify 10-Year CBA (2011), *available at* www.nba.com. According to well-respected labor expert and sports law professor William B. Gould IV, "What appeared to be a rout of the players in November emerged as a reasonable face-saving compromise." Gould, W.B., IV (2012). The 2011 Basketball Lockout: The Union Lives to Fight Another Day—Just Barely, *Stanford Law Review*, at page 56. According to another sports law scholar, "Player concessions were predictable because the NBA's economic structure separately needed an overhaul. The magnitude of such concessions, however, was startling." Parlow, M.J. (2014). Lessons from the NBA Lockout: Union Democracy, Public

Support, and the Folly of the National Basketball Players Association, *Oklahoma Law Review*, at page 1.

74 Gould, W.B., IV (2012). The 2011 Basketball Lockout: The Union Lives to Fight Another Day—Just Barely, *Stanford Law Review*, at page 56.

75 Berri, D.J. (2012). Did the Players Give Up Money to Make the NBA Better? Exploring the 2011 Collective Bargaining Agreement in the National Basketball Association, *International Journal of Sport Finance*, at page 169.

76 Feldman, G. (2011). The Nuclear Winter is Over: The New CBA, and How the Lawyers Saved the Day (Sort Of), *Grantland* (explaining that, as soon as the players got the owners to make a few concessions on system issues, they agreed to settle the lawsuit and re-form the players association in order to agree to terms on a new CBA).

77 *See* NBA CBA (2011), Article XXXIX, Section 1 (providing that "This Agreement shall be effective from December 8, 2011 and, unless terminated pursuant to the provisions of this Article XXXIX, shall continue in full force and effect through June 30, 2021").

78 *See* NBA CBA (2011), Article XXXIX, Section 2 (providing that "The NBA and the Players Association shall each have the option to terminate this Agreement on June 30, 2017 by serving written notice of its exercise of such option on the other party on or before December 15, 2016").

79 Several NBA collective bargaining agreement experts such as Larry Coon expected the players to opt out. In April 2014, Larry Coon wrote: "My prediction is that the players will opt-out of the agreement in 2017." Coon, L. (2014). New Cap, Tax and Lockout Projections, *available at* www.cbafaq.com.

80 Official Release—League, NBA Players Reach Tentative Agreement on New Collective Bargaining Agreement (2016), *available at* www.nba.com.

81 *See* Parlow, M.J. (2010). The NBA and the Great Recession: Implications for the Upcoming Collective Bargaining Agreement Renegotiation, *DePaul Journal of Sports Law & Contemporary Problems*, at page 195 (writing that because of the overall state of the economy in 2009 and 2010, the NBA was in a "precarious economic state" and therefore anticipated a "contentious, but necessary, renegotiation of the NBA's collective bargaining agreement"). For example, in February 2010, then-current NBA commissioner David Stern projected that the NBA would lose approximately $400 million during the 2009–2010 season. Professor Matthew Parlow anticipated that negotiations between players and team owners in 2010 and 2011 would center on the following concepts: allocation of BRI, salary cap, luxury tax, player contract provisions and a team revenue sharing system.

82 NBA owners viewed decreasing player salaries as a mechanism to increase team competitive balance in the league. *See* Berri, D.J. (2012). Did the Players Give Up Money to Make the NBA Better? Exploring the 2011 Collective Bargaining Agreement in the National Basketball Association, *International Journal of Sport Finance*, at page 158.

83 *See* NBA CBA (2005), Article VII, Section 2(e)(1) ("In the event that for any Salary Cap Year Total Salaries and Benefits is less than 57% of BRI, the difference shall be paid by the NBA to the Players Association no later than thirty days following the completion of the Audit Report for such Salary Cap Year for distribution to all NBA players who were on an NBA roster during the Season covered by such Salary Cap Year on such proportional basis as may be reasonably determined by the Players Association"). *See also* NBA CBA (2005), Article VII, Section 12(b)(3) (providing that the Designated Percentage for each Salary Cap Year is 57%, subject

to a few limited exceptions that would increase the Designated Percentage up to a maximum of 58%).

84 *See* Letter from Billy Hunter and Derek Fisher to All NBA Players (October 2011) (providing that, "This offer—measured against our current system which guarantees us 57% of BRI—shifts an average of $185 million per year to the owners' side, for a total of $1.1 billion over six years. We feel this offer —which would involve no rollbacks of existing contracts and maintain the current Salary Cap and Luxury Tax levels—is fair and addresses the owners' complaints").

85 Letter from Billy Hunter and Derek Fisher to All NBA Players (October 2011).

86 Memorandum from Commissioner David Stern to NBA Players (November 2011).

87 *See* NBA CBA (2011), Article VII, Section 12(b)(3) (indicating that "The Designated Share for the 2011–12 Salary Cap Year shall equal 51.15% of BRI").

88 *See* NBA CBA (2011), Article VII, Section 12(b)(3) (providing that "in no event shall the Designated Share for any Salary Cap Year commencing with the 2012–13 Salary Cap Year be less than 49% of BRI or greater than 51% of BRI").

89 *See* Taubin, L. (2012). Welcome to the Real 2011 NBA Lockout: Where Owner-Friendly Tax Provisions and Non-Monetized Benefits Color the Lockout Landscape, *Cardozo Public Law, Policy, and Ethics Journal*, at pages 140–141.

90 *See* NBA CBA (2011), Article VII, Section 2 (providing that "The Salary Cap for the 2011–12 Salary Cap Year will equal $58.044 million"). The salary cap for future seasons under the 2011 CBA would equal at least $58.044 million. The salary cap could also increase based on a formula that involved projected BRI. The salary cap has indeed increased since the 2011–2012 NBA season. For example, the NBA salary cap significantly increased from $70 million in 2015–2016 to more than $94 million in 2016–2017 based primarily on the NBA's new league media rights deals (which are discussed in further detail within this chapter). *See also* Lowe, Z. (2014). How the NBA's New TV Deal Could Blow Up the Salary Cap, *Grantland* (commenting that, "The importance of the league's cap situation cannot be overstated. It has been the single biggest topic of conversation among team executives for the last year. The salary cap rises and falls hand in hand with league revenues, and this TV contract will be the largest injection of revenues in NBA history"). In addition, the salary cap for the 2019–2020 NBA season exceeded $109 million.

91 *See* NBA CBA (2005), Article VII, Section 2(b)(1) (indicating that "For each Salary Cap Year during the term of this Agreement, there shall be a Minimum Team Salary equal to 75% of the Salary Cap for such Salary Cap Year. The Minimum Team Salary for the 2005–06 Salary Cap Year for all Teams other than the Charlotte Bobcats shall be deemed to be $37.125 million. The Minimum Team Salary for the 2005–06 Salary Cap Year for the Charlotte Bobcats shall be deemed to be $27.844 million").

92 *See* NBA CBA (2011), Article VII, Section 2(b)(1) (requiring that "For the 2011–12 Salary Cap Year, there shall be a Minimum Team Salary equal to $46.435 million. For the 2012–13 Salary Cap Year, there shall be a Minimum Team Salary equal to 85% of the Salary Cap for such Salary Cap Year. For each Salary Cap Year thereafter during the term of this Agreement, there shall be a Minimum Team Salary equal to 90% of the Salary Cap for such Salary Cap Year").

93 Letter from Billy Hunter and Derek Fisher to All NBA Players (October 2011).

94 *See* Memorandum from Commissioner David Stern to NBA Players (November 2011) (noting the NBA's "move away from a 'hard' salary cap").

95 *See* NBA CBA (2005), Article VII, Section 6(e) (providing that "A Team may sign one or more Player Contracts during each Salary Cap Year, not to exceed five

Seasons in length, that, in the aggregate, provide for Salaries and Unlikely Bonuses in the first Salary Cap Year totaling up to 108% of the Average Player Salary for the prior Salary Cap Year").

96 *See* NBA CBA (2011), Article VII, Section 6(e).

97 *See* NBA CBA (2011), Article VII, Section 6(f).

98 *See* NBA CBA (2011), Article VII, Section 6(g).

99 The luxury tax model, which consists of a complicated combination of escrow, tax and distribution components, attempts to encourage NBA teams to spend less on player salaries with the ultimate goal of increasing the profitability of the league as a whole. *See* Kaplan, R.A. (2004). The NBA Luxury Tax Model: A Misguided Regulatory Regime, *Columbia Law Review*, at page 1617. *See also* Parlow, M.J. (2014). Lessons from the NBA Lockout: Union Democracy, Public Support, and the Folly of the National Basketball Players Association, *Oklahoma Law Review*, at page 10 (noting that the luxury tax system "may wind up creating significant financial disincentives for teams that choose not to exceed the luxury tax threshold. If enough teams seek to avoid paying the new luxury tax, there will be less money to distribute through revenue sharing than was originally estimated").

100 *See* NBA CBA (2005), Article VII, Section 12(f)(1) (explaining that "Each Team whose Team Salary exceeds the Tax Level for any Salary Cap Year shall be required to pay a tax to the NBA equal to the amount by which the Team's Team Salary exceeds the Tax Level").

101 *See* NBA CBA (2011), Article VII, Section 12(f)(1).

102 *See* NBA CBA (2011), Article VII, Sections 12(f)(1)(iii) and 12(f)(1)(iv).

103 The 2011 CBA contains additional rules that attempt to control payroll spending by all teams. For example, starting with the 2013–2014 NBA season, teams are not allowed to engage in sign-and-trade transactions if the trade would result in the proposed acquiring team in the transaction exceeding the luxury by more than $4 million; likewise, any team that is involved in a sign-and-trade deal during a particular NBA season is not permitted to exceed the luxury tax threshold amount by more than $4 million at any point during that season. *See* NBA CBA (2011), Article VII, Section 8(e).

104 *See* NBA CBA (2011), Article VII, Section 12(g)(2)(1) (explaining that "The NBA may elect to distribute up to 50% of such amounts to one or more Teams based in whole or in part on the fact that such Team(s) did not owe a tax for such Salary Cap Year (e.g., the NBA could elect to distribute 50% of such amounts in equal shares to all non-taxpayers in such Salary Cap Year")).

105 *See* Associated Press (2011). NBA Owners No Longer Insist on Non-Guaranteed Contracts, *available at* www.nba.com (confirming that "NBA owners relaxed their insistence on non-guaranteed contracts ... but players cautioned that isn't enough because the league [was] still seeking a hard salary cap").

106 *See* NBA CBA (2005), Article VII, Section 5(c).

107 *See* NBA CBA (2005), Article VII, Section 6(b).

108 *See* NBA CBA (2011), Article VII, Sections 5(c) and 6(b). *See also* NBA CBA (2011), Article II, Section 7.

109 *See* NBA CBA (2011), Article VII, Section 12(j).

110 *See* NBA CBA (2011), Article XI. During the next round of collective bargaining, the league and its players might want to address potential "integrity of the game" situations that could potentially evolve from the new performance-based qualifying offer system as well as performance-based incentives in player contracts. For example, a

team might be financially incentivized to limit the number of minutes for a fourth-year player or strategically bring the player off the bench after the first few minutes of a game if that player is close to meeting the starter criteria during the final few weeks of the season. Similarly, during the 2016–2017 season, NBA player Maurice Harkless candidly acknowledged that he intentionally did not attempt a three-point shot during the final game of the regular season, because if he missed one three-point shot during that game without making any three-pointers, his overall season percentage for three-point shooting would have dropped to 34.8%. Harkless had a $500,000 performance incentive/bonus in his player contract if he shot 35% or better from three-point range during the 2016–2017 regular season.

111 *See* NBA CBA (2017), Article XI, Section 5 (indicating that, under the 2017 CBA, the period for a team with a right of first refusal to match an offer sheet was shortened from three days under the 2011 CBA to two days).

112 *See* NBA CBA (2011), Article XI, Section 5(e).

113 Adjustments to the salary cap and minimum team salary requirements involve a multi-step calculation formula. Article VII, Section 2(d) of the 2011 CBA provides the following illustrative calculation example: "Assume Total Salaries and Benefits for the 2013–14 Season are $2.27 billion and the Designated Share is $2.1 billion resulting in an Overage of $170 million (which equals 7.5% of Total Salaries and Benefits). Assume Projected BRI for the 2014–15 Season ($4.41 billion) exceeds actual BRI for the 2013–14 Season ($4.2 billion) by 5%. Assume there are 30 Teams in the NBA in 2014–15. The Salary Cap for the 2014–15 Season would be reduced by $1.1 million ((7.5% of Total Salaries and Benefits ($170 million) less 6% of Total Salaries and Benefits ($136 million)) divided by 30)."

114 Official Release—NBA Board of Governors Ratifies 10-Year CBA (2011), *available at* www.nba.com. *See also* Official Release—Summary of Principal Deal Terms (2011), *available at* www.nba.com. The escrow system is designed to serve as a form of insurance against player salaries rising above a specified percentage of league revenue. *See* Kaplan, R.A. (2004). The NBA Luxury Tax Model: A Misguided Regulatory Regime, *Columbia Law Review*, at page 1633.

115 This summary of key deal terms is not meant to provide an exhaustive, comprehensive or all-inclusive list of every principal deal point agreed to and included within the 2011 CBA. Instead, the summary is meant to spotlight some of the core fundamental provisions within the 2011 CBA.

116 Feldman, G. (2011). The Nuclear Winter is Over: The New CBA, and How the Lawyers Saved the Day (Sort Of), *Grantland*.

117 Feldman, G. (2011). The Nuclear Winter is Over: The New CBA, and How the Lawyers Saved the Day (Sort Of), *Grantland*.

118 Berri, D.J. (2012). Did the Players Give Up Money to Make the NBA Better? Exploring the 2011 Collective Bargaining Agreement in the National Basketball Association, *International Journal of Sport Finance*, at page 167.

119 Parlow, M.J. (2017). Lessons from the NBA Lockout: Union Democracy, Public Support, and the Folly of the National Basketball Players Association, *Oklahoma Law Review*, at pages 4, 13 (explaining that, "Commentators posit various theories as to why the NBPA wound up with a relatively undesirable deal in the 2011 [CBA]. These include the financial strain that the lockout inflicted on players, the overestimation of the impact of NBA players playing overseas, and the players' emotional reactions to the collective bargaining negotiations, coupled with the impact racial overtones had on the process").

120 *See* Staudohar, P.D. (2012). The Basketball Lockout of 2011, *Monthly Labor Review*, at page 28.

121 Kaplan, R.A. (2004). The NBA Luxury Tax Model: A Misguided Regulatory Regime, *Columbia Law Review*, at page 1650.

122 Mahoney, B. (2014). Silver: Premature to Say Union Will Opt Out of CBA, *Associated Press* (Klempner also stated: "Our league's recently reported economic successes come as no surprise to the players").

123 Mahoney, B. (2014). Silver: Premature to Say Union Will Opt Out of CBA, *Associated Press* (Silver further opined: "I think it's premature, frankly, for either side to be making determinations about how well this deal has or hasn't worked.... So I don't really buy into sort of that speculation that they are already planning to opt out or that we are thinking about it").

124 Official Release—NBA Commences Lockout of Its Players (2011), *available at* www.nba.com.

125 *See* NBA CBA (2011), Article II, Section 3(d). The default payment schedule was 24 semi-monthly installments over a 12-month period. However, players had the option to request payment over a period of six months or 18 months instead of 12 months.

126 Soshnick, S. (2014). LeBron Advised to Take Less Money in More Paychecks by Union, *Bloomberg*. *See also* Amick, S. and Zillgitt, J. (2014). NBA Union Wants Players to Prepare for Work Stoppage, *USA Today*.

127 Mahoney, B. (2014). Silver: Premature to Say Union Will Opt Out of CBA, *Associated Press*.

128 Mahoney, B. (2014). Silver: Premature to Say Union Will Opt Out of CBA, *Associated Press*. According to Charles Grantham, executive director of the NBPA from 1988–1995, "Ideally, whether labor or management, you begin work on the next negotiation the day after you sign the last agreement." Deveney, S. (2014). The Baseline: Another Lockout Ahead? 'We Know the Storm Is Coming,' *Sporting News*. In July 2014, Michele Roberts also made the following comments: "I understand that there's going to be some level of winning and losing in any big negotiation. In the end, I want my clients to be happy. If my clients got the best deal they could under the circumstances, I would consider it a win. I would consider it a catastrophe—and it never would happen—if my clients felt shortchanged in a negotiation." Gregory, S. (2014). Meet the First Woman to Run a Major Pro Sports Union, *Time Magazine*.

129 *See* Staudohar, P.D. (2012). The Basketball Lockout of 2011, *Monthly Labor Review*, at page 30 ("Although Stern led the owners, much of the face-to-face negotiation at the bargaining table was handled by deputy commissioner Adam Silver").

130 *See* Fagan, K. (2014). Impact 25: NBA Union Chief Michele Roberts Knows Exactly What She's Doing, *available at* www.espn.com (writing that "Roberts is a master at controlling narrative, a skill that will almost definitely be tested in the coming years, when the NBA and players association are back at the negotiating table"). For a discussion on how the NBPA's arguable deficiencies in union democracy, intra-union communications and public relations undermined its bargaining position and adversely impacted its negotiation efforts in 2010–2011, *see* Parlow, M.J. (2014). Lessons from the NBA Lockout: Union Democracy, Public Support, and the Folly of the National Basketball Players Association, *Oklahoma Law Review*, at pages 46–47 (expressing the viewpoint that, during the negotiation process for the 2011 CBA, "the NBPA's public relations campaign was flawed for a

variety of reasons ... the NBPA was not well prepared for the lockout and their media strategy was ill-conceived and poorly executed. While the union leadership attempted to educate members about their public relations approach, players failed to promote a uniform message and said—or tweeted—questionable things that reinforced existing negative public perceptions of the players. Moreover, even when the players were on message, their public relations themes seemed oblivious to the economic climate ... even when the players had good arguments or facts on their side, their messages did not resonate with the public. The players' public relations efforts were ultimately ineffective and thus did not give the union the leverage it sought in its collective bargaining").

131   Some media members wrote that is was imperative for Michele Roberts to "come across as a strong figure to the players, unify them, and, as well, influence public opinion." Keh, A. and Araton, H. (2014). Establishing Her Position in the Post, the *New York Times*.

132   Keh, A. and Araton, H. (2014). Establishing Her Position in the Post, the *New York Times* (quoting labor expert and sports law professor William B. Gould IV).

133   *See* Official Release—Adam Silver's Statement About NBPA Appointment New Executive Director (2014), *available at* www.nba.com ("On behalf of the NBA, I would like to congratulate Michele Roberts on her appointment as the NBPA's new Executive Director and look forward to working with her and the NBPA Executive Committee to ensure the continued health and growth of our game. The partnership between our players and teams is the backbone of the league, and we are eager to continue working with the Players Association to build this relationship").

134   Deveney, S. (2014). The Baseline: Another Lockout Ahead? 'We Know the Storm Is Coming,' *Sporting News* (One NBA player agent further commented: "She's serious, she is impressive. She is coming at this from an outsider's perspective. With Billy, he accepted that the system we have is what it is, and all we can do is try to protect as much ground as possible. Michele is a clean slate, she flat-out sees some of the things we accept as wrong").

135   Deveney, S. (2014). The Baseline: Another Lockout Ahead? 'We Know the Storm Is Coming,' *Sporting News*.

136   *See* Youngmisuk, O. (2014). Commish: 'Premature' to Worry, *available at* www.espn.com.

137   Torre, P.S. (2014). NBPA Director: 'Let's Stop Pretending,' *available at* www.espn.com. When Michele Roberts criticized several aspects of the NBA business model in November 2014, Commissioner Silver responded: "We will address all of these topics and others with the Players Association at the appropriate time." NBA Commissioner Adam Silver Statement (2014), *available at* www.nba.com.

138   Winderman, I. (2014). Fight to Avert 2017 NBA Lockout Starts Now, *Sun Sentinel*.

139   Interview by Andy Katz (ESPN reporter and journalist) with Adam Silver (NBA commissioner) (2014). *ESPN Outside the Lines*. In a separate interview with espnW, Commissioner Silver acknowledged that "no one at the NBA is underestimating [Roberts].... She's made it clear she will be a strong advocate for the players." Fagan, K. (2014). Impact 25: NBA Union Chief Michele Roberts Knows Exactly What She's Doing, *available at* www.espn.com.

140   Interview by Andy Katz (ESPN reporter and journalist) with Adam Silver (NBA commissioner) (2014). *ESPN Outside the Lines*.

141   Fagan, K. (2014). Impact 25: NBA Union Chief Michele Roberts Knows Exactly What She's Doing, *available at* www.espn.com.

142 *See* Keh, A. and Araton, H. (2014). Establishing Her Position in the Post, the *New York Times* (explaining that any substantive negotiations with the league will take place in private, but Roberts understands the importance of "shaping the perceptions of the NBA" and protecting "the image of the players" who Roberts believed were labeled as "money hungry" during the 2010–2011 collective bargaining process).

143 Keh, A. and Araton, H. (2014). Establishing Her Position in the Post, the *New York Times*. *See also* Fagan, K. (2014). Impact 25: NBA Union Chief Michele Roberts Knows Exactly What She's Doing, *available at* www.espn.com (quoting Michele Roberts: "The league's narrative was so powerful in 2011 that it even had the fans saying, 'Share the money. Don't stop playing. You make a lot of money.' I remember thinking, 'Everyone believes the players make too much money'").

144 *See* Draper, K. (2018). Michele Roberts on NBA Competitive Imbalance: Don't Blame the Players, the *New York Times* (explaining that the NBA proposal would prevent teams from signing players to inflated contracts merely because those players had the good fortune of becoming free agents in July 2016).

145 Payne, M. (2014). NBA Union Chief Michele Roberts Questions Commissioner Adam Silver's Assertions that One-Third of NBA Teams Are Unprofitable, the *Washington Post*.

146 Official Release—NBA Statement Regarding the Salary Cap (2015), *available at* www.nba.com. *See also* Interview by Rachel Nichols (ESPN reporter and journalist) with Adam Silver (NBA Commissioner) (2016), *available at* www.espn.com (quoting Adam Silver: "The fact that all of this cap room is going to come in at once and so we are going to have roughly a $20 million increase from about $70 million to $90 million in the cap in one summer is not how we would have constructed it. Having said that, that [*sic*] players make decisions for lots of reasons"). In February 2018, Michele Roberts was asked if she has ever reconsidered the stance of the NBPA related to the 2015 discussion with the NBA about the salary cap smoothing concept. Roberts emphatically responded: "There was going to be no smoothing of the owners' profits at all. They were going to enjoy real money that reflected where we were financially as a game. Why in the world would players pretend that the game was not making as much money and therefore have smaller contracts? It was an absurd suggestion, I thought personally"). Feldman, D. (2018). Michele Roberts: Cap Smoothing 'Disgraceful Request' by NBA, *available at* www.nbcsports.com. Michele Roberts also remarked: "Agreeing to artificially lower the salary cap 'offends our core.' It would be quite counterintuitive for the union to ever agree to lower, as opposed to raise, the salary cap. If we ever were to do so, there would have to be a [darn] good reason, inarguable and uncontroverted." Draper, K. (2018). Michele Roberts on NBA Competitive Imbalance: Don't Blame the Players, the *New York Times*.

147 This statement by Adam Silver was not a part of an official NBA release, but rather was published by several media outlets. *See generally* Arnovitz, K. (2015). Why Bigger Pie is Not Big Enough for All, *available at* www.espn.com. *See also* Davis, S. (2015). NBA Commissioner Adam Silver Says A 'Significant Number' of Teams are Losing Money, *Business Insider*.

148 Official Release—Statement from NBPA Executive Director Michele Roberts (2015), *available at* www.nbpa.com.

149 Fitzgerald, M. (2015). Top Takeaways from Adam Silver's Board of Governors Press Conference, *available at* www.bleacherreport.com.

150 Torre, P.S. (2014). NBPA Director: 'Let's Stop Pretending,' *available at* www.espn.com.

151 Soshnick, S. (2014). LeBron James Will Reap $50 Million More From TV Deals, *Bloomberg*.

152 Araton, H. (2014). Owners Can't Line Their Pockets Now and Cry Poverty Later, LeBron James Says, *New York Times*.

153 Berger, K. (2014). Adam Silver: 'My Preference Would Be to Have a Harder Cap,' *CBS Sports*.

154 Torre, P.S. (2014). NBPA Director: 'Let's Stop Pretending,' *available at* www. espn.com.

155 NBA Commissioner Adam Silver Statement (2014), *available at* www.nba.com.

156 Torre, P.S. (2014). NBPA Director: 'Let's Stop Pretending,' *available at* www. espn.com.

157 *See* NBA CBA (2011), Article XI, Section 4.

158 To learn more about a proposed franchise player designation system that would complement and perhaps even improve the NBA's restricted free agency system and also partially replace the NBA's current qualifying offer system, *see* Bukstein, S. and Eisenberg, J. (2015). Implementing a Franchise Player Designation System in the NBA, *Harvard Journal of Sports and Entertainment Law*. Bukstein and Eisenberg proposed that the NBA adopt a franchise player designation system in specifically defined circumstances—for first-round picks who last played under a four-year rookie salary scale contract and for players who last played under a multi-year contract signed in free agency with an average annual salary of at least $10 million.

159 *See* NBA CBA (2011), Article XI, Section 1(c) for a description of the qualifying offer process.

160 The October 1 deadline is 90 days after the date by which the qualifying offer must be made, and just one day before the start of a team's training camp for the upcoming season. Under the existing rules, a qualifying offer may be unilaterally withdrawn by the team at any time through July 23 following its issuance. If the qualifying offer is not withdrawn on or before July 23, it may be withdrawn thereafter but only if the player agrees in writing to the withdrawal. If a qualifying offer is withdrawn, the player immediately becomes an unrestricted free agent. *See* NBA CBA (2011), Article XI, Section 4(c). Note that, based on the terms of the 2017 CBA, the July 23 deadline for a team to unilaterally withdraw a qualifying offer was changed to July 13. *See* NBA CBA (2017), Article XI, Section 4(c).

161 *See* Helin, K. (2011). NBA Proposes Franchise Tag, Non-Guaranteed Contracts, *Sports Illustrated. See also* Ford, C. (2011). Franchise Player Tag in the NBA?, *available at* www.espn.com.

162 Klosterman, C. (2014). Rookie of the Year: Adam Silver, *GQ Magazine*.

163 Klosterman, C. (2014). Rookie of the Year: Adam Silver, *GQ Magazine*.

164 Torre, P.S. (2014). NBPA Director: 'Let's Stop Pretending,' *available at* www. espn.com. *Chapter 3* includes a discussion of potential future topics of collective bargaining between the league and its players. Fascinatingly enough, the NBA has dramatically shifted its perspective and position regarding eligibility for the NBA draft. In February 2019, the NBA submitted an official proposal to the NBPA that proposed lowering the draft-eligible age from 19 to 18 years of age potentially commencing with the 2022 NBA draft. It is important to note that the NBA and NBPA are permitted to modify a specific term/provision within the CBA at any time. In other words, the league and its players do not need to wait until expiration of the current 2017 CBA to modify the NBA draft eligibility rule.

165 Mahoney, B. (2014). Silver: NBA Will Review Domestic Violence Policies, *Associated Press*.

166 *See* NBA CBA (2011), Article VI, Section 7 (providing that "When a player is convicted of (including a plea of guilty, no contest, or nolo contendere to) a violent felony, he shall immediately be suspended by the NBA for a minimum of ten games").

167 Amick, S. (2014). NBPA Chief: NBA Tried to 'Out-Muscle' NFL with Jeffrey Taylor Suspension, *USA Today*.

168 Amick, S. (2014). NBPA Chief: NBA Tried to 'Out-Muscle' NFL with Jeffrey Taylor Suspension, *USA Today*. *See also* Keh, A. and Araton, H. (2014). Establishing Her Position in the Post, the *New York Times* (further quoting Michele Roberts: "Whether or not the union responds to what it perceives as a violation of the CBA, that's not the player's call, that's the union's responsibility. The point needed to be made to the league and the public").

169 McCann, M.A. (2014). Why the NBA Won't Touch Its Domestic Violence Policies Anytime Soon, *Sports Illustrated*.

170 Official Release—NBA and NBPA Statement Regarding Today's Meeting (2015), *available at* www.nba.com.

171 Badenhausen, K. (2016). How the NBA Secured a New Deal with $10 Million Player Salaries, *Forbes* (expressing the viewpoint that, "by the time Roberts and Silver got to the table, most of the issues had been resolved").

172 Interview by Rachel Nichols (ESPN reporter and journalist) with Adam Silver (NBA Commissioner) (2016), *available at* www.espn.com.

173 Interview by CJ McCollum (NBA player and aspiring journalist) with Adam Silver (NBA commissioner) (2016), *available at* www.theplayerstribune.com.

174 Interview by CJ McCollum (NBA player and aspiring journalist) with Adam Silver (NBA commissioner) (2016), *available at* www.theplayerstribune.com (Commissioner Silver further explained that the goal of the league "from the fan standpoint would be, just for them to one day hear, 'We have a new deal,' or an extension of the current deal and everybody's focused on the game").

175 Washburn, G. (2016). NBA Union Chief Optimistic Sides Will Avoid Lockout, *Boston Globe*.

176 Washburn, G. (2016). NBA Union Chief Optimistic Sides Will Avoid Lockout, *Boston Globe* (providing the following additional thoughts from Michele Roberts in August 2016: "I've heard Adam proclaim his optimism. I've proclaimed mine, so I would like to sooner rather than later be able to have a press conference where we both stand together and announce together that we have a deal and there will be no work stoppage. There will be no lockout. Having said that, I've got to be ready for anything. But I am optimistic").

177 Blinebury, F. (2016). Silver Optimistic New CBA Will Be Reached Before Deadline, *available at* www.nba.com. Blinebury, F. (2016). Adam Silver Says Collective Bargaining Talks to Continue Next Week, *available at* www.nba.com. *See also* Aldridge, D. (2016). It's Early—Very Early—But Signs Encouraging in NBA Labor Talks, *available at* www.nba.com (writing that, "A new deal may not necessarily involve a great restructuring of the BRI split. The players seem to be doing rather well financially under the current system").

178 Aldridge, D. (2016). Nothing Finalized Yet, But Labor Peace Looking More and More Possible in NBA, *available at* www.nba.com.

179 Wertheim, J. (2016). Michele Roberts: I Wouldn't Mind 'Routing the League,' *Sports Illustrated* (further quoting Michele Roberts as saying: "I wouldn't mind

routing the league.... Having said that, every negotiation—most negotiations I should say—end up with each side saying, 'I wanted more or I gave away more than what I wanted to give away.' That's what the nature of negotiation is").

180 O'Connor, K. (2016). The Changes to Expect in the NBA's Upcoming Collective Bargaining Agreement, *available at* www.theringer.com.

181 Official Release—NBA Players and Board of Governors Ratify New Collective Bargaining Agreement (2016), *available at* www.nba.com.

182 Official Release—New NBA Collective Bargaining Agreement Signed (2017), *available at* www.nba.com.

183 Aldridge, D. (2016). NBA, NBPA Reach Tentative Seven-Year CBA, *available at* www.nba.com.

184 Coon, L. (2017). NBA Salary CAP FAQ: 2017 Collective Bargaining Agreement, *available at* www.cbafaq.com.

185 McCann, M. (2016). Biggest Takeaways: The NBA's New CBA Deal, *Sports Illustrated* (emphasizing the "continuous and productive negotiation sessions" between team owners and players).

186 The NBA released a document that provided a detailed yet succinct overview of principal deal terms. This "Principal Deal Points" document listed the following additional unchanged elements from the 2011 CBA: (1) The salary cap and tax structure will remain the same, including the calculation of cap/tax levels, use of salary cap exceptions, tax rates and transaction limits on teams over the tax apron; (2) the escrow system will remain the same; (3) existing rules on maximum free agent contract length will be retained; and (4) restricted free agency will remain in place with certain process-related changes.

187 *See* NBA CBA (2017), Article VII, Section 6 (indicating that the revised amounts will increase or decrease each successive NBA season starting with the 2018–2019 season based on corresponding percentage increases or decreases to the salary cap).

188 *See* NBA CBA (2017), Article VIII. The following examples indicate select rookie scale contract amounts for players drafted during the June 2019 NBA draft who were therefore "rookies" during the 2019–2020 season: $8.1 million for first draft pick, $3.5 million for 10th draft pick, $2.1 million for 20th draft pick and $1.6 million for 30th draft pick. *See* NBA CBA (2017), Exhibit B-3. Second round draft picks are not automatically guaranteed an NBA contract. No formal rookie scale applies to second round picks. NBA teams must use cap space or a salary cap exception to sign second round picks. For instance, a team could sign a second round pick to a two-year deal at the minimum salary amount or could sign a second round pick to a three-year contract by utilizing part of the team's mid-level exception.

189 *See* NBA CBA (2017), Article VII, Sections 6(d) and 6(m)(3).

190 "Early Qualifying Veteran Free Agent" means a Veteran Free Agent who, prior to becoming a Veteran Free Agent, played under one or more player contracts covering some or all of each of the two preceding seasons, and who either played exclusively with his prior team during such two seasons, or, if he played for more than one team during such period, changed teams only by means of trade, by means of assignment via the NBA's waiver procedures, or by signing with his prior team during the first of the two seasons. *See* NBA CBA (2017), Article I, Section 1(u).

191 *See* NBA CBA (2017), Article VII, Section 5(c).

192 *See* NBA CBA (2017), Article VII, Section 8. The 2017 CBA contains a set of detailed rules related to player trades. The applicable trade range formula regarding allowable outgoing salaries and incoming salaries is based in part on whether a team is a taxpaying

team (that is, total player salaries on a team after the trade would exceed luxury tax level) or a non-taxpaying team (that is, a team whose salary would exceed the salary cap amount but not the luxury tax threshold after the trade). For example, CBA Article VII, Section 6(j) provides the following nuanced rules related to the application of three different potential trade ranges for a non-taxpaying team: A team whose post-assignment team salary would be equal to or less than the luxury tax level for the then-current salary cap year may replace a traded player with one or more replacement players whose player contracts are acquired simultaneously and whose post-assignment salaries for the then-current salary cap year, in the aggregate, are no more than an amount equal to the greater of: (1) the lesser of (A) 175% of the pre-trade salary of the traded player plus $100,000, or (B) 100% of the pre-trade salary of the traded player plus $5 million; or (2) 125% of the pre-trade salary of the traded player, plus $100,000.

193 *See* NBA CBA (2017), Article II, Section 7. *See also* NBA CBA (2017), Article VII, Section 7(a). *See also* NBA CBA (2017), Article IX, Section 1. *See also* Official Release—2017 NBA Collective Bargaining Agreement: Principal Deal Points (2017), *available at* www.nba.com.

194 *See* NBA CBA (2017), Article II, Section 7. *See also* NBA CBA (2017), Article VII, Section 7(b). *See also* NBA CBA (2017), Article IX, Section 1. *See also* Official Release—2017 NBA Collective Bargaining Agreement: Principal Deal Points (2017), *available at* www.nba.com.

195 *See* NBA CBA (2017), Article II, Section 11. The NBA's development league was rebranded from the D-League (Development League) to the G League ("Gatorade League") in June 2017 as a result of a corporate partnership deal between the NBA and Gatorade. NBA G League players could potentially earn more than $410,000 during the 2019–2020 season. For example, if a G League player spent the entire 2019–2020 season in the development league on a two-way contract, maximized his allowable time with the affiliated NBA team and his contract was not converted to a standard NBA player contract at any point during the season, then that player would earn the following amounts: (1) $350,175 for 69 NBA days of service (45 days of service during NBA regular season, six days of service before start of G League training camp and 18 days after conclusion of G League regular season at a daily compensation rate of $5,075 per day); and (2) additional base compensation of $60,480 for 108 G League days of service (at a daily rate of $560 per day). *See* NBA CBA (2017), Article II, Section 11(b).

196 *See* NBA CBA (2017), Article XXXIII, Section 9.

197 *See* NBA CBA (2017), Article VI, Section 4.

198 *See* NBA CBA (2017), Article VI, Section 5.

199 *See* NBA CBA (2017), Article VI, Section 6.

200 *See* NBA CBA (2017), Article XXXVI, Sections 1 and 2.

201 National Basketball Players Association—THINK450 (https://nbpa.com/think450). THINK450 is the "innovation engine of the NBPA."

202 Beer, J. (2018). NBA Players Union Unveils New Marketing Rights Group Think450, *Fast Company* (explaining that that NBPA is "bullish on the opportunity for THINK450 to market players beyond the uniform. NBA players are among the most active on social media, the most recognizable in culture, so brand partnerships are as easy to imagine off the court as on the court").

203 *See* NBA CBA (2017), Article II, Section 8(a). *See also* NBA CBA (2017), Article XXXVII, Section 1. *See also* NBA CBA (2017), Exhibit A—Uniform Player Contract, Sections 13(a) and 13(d).

204 *See* Official Release—2017 NBA Collective Bargaining Agreement: Principal Deal Points (2017), *available at* www.nba.com. *See also* NBA CBA (2017), Article IV, Section 3(a).

205 *See* NBA CBA (2017), Article XXII, Section 12.

206 *See* NBA CBA (2017), Article XXIX, Section 11. *See also* Official Release—2017 NBA Collective Bargaining Agreement: Principal Deal Points (2017), *available at* www.nba.com.

207 *See* NBA CBA (2017), Article XLI, Section 6.

3   Collective bargaining in the NBA

Part 2

Overview of chapter contents

This chapter anticipates the next round of collective bargaining in the NBA, and previews some of the existing (and anticipated) challenges and opportunities that players and team owners will potentially face and hopefully work together in the years ahead to negotiate, solve and resolve. This chapter also details numerous current business and governance issues within the NBA, including contract tampering (having unauthorized conversations/communications), circumvention of CBA rules (entering into unauthorized contracts, or taking steps to enter into unauthorized contracts), sports betting and the league revenue sharing plan.

The future of collective bargaining in the NBA

Adam Silver and Michele Roberts will continue to be responsible for leading the league, its member teams and NBA players in future collective bargaining negotiations for the foreseeable future.[1] In June 2018, Adam Silver's contract was extended through the 2023–2024 NBA season. Less than a month later, in July 2018, Michele Roberts was re-elected as NBPA executive director for another four-year term.

Since agreeing to terms for the 2017 CBA, Adam Silver and Michele Roberts have collaborated on a series of impactful initiatives related to player programming. For example, in September 2018, the NBA and NBPA sent a letter to all NBA players expressing support for player civic engagement. The letter also encouraged NBA players to utilize newly-enhanced mental wellness programs and other resources for personal development. The following excerpt is from the letter written by Adam Silver and Michele Roberts and distributed to all league players:

> We continue to support your efforts to bring together families, community leaders and law enforcement to rebuild trust in our neighborhoods; mentor and empower young people; encourage civic engagement; and amplify the voices of organizations that champion the values of equality, diversity and inclusion. We're also offering more resources for your own personal development. Each of our offices has newly-enhanced mental wellness programs,

which we encourage you to use to manage stress, anxiety and other challenges. It's a critical step that can also encourage teammates and fans alike to understand that it's a sign of strength, not weakness, to ask for help. Above all, our partnership shows that we are one family. We may not always agree on every issue, but we still look out for one another. We listen and learn from each other. And we understand that we're all part of something bigger than just a game.[2]

In August 2019, the NBA announced an expanded set of player mental health guidelines for the 2019–2020 season. All NBA teams were required to: (1) hire at least one full-time licensed mental health professional (psychologist or behavioral therapist) who has experience in assessing and treating clinical mental health issues; (2) identify a licensed psychiatrist available to help players manage any mental health concerns; (3) enact a written action plan for mental health emergencies; and (4) inform players and staff members how the team will ensure privacy and confidentiality of mental health matters.[3]

Similar to collaborating in order to address issues related to player community involvement and player mental health, the NBA and NBPA can also hopefully work together to address some or all of the following challenges and opportunities in the months and years ahead.

NBA draft initial eligibility requirements

The 2017 CBA contains the following initial eligibility criteria for NBA hopefuls: (1) The player is or will be at least 19 years of age during the calendar year in which the draft is held; and (2) With respect to a player who is not an international player, at least one NBA season has elapsed since the player's graduation from high school (or, if the player did not graduate from high school, at least one year has elapsed since the graduation of the class with which the player would have graduated had he graduated from high school).[4] The NBA has dramatically shifted its perspective and position regarding eligibility for the NBA draft. Even though initially opposed to lowering the draft-eligible age and actually inclined to raise the draft-eligible age from 19 years to 20 years, Commissioner Silver eventually developed a different perspective on this issue. For instance, in February 2017—just over a month after the 2017 CBA was signed—Commissioner Silver made the following remarks:

> I think both of us, while our traditional positions have been the league would like to raise the minimum age from 19 to 20, and at least Michele's stated position is that she would like to lower it from 19 to 18, I think there is an acknowledgement that the issue is far more complex than that. And it requires sort of all the constituent groups to be at the table. And I will say— and maybe it's a little bit of a different position from my standpoint—I think rather than standing here and saying the league's goal is to get from 19 to 20, I think I have a better understanding of the issue now as well, as I

talk to some of the young players who are coming into our league who have only completed a portion of their freshman year in college and have a better understanding of what the conditions are for them both academically and in terms of their basketball requirement.[5]

In October 2017, the National Collegiate Athletic Association (NCAA) established an independent Commission on College Basketball to assess the state of college basketball as well as to recommend transformational changes that would address multiple issues and challenges within the sport. One recommendation made by the Commission on College Basketball in April 2018 encouraged the NBA and NBPA to once again make 18-year-olds eligible for the NBA draft, so that high school players who are drafted may proceed directly to the NBA and bypass participation in college basketball. The report issued by the Commission on College Basketball also clarified that "the NCAA lacks the legal power to change one-and-done on its own; the power to make this change lies exclusively with the NBA and the NBPA."[6] The report also concluded that the existing "one-and-done" draft eligibility system "has played a significant role in corrupting and destabilizing college basketball, restricting the freedom of choice of players, and undermining the relationship of college basketball to the mission of higher education.... The recent commitment of the NBA to improve the G League may enhance its appeal as a professional option for elite players who are 18 and do not wish to attend college."[7]

At the annual NBA Board of Governors meeting in July 2018, Commissioner Silver made the following comments about the NBA draft eligibility framework:

> We presented the pros and cons on going from 19 to 18. In conjunction with that presentation, we discussed a lot about the development of younger players prior to them coming into the professional ranks. We've had several discussions with both the NCAA and USA Basketball about engaging with them, with players beginning roughly at 14 years old, and especially with those elite players who we know statistically have a high likelihood when they are identified at that age of being top-tier players coming into the league. So, I think the next step will be to sit down with the players association. Of course, it has to be collectively bargained if we are going to lower the age. That's something we will begin to discuss with [the players].[8]

In February 2019, the NBA submitted an official proposal to the NBPA that proposed lowering the draft-eligible age from 19 to 18 years of age potentially commencing with the 2022 NBA draft. This new approach of allowing 18-year-old basketball players to enter the NBA draft would replace the current "one-and-done" rule in the 2017 CBA—a rule that has been in effect since the 2006 NBA draft. It is important to note that the NBA and NBPA are permitted to modify a specific term/provision within the CBA at any time. In other words, the league and its players do not need to wait until expiration of the current 2017 CBA to modify the NBA draft eligibility rule.[9]

Although NBA and NBPA representatives continued to remain hopeful about agreeing to a modification of the draft eligibility rule that presently exists within the 2017 CBA, by April 2019 a few minor areas of potential disagreement and compromise surfaced. For example, the NBA requested that the NBPA agree to require that draft prospects who bypass college provide NBA teams with medical information in order to create maximum medical transparency regarding the pool of younger players. The NBPA reportedly received feedback from NBA player agents before letting the league know that the players association preferred not to require that 18-year-old draft picks supply medical records. In addition, the NBA expressed interest in requiring that 18-year-old draft prospects attend and participate at the NBA pre-draft combine.[10] Collaborating and reaching consensus on an issue such as lowering the draft-eligible age—an issue that previously represented a source of contention and tension between the league and the NBPA—certainly functions as another positive indicator for the future of collective bargaining between players and team owners.

Refining the definition of BRI

NBA players might decide to collaborate with team owners to further clarify certain aspects of the current definition of BRI as well as to expand or revise other elements of the BRI definition. For example, under the 2017 CBA, "proceeds from the sale or rental of real estate" by NBA teams is expressly excluded from the definition of BRI, as are proceeds from businesses outside the arena besides team-operated stores (for example, restaurants, casinos, hotels and retail businesses).[11] In recent years, numerous NBA teams such as the Orlando Magic and Golden State Warriors have been involved with mixed use real estate developments surrounding the basketball arena that include a combination of commercial space, retail stores, residential housing along with sports and entertainment elements.[12]

In the words of former NBA commissioner David Stern, "The franchise is a media company. It is a digital company. It holds a key to a demographic. And it's also an epicenter for real estate development."[13] As explained by Atlanta Hawks CEO Steve Koonin, "Teams have traditional revenue streams—sponsorship, ticket sales, media rights and what you can generate inside your arena. Those can grow over time, but real estate development can represent a hedge against future uncertainty in all of these revenue areas."[14] Gary Arrick, CFO of the NBPA, believes that revenue generated from these real estate development projects adjacent to NBA team arenas should be shared with the players. Arrick explained that, in his view, "Irrespective of what the current CBA says, it's a reasonable argument that the players should share in some fashion in all revenue generated by the game—whether directly or indirectly. We are not arguing that ownership isn't putting up the capital and taking the risk. But we would argue there should be some recognition of the players in these additional revenue streams, including real estate income streams [and] increases in franchise value."[15]

Contract length and compensation guarantees

NBA players might request that salaries under existing player contracts increase based on specified future increases in league revenues in addition to increasing the overall future team salary cap amount based on actual increases in BRI.[16] NBA players might also focus on player mobility items such as a player having the ability to select his new team if multiple teams claim that player off of waivers as well as players having both an early termination option and a player option in the final two years of a maximum salary contract. NBA owners might push for a limit on the number of guaranteed years in player contracts (for example, three guaranteed years in a five-year contract) and might also request that player contracts contain "conditional guarantees" based on factors such as meeting a minimum "games/minutes played" threshold.

In addition, NBA players and the league could collaboratively conclude that specific types of player contracts—for example, "supermax" contracts in which players can earn up to 35% of the salary cap—should count less for salary cap purposes as compared with the pure cash value of the deals. This framework would provide teams with the ability to retain star players while also preserving some salary cap flexibility for future player transactions. For example, during the 2019–2020 season, the Washington Wizards were required to pay injured player John Wall $38.2 million—an amount equal to 35% of the $109.14 million salary cap. Perhaps the league and its players might agree that these supermax deals should only count as "25% of the salary cap" for salary cap calculation purposes, which would result in the contract for John Wall counting $38.2 million for cash purposes during the 2019–2020 season but only counting $27.3 million for salary cap application purposes—the end result would be an additional $10.9 million in salary cap space/flexibility for the Wizards to spend on one or more players who could add value to the team while John Wall recovered from surgery on his left Achilles tendon. In addition, the league and players could also discuss adjustments to the "supermax cash vs. cap" concept based on the overall productivity/performance of the supermax player. For example, if a player like John Wall failed to play a certain number of minutes during the 2019–2020 season (or failed to achieve certain other statistical metrics related to quantifiable variables such as average points per game), the value of his contract might only count as 15% or 20% of the salary cap instead of the actual cash value of his contract (35% of the salary cap). Again, this concept focuses on encouraging teams to take risks by offering star players supermax contracts while simultaneously preserving future salary cap flexibility for a team in the event that a supermax player suffers a serious injury and/or severely underperforms during one or more years of the supermax deal.[17]

Wearable biometric tracking systems and subsequent use of player data

The 2017 CBA defines wearables as any "device worn by an individual that measures movement information (such as distance, velocity, acceleration, deceleration, jumps, changes of direction, and player load calculated from such information and/or height/weight), biometric information (such as heart rate, heart rate variability, skin temperature, blood oxygen, hydration, lactate, and/or glucose), or other health, fitness, and performance information."[18] Immediately after the league and the NBPA reached agreement on the 2017 CBA, a joint advisory wearables committee was formed. The committee consists of three representatives appointed by the NBA and three representatives appointed by the NBPA. The wearables committee is responsible for: (1) reviewing all requests by individual teams, the NBA or the NBPA to approve a wearable device for use by players (with the standard being whether the functionality of the wearable device has been validated and whether the wearable device would be potentially harmful to anyone including the player if used as intended); and (2) establishing cybersecurity standards for the storage of data collected from wearables.

In addition, NBA teams are permitted to request that a player utilize wearable devices on a voluntary basis in practice (but not during actual NBA games). Before a team is allowed to request that a player use an approved wearable device, the team must provide the player with a confidential written explanation that details: (1) what the wearable device will measure; (2) the meaning of each measurement; and (3) the benefits to the player in the team obtaining the movement data and/or biometric data (for example, the data will allow the team to develop an optimized muscle recovery strategy along with optimal utilization of the player's skill set on the basketball court). NBA players retain the right to decline (or discontinue) the use of a wearable device at any time, and must also have full access to any data collected from approved wearables. The data collected from a wearable worn by a player at the request of a team may be used for player health and performance purposes along with team on-court tactical and strategic purposes. The data may not be considered, used, discussed or referenced for any other purpose such as any commercial purpose or in negotiations regarding a prospective player contract. Any NBA team that engages in an unauthorized use of player movement data or biometric data will be subject to a fine of up to $250,000. When negotiating terms for the 2017 CBA, the NBA and the NBPA also agreed "to continue to discuss in good faith the use of wearables in games and the commercialization of data from wearables."[19]

Questions and issues related to wearables for the NBA and NBPA to consider during future bargaining sessions include the following:

- How can the league and the NBPA ensure that biometric data collected via wearable devices is not being utilized as intel/leverage by team executives for future contract negotiations?

- What quality control systems should be developed to guarantee the accuracy and reliability of movement data and biometric data produced by wearables?
- If players agree to a one-year pilot test of playing in regular season games with wearable devices, what steps will be developed to ensure the integrity of the game along with player safety?
- When players are traded, what happens with biometric data collected by a former team (for example, can that data now be used in scouting reports by the former team to develop game strategy)?
- If player biometric data is eventually sold to external companies, how will the league and its players share in resultant revenue?
- How can the league and the NBPA monitor and manage other potential misuses of player biometric data?
- Should NBA game basketballs integrate data tracking capabilities?[20]

Competitive balance among all teams in league

Facilitating and maintaining competitive balance is not a new issue of concern for team owners and players, but rather functions as an ongoing challenge within professional sports leagues such as the NBA. One issue related to competitive balance that existed prior to the NBA and NBPA finalizing the 2017 CBA relates to the formation of "super teams" within the league. In July 2016, during an annual press conference at the Las Vegas Summer League, Commissioner Silver provided the following detailed insight and input regarding the importance of competitive balance:

> I think we can make the system even better and I think it is critically important that fans of every market have that belief that if their team is well managed—that they can compete. And, certainly, it's important to me that markets in this league, those that are perceived as small, those that are larger, all feel that they have an equal chance. And my sense is that some of the player movements we just saw isn't necessarily a function of market size— it's clearly a case of one particular player's desire to be in a situation with a group of players who have already proven that they can win. And by the way I don't mean to be so cryptic, in the case of Kevin Durant I absolutely respect his decision once he becomes a free agent to make a choice that is available to him and in this case he operated 100% within the way of the system and same with Golden State. Having said that, I do think to maintain those principles that I discussed in terms of creating a league in which every team has the opportunity to compete, we do need to re-examine some of the elements of our system so that I'm not here next year or the year after again talking about anomalies. There are certain things, corrections, we believe we can make in the system. Of course [we are] going to negotiate here with the union but it requires two parties to make those changes and I think we have had very productive discussions with the union so far and we will continue to do so.[21]

Two years later, in July 2018, Commissioner Silver once again addressed the enduring issue of competitive balance within the NBA:

> I don't necessarily think it's per se bad that the Warriors are so dominant. As I've said before, we're not trying to create some forced parity. What we really focus on is parity of opportunity, and a fair point can be made in a tax system when certain teams are spending significantly more than others that that is not parity of opportunity. Also, certain teams have advantages that other teams don't based on the resources in the market, the wealth of the market, and they may be in a position to go deeper into the tax than another team does.... I don't have anything precise in mind other than engaging with the Players Association and talking about how we can improve things. There is always the next collective bargaining agreement, but I think in addition that we have developed a certain rapport with the Players Association where I feel we can talk about anything at any time.[22]

Playoff format and number of regular season games

In 2018, the NBA began to brainstorm potential future changes to the current playoff seeding system. One proposed concept involved selecting the 16 teams with the best records in the league for playoff participation, as compared with the current system in which the top eight teams from each of the Eastern Conference and Western Conference participate in the playoffs. Another complementary concept that recently surfaced related to having a "play-in" tournament before the official playoffs, which would be somewhat similar to the two "wild card" games in Major League Baseball's postseason. Commissioner Silver explained that travel serves as the primary potential hurdle to these playoff overhauling proposals. The NBA estimates an increase of about 40,000 miles of travel during the postseason if the league eliminated its current conference format and simply invited the top 16 teams in the league to participate in the playoffs. Commissioner Silver commented, "The obstacle is travel, and it's not tradition in my mind, at least ... that as we've added an extra week to the regular season, as we've tried to reduce the number of back-to-backs, that we are concerned about teams crisscrossing the country in the first round, for example. We are just concerned about the overall travel that we would have in the top 16 teams.... It's still my hope that we're going to figure out ways. Maybe ultimately you have to add even more days to the season to spread it out a little bit more to deal with the travel. Maybe air travel will get better. All things we'll keep looking at."[23]

In June 2016, NBA player CJ McCollum interviewed Commissioner Silver. During the interview, Commissioner Silver acknowledged, "I know it is one of the topics that the players association is talking about, the length of the preseason and the number of games we play in the preseason."[24] The 2017 CBA reduced the number of permitted preseason (exhibition) games per team from eight games to six games; in addition, the overall time period for training camp and the preseason was shortened by seven days.[25] Hopefully the NBA and the NBPA can similarly work together to develop an innovative framework that would provide players with additional days of rest (lessening overall player workloads), further reduce the number of back-to-back games, and optimize fan engagement throughout the regular season (perhaps by implementing a mid-season tournament).

In 2019, Commissioner Silver provided the following insight: "Sometimes it's science, but sometimes it's art. I think a fair point from fans could be if ultimately the science suggests that 82 games is too many games for these players, maybe you shouldn't have an 82-game season. I accept that, and that's something we'll continue to look at. We and the players have a common interest in maximizing viewership and maximizing interest. I'm a traditionalist on one hand, but on the other hand [the current 82 game format] is 50 years old or so … and there is nothing magical about it."[26] In 2019, the NBA indicated a willingness to consider a major overhaul to NBA All-Star Weekend, which could include revamping or perhaps even replacing the actual All-Star Game. During a press conference in March 2019, Commissioner Silver directly admitted, "The All-Star Game didn't work."[27] The league and its players have many synergistically interconnected issues to discuss and address in the years ahead related to the number of preseason and regular season games, playoff format/framework, NBA All-Star Weekend and similar items involving other league and team events.

Current (and anticipated) business and league governance challenges and opportunities

The NBA has approved and implemented a series of new rules and revamped policies after agreeing to terms in the 2017 CBA. For instance, in September 2017 the NBA Board of Governors approved changes to the NBA draft lottery system. The new lottery system rules became effective starting with the June 2019 NBA draft. The main emphasis of the NBA draft lottery system reform is to even out the odds of landing the first pick in the NBA draft for the teams with the lowest winning percentage during the prior year. Based on the new lottery system, the three teams with the worst record will now each have a 14% chance of being awarded the top draft pick; prior to the 2019 NBA draft, the team with the lowest winning percentage had a 25% chance of winning the draft lottery as compared with a 19.9% chance for the team with the second worst record the prior season and a 15.6% chance for the team with the third worst record. As a result, the new draft lottery system will hopefully discourage "tanking" (that is, losing games intentionally as a result of teams not playing with full effort on the basketball court, general managers trading away the most talented player(s) on the team, or coaches intentionally resting star players at the end of the season). As explained by Byron Spruell, NBA president of league operations, "NBA draft lottery reform is a meaningful step in our continuous effort to enhance the quality of our games. These changes were necessary to improve the competitive incentives for our teams."[28]

Also, in September 2017, the NBA Board of Governors agreed on a policy related to teams deciding to intentionally rest (not allocating any game playing minutes to) healthy players—that is, players who are not injured intentionally not playing in a game ostensibly in order to focus on "load management." The NBA provided teams with the following guidance for the new policy related to resting healthy players, which was initially implemented and enforced during the 2017–2018 NBA season:

- Teams are prohibited from resting healthy players for any high-profile, nationally televised game—any violation of this provision will constitute conduct prejudicial or detrimental to the NBA and result in a fine of at least $100,000;
- Absent unusual circumstances, a team should not rest multiple healthy players for the same game or rest healthy players when playing on the road;
- In situations when teams decide to rest healthy players, the players should be visible and available to interact with fans; and
- Any team that violates this policy, or otherwise rests a healthy player in circumstances that are prejudicial or detrimental to the league, is subject to discipline by the NBA.[29]

Another example of a recent rule change approved by the NBA Board of Governors involves the introduction of a "Coach's Challenge" to trigger instant replay review of a limited set of referee calls. This new rule was adopted on a one-year trial basis during the 2019–2020 season. According to Byron Spruell, NBA president of league operations, "Giving head coaches a voice will enhance the confidence in our replay process among teams and fans and add a new, exciting strategic element to our game."[30] Key aspects of the "Coach's Challenge" concept include the following:

- Each team is entitled to one challenge during every regular season and postseason game (regardless of whether the challenge by the head coach is ultimately successful)
- A team can use its challenge in the following instances: (1) a called personal foul charged to its own team; (2) a called out-of-bounds violation; or (3) a called goaltending or basket interference violation
  - A team can use its challenge on a called personal foul at any point in the game
  - In the last two minutes of the fourth period or the last two minutes of any overtime period, a called out-of-bounds violation or called goaltending/basket interference violation will not be challengeable by the coach and instead any review will be exclusively prompted by on-court referees.[31]

In addition to adopting the above-mentioned new rules and revising existing rules, which did not require collective bargaining with players, team owners and

Commissioner Silver might also decide to continue addressing (and also start focusing on) various league governance and systematic issues related to basketball operations that likewise do not require formal collective bargaining sessions with—or approval from—players in the league.[32] The following examples attempt to provide an overview of various current (and anticipated) business and governance challenges and opportunities within the NBA.

Tampering with player contracts (impermissible contact between teams and players), player trade demands, free agency communications and circumvention of CBA rules

In December 2018, Commissioner Silver issued a memo to all league teams reminding each team that "conduct that interferes with contractual employment relationships is prohibited … [teams should] refrain from any conduct—including public statements—that could be viewed as targeting or expressing interest in another team's player."[33] Commissioner Silver's memo to all teams was an inevitable natural byproduct of several situations involving tampering that transpired throughout previous NBA seasons. For example, in August 2017 the NBA fined the Los Angeles Lakers $500,000 for violating the league's anti-tampering rule. According to the official NBA press release related to this situation, "The conduct at issue involved communications by Lakers General Manager Rob Pelinka with the agent representing Paul George that constituted a prohibited expression of interest in the player while he was under contract…. The NBA's anti-tampering rule prohibits teams from interfering with other teams' contractual relationships with NBA players, including by publicly expressing interest in a player who is currently under contract with another team or informing the agent of another team's player of interest by one's own team in that player."[34]

Other similar examples of tampering commonly involve one or more NBA players encouraging/inducing another player presently under contract with a different NBA team to request a trade from his current team, or an NBA player publicly requesting/demanding a trade from his current team. For example, in January 2019, the NBA fined Anthony Davis $50,000 for violating a collectively-bargained rule prohibiting players or their representatives from making public trade demands; more specifically, the fine was for statements that were made by Davis' agent, Rich Paul, in an intentional effort to undermine the contractual relationship between Davis and the New Orleans Pelicans.[35] Commissioner Silver candidly expressed that trade demands "are disheartening to the team, they are disheartening to the community, and they don't serve the player well. That is an issue that needs to be addressed, and there is not a simple solution. Players have leverage and economic power of their own. But that is what collective bargaining agreements are for—to sit down and come up with a set of rules that are sensible and fair for everyone."[36]

Similar issues have recently surfaced relating to teams reaching out to prospective free agents before the official date and time at which teams are officially permitted to begin recruiting and negotiating with free agents. For example, during the 2019 summer free agency period, multiple player signings (for example, Kemba Walker signing with the Boston Celtics and Kyrie Irving signing with the Brooklyn Nets) were "unofficially" announced before the official start of free agency; this meant that teams and players had engaged in contract negotiations prior to the technical starting point of free agency.[37] Commissioner Silver acknowledged, "We always knew there was some leakage and slippage around those deadlines. We need to revisit and reset those rules. It's pointless to have rules that we can't enforce. It hurts the perception of integrity around the league."[38] In part as a result of these known integrity-related challenges with respect to teams unscrupulously communicating with free agents, the NBA slightly amended its rules so that teams and players are now permitted to begin free agent negotiations at 6:00 p.m. Eastern Standard Time on June 30 each summer—six hours earlier than the previous start time of 12:01 a.m. Eastern Standard Time on July 1.[39] However, the NBA fully understands that this issue of teams reaching out to players before the official start of free agency in order to create negotiation leverage represents an evolving and difficult issue to completely solve or resolve.

Another connected area of collective concern among NBA teams relates to salary cap circumvention when teams sign free agents each year in July. The 2017 CBA contains extensive regulations and prohibitions related to circumvention. For instance, teams are not allowed to: (1) enter into a sponsorship agreement with a company and subsequently direct payments to be made directly to a player on the team; (2) make a financial inducement to any NBA player not currently under contract with the team; (3) provide players on the team with any compensation, consideration or anything else of value that extends beyond what is allowed to be included within the player's contract and as other player benefits (for example, hotels, meals and per diem) based on the CBA rules; and (4) make any promises or guarantees about future prospective contract extensions or renegotiations other than as expressly permitted by the 2017 CBA.[40]

As explained by Professor Michael McCann, "The conferral of financial benefits to players, or their representatives, in ways that extend beyond the terms of a player's contract constitutes illicit compensation under league rules. Unauthorized compensation is a similar and related problem to tampering. Both are about teams negotiating with players to gain an unfair advantage over rivals. Yet unauthorized compensation is more disturbing and consequential. It concerns money changing hands rather than mere communications."[41] For example, in August 2015, the NBA fined the Los Angeles Clippers $250,000 for violating NBA rules prohibiting teams from offering players unauthorized business or investment opportunities. According to the official NBA press release related to this situation, "The violation involved a presentation made by the Clippers to free agent DeAndre Jordan on July 2 that improperly included a potential third-party endorsement opportunity for the player…. The NBA's anti-circumvention rules prohibit teams from, among other things, providing or arranging for others to provide any form of compensation to a player unless such compensation is included in a player contract or otherwise expressly permitted under the CBA."[42]

A similar situation emerged during the free agency period in July 2019. A series of similar (yet not completely verified) media reports indicated that Kawhi Leonard's uncle and advisor, Dennis Robertson, demanded various benefits—including guaranteed endorsement deal money and free housing—from several teams during preliminary contract negotiations on Kawhi's behalf.[43]

In recent years, some NBA teams have attempted to develop clever salary cap management strategies that technically adhere to player contract rules but also presumably violate "the spirit" (i.e., the overall purpose and intentions) of the CBA. For example, before the 2019–2020 season, the Houston Rockets signed NBA veteran player Nene to a new two-year contract purportedly worth $20 million over the two seasons with base compensation of about $2.56 million for the 2019–2020 season (minimum salary amount required under Article II, Section 6 of the 2017 CBA for a player like Nene with more than ten years of experience in the NBA). In addition to Nene's base compensation, the Houston Rockets also included several "likely bonuses" totaling more than $7 million per season in Nene's contract primarily based on number of games played. However, in order to earn this bonus money in each of the two seasons of the new contract, the team(s) Nene played for during each such season would need to individually win at least 52 games. Because the Houston Rockets won 53 games during the 2018–2019 season, winning 52 games would be considered "likely" for bonus purposes in Nene's contract with the Rockets. However, before signing Nene, the Houston Rockets seemed to already have a plan in place to trade Nene to a team such as the Memphis Grizzlies that was not very likely to win 52 games during the 2019–2020 season. A team like the Grizzlies would plausibly have been willing to trade a player like Andre Iguodala to the Rockets in exchange for Nene (plus at least about $3.7 million more in outgoing salary from the Rockets) in order to reduce the team's total cash obligations with respect to player payroll for the 2019–2020 season. Including the "likely bonuses" within Nene's contract in a trade would have helped to facilitate a deal for a player such as Andre Iguodala along with creating a valuable trade exception for the Rockets based on the trade rules in the 2017 CBA. However, both the NBA and the NBPA agreed that the Rockets would not be permitted to count the "likely bonuses" in Nene's contract for outgoing salary calculation/matching purposes during any future trade. Even though the Nene contract concept devised by the Rockets technically falls within the parameters of the 2017 CBA rules, the league and the NBPA both reviewed the contract after it was filed with the NBA and subsequently determined that the contract concept violated the spirit of the CBA rules. Therefore, the proposed "likely bonus" concept was not approved for outgoing salary calculation/matching purposes with respect to any potential future trade because it was deemed to be an attempt to circumvent the salary cap principles in the 2017 CBA. As a result, the Rockets could be in a situation where the team would owe Nene approximately $2.4 million in bonus money in addition to his $2.56 million base salary if: (1) the Rockets win at least 52 games during the 2019–2020 season; (2) Nene plays in at least ten of 82 regular season games; and (3) the Rockets are unable to trade Nene before the

February trade deadline. Similarly, the Rockets would owe Nene $10 million total for the 2019–2020 season if: (1) the Rockets win at least 52 games during the 2019–2020 season; (2) Nene plays in at least 40 of 82 regular season games; and (3) the Rockets are unable to trade Nene before the February trade deadline. This contract situation involving the Houston Rockets demonstrates the potential pitfalls of violating "the spirit of the CBA."[44]

In September 2019, Commissioner Silver provided all NBA teams with another memo, which addressed what the league considered to be a "widespread perception that many of the league's rules are being broken on a frequent basis" when it comes to tampering, salary cap matters and the timing of free agency discussions.[45] As detailed in the memo, tampering with players or team personnel could result in a fine as high as $10 million (double the previous $5 million limit). Similarly, if a team enters into an unauthorized (improper) deal with a player, the team can be fined up to $6 million—and the player can also be assessed with a $250,000 fine. In addition, any statements or conduct detrimental to the integrity of the NBA could now result in a $5 million fine (up from the previous ceiling of $1 million), and a rule violation with no specific predetermined penalty could merit a $10 million fine (up from $2.5 million previously).[46] The league also proposed—and then officially approved—additional penalties for tampering and CBA rule circumvention, including the forfeiture or transfer of draft picks, suspensions of team executives, voiding of contracts and prohibiting teams from signing the person(s) that the team tampered with in circumvention of the CBA rules.

Also, in September 2019, the NBA Board of Governors formally approved the following stringent package of measures and requirements in order to more effectively encourage transparency and enforce compliance with league tampering and salary cap circumvention rules:

- A requirement that a team report, within 24 hours, any instance of an agent or player representative asking for an unauthorized benefit that is not allowed by the 2017 CBA;
- A requirement that teams preserve and do not delete emails, text and other communications with NBA players and NBA player agents for one year;
- A requirement that a representative from each organization verify that the team followed all applicable NBA rules and regulations related to negotiating with and signing free agents—each team governor/owner must also personally certify that every player contract complies with all established and relevant NBA rules;
- The development of new channels for teams and team employees to anonymously report rules violations or tampering;
- The development of rules to prevent players from inducing other NBA players under contract to request trades; and
- The initiation of annual investigatory audits of five randomly selected NBA teams each year to assess compliance with the new system rules (for example, auditing the communications between basketball operations representatives

such as general managers at different NBA teams as well as auditing the communications between NBA front office personal and player agents).[47]

When asked about the strict new compliance and integrity related measures, Commissioner Silver responded, "We need to ensure that we are creating a culture of compliance in this league and that our teams want to know that they are competing on a level playing field, and frankly don't want to feel disadvantaged if they are adhering to our existing rules.... The ultimate goal here is to ensure compliance and to ensure that there is that appropriate tension that exists at the team. So, there is sort of a significant threat that if a team doesn't comply, that there will be consequences."[48] Commissioner Silver also commented on his viewpoint that NBA players also support rules and policies that underscore the importance of competitive balance: "What gets lost sometimes is that for the 450 players or so in the league, they want a competitive landscape as well. They don't necessarily want a system where there is a sense that certain teams have a competitive advantage over other teams, because then you are just benefiting the players that happen to be on those teams."[49]

Relatedly, a few days later during September 2019, NBPA executive director Michele Roberts expressed her perspective on the apparent perception of some team and league executives that a select group of current NBA star players have too much power and, as a result, are able to essentially force a trade from their current team:

> There's just a perception that owners have rights and players don't.... No one has said a word about what happens when the team precipitously trades a man, especially a family man, and the consequences that that has on him. We spend so much time criticizing a player's decision to move but no time wondering or thinking is anything contoured about a team's decision to move a player. Teams want to maintain some competitive advantage.... So there's some structural issues that have to be acknowledged. What I think has to happen is we have to somehow stop the chatter that I think is growing in intensity about the problem of player movement. I don't see it as a problem any more than I would see a lawyer deciding to work in another firm as a problem. I thought that that was something we were supposed to be able to do in this country. And as long as if you comply with the rules, then I mean if a player says, "Look, you asked me a question. No, I don't want to play for New Orleans anymore. I don't like the management for me. Is it working? I don't like the direction of the team."[50]

Commissioner Silver and team owners will continue to collaborate in order to address issues related to player movement (trades), contract tampering and salary cap circumvention. Commissioner Silver is a realist, as reflected by the following comment: "The one strong conviction I have is that we should not have rules that are not strictly enforced. We know that is the case right now. Whether that is by virtue of practice, whether it's because the world around us has changed, whether it's because players have power that they didn't used to have, I'm not so sure."[51]

Sports betting

The definition of BRI in the 2017 CBA includes revenue generated from sponsorships as well as revenue generated from gambling on NBA games (excluding revenues generated by team-owned casinos or other gambling businesses whose total revenues are not predominantly derived from gambling on NBA games).[52] Therefore, both the league and its players have financial incentive to optimize revenue from sources such as fans betting on the outcome of NBA games.

In January 2018, NBA assistant general counsel Dan Spillane represented the NBA at a hearing in front of the New York State Senate Standing Committee on Racing, Gaming and Wagering. The NBA's written statement explained that, "The NBA's position on sports betting has evolved in recent years. For decades, the NBA, along with the other major professional sports leagues, opposed the expansion of legal sports betting.... We have studied these issues at length. Our conclusion is that the time has come for a different approach that gives sports fans a safe and legal way to wager on sporting events while protecting the integrity of the underlying competitions."[53] This written statement indicated that the NBA supported a federal approach to regulating sports betting because—based on the viewpoint of league executives—a federal approach would be the simplest way to create clear and uniform protections for the integrity of NBA games. However, the NBA indicated that the league would not oppose state-by-state legislation that included requisite safeguards and oversight. In its written testimony, the NBA detailed the following aspects of a potential sports betting regulatory structure that the league hoped would be incorporated into any federal or state legislation that attempted to regulate betting on NBA games:

- Legislation should enable the detection and prevention of improper conduct relating to sports betting;
- Legislation should recognize that professional sports leagues provide the foundation for sports betting while bearing the risks that sports betting imposes (even when regulated)
  - Because professional sports leagues such as the NBA will need to invest more in compliance and enforcement, including bet monitoring, investigations and education, any legislation should compensate leagues for the risk and expense created by sports betting and the commercial value the sports product creates for betting operators—the NBA believed it is reasonable for operators to pay each professional sports league 1% of the total amount bet on league games as an integrity (royalty) fee;
- Legislation should allow professional sports leagues such as the NBA to restrict wagering on their own games/events (each league needs the ability to approve the types of wagering that are offered); and

- Legislation should incorporate consumer protections for bettors, including a rigorous licensing program to ensure operators are properly vetted, along with age restrictions, self-exclusion programs and other measures to address problem gambling and regulations of gambling advertising to protect vulnerable persons.[54]

The following month, in February 2018, the NBA and Major League Baseball (MLB) distributed a one-page joint statement to various lawmakers and other sports betting constituents. This document, labeled "Protecting the Integrity of Sports in a Regulated Sports Betting Market," supplemented the NBA's written statement for New York legislators. For example, the NBA and MLB document explained that, "Any law that legalizes sports betting has to put consumer safety and sports integrity first, and recognize that without our games and fans, sports betting could not exist." In addition to repeating many of the concepts listed in the written statement prepared for the New York sports betting committee, the NBA and MLB listed the following supplementary essential principles related to ensuring fair and safe sports betting:

- Betting operators must immediately report abnormal betting patterns and suspicious activity, cooperate with investigations by regulators and leagues, and make betting information available for integrity monitoring purposes;
- Requiring the use of official league real-time data will ensure the accuracy and consistency of betting outcomes for fans; and
- Legislation should authorize betting on Internet and mobile platforms, because limiting betting to just a handful of in-person locations will allow the offshore black market to continue to flourish—defeating a major purpose of legalizing and regulating sports betting.[55]

In May 2018, the United States Supreme Court determined that one particular federal gambling statute—the Professional and Amateur Sports Protection Act of 1992 (PASPA)—violated the 10th Amendment of the United States Constitution (often known as the "commandeering clause") because PASPA illegally empowered the federal government to order certain states to take specific actions to disallow/prohibit sports gambling. As a result, that specific federal statute is no longer enforceable against states, businesses or individuals—therefore, individual states are now permitted to develop legislation that would legalize/authorize and regulate sports gambling within that specific state.[56]

The NBA quickly issued a press release following the Supreme Court's decision to overturn PASPA. The NBA press release included the following statement from Commissioner Silver: "Today's decision by the Supreme Court opens the door for states to pass laws legalizing sports betting. We remain in favor of a federal framework that would provide a uniform approach to sports gambling in states that choose to permit it, but we will remain active in ongoing discussions with state legislatures. Regardless of the particulars of any future sports betting law, the integrity of our game remains our highest priority."[57] Likewise, the NBPA also issued an official statement that read: "Today's decision by the Supreme Court will significantly impact our sport—indeed, all sports in this country. The NBPA will, often in conjunction with the other sports unions, work to ensure that our players' rights are protected and promoted as we venture into this new territory."[58]

In July 2018, Commissioner Silver indicated that, "In addition to working with the state legislatures, we're also talking directly to the gaming establishments about entering into commercial deals. My view is we should be compensated for our intellectual property, but we can do that directly, again, with commercial relationships with gaming establishments."[59] In October 2018, the NBA announced a new three-year collaborative partnership with MGM Resorts International. As part of the partnership, MGM Resorts will function as the "Official Gaming Partner" of the NBA, and will therefore be allowed to utilize official NBA data, league trademarks and branding (on a non-exclusive basis) across MGM Resorts' land-based and digital sports betting offerings throughout the United States. Commissioner Silver made the following comment about this innovative new collaborative partnership: "As the landscape for sports betting in the U.S. continues to evolve at a rapid pace, MGM Resorts is a proven gaming leader for us to work with on this groundbreaking partnership. Our collaboration will result in the best possible gaming and entertainment experience for consumers through the use of accurate, real-time NBA and WNBA data, and our collective efforts to maintain and enhance the integrity of our games."[60]

By December 2018, the NBA was able to enter into sponsorship deals with two additional "Authorized Gaming Operators"—The Stars Group and FanDuel. Scott Kaufman-Ross, head of fantasy and gaming within the NBA league office, explained that the partnership between the NBA and The Stars Group would "be another way to create authentic fan engagement with league logos and official NBA betting data, while leveraging Stars' global expertise to further optimize the fan experience."[61] Kaufman-Ross similarly commented that the fundamental focus of the NBA's new dynamic partnership with FanDuel has been on "innovation around the fan experience, and we are excited to extend it to include sports betting."[62]

As demonstrated by the NBA's sponsorship deals with MGM Resorts, The Stars Group and FanDuel, professional sports leagues such as the NBA have already figured out a way to generate sizable revenue directly from betting operators in the form of sponsorships, advertising and product fees.[63] In addition, increased fan engagement with a league such as the NBA as a result of authorized sports betting could function as another significant source of new revenue. In October 2018, the American Gaming Association issued a report on projected sports betting related revenue for each of the major professional sports leagues in the United States. The American Gaming Association estimated that sports betting could eventually add approximately $585 million annually to total NBA league revenue.[64]

In addition to focusing on optimizing revenue from sports betting collaborative partnerships, Commissioner Silver, team owners and players within the league have also emphasized that protecting the integrity of the game of basketball is also of paramount importance. In February 2019, the NBA issued a statement detailing the league's sports betting focused initiatives:

- During the 2018–2019 season, all players, referees, and team and league employees underwent live training sessions on the NBA Gaming Policy;
- Posters, brochures and other informative educational materials were also distributed widely across team arenas and league offices;
- The league has entered into commercial agreements with gaming operators that include a range of integrity-related measures, such as data sharing for integrity monitoring purposes, screening of league insiders and cooperation requirements for league integrity investigations;
- The league has deepened its existing relationships and created new relationships with gambling regulators, operators, and experts to improve and increase the flow of information about gambling (including relating to unusual activity); and
- The league has hired (and is continuing to hire) additional personnel in the areas of compliance, integrity and investigations.[65]

The NBA will unquestionably continue to monitor the evolving sports betting landscape in the United States in order to identify additional economic opportunities as well as to ensure that the league is doing everything possible to protect the integrity of the sport.

NBA revenue sharing plan among teams in the league

The NBA revenue sharing plan operates in conjunction with certain elements of the CBA (for example, the luxury tax system) in order to address potential economic disparity among teams within the league. The revenue sharing plan is designed to help redistribute money from high-revenue teams (generally in big markets) to lower revenue teams (generally in small markets) in order to ensure that all teams in the league have the financial ability to keep up with the consistently growing salary cap.[66]

NBA owners are permitted to unilaterally implement and make changes to the league's revenue sharing plan. Prior to the 2011 NBA collective bargaining agreement, revenue sharing was somewhat limited. The league's luxury tax, which required teams who exceeded a certain payroll threshold to pay a "fine," was the primary funding source for league revenue sharing during the 2005 CBA. When the 2011 CBA was ratified in December 2011, the NBA Board of Governors also voted to approve a new revenue sharing plan that substantially increased the funds previously shared among NBA teams in part by including local team revenue in the revenue sharing equation.

Then-current NBA commissioner David Stern commented, "The [Board of Governors] realized that it was imperative that our revenue sharing program be improved. We have found a solution that should provide our league with better competitive balance."[67] David Stern also explained that net transfers under the revamped league revenue sharing system would be "a multiple of what they were under the old deal of revenue sharing."[68] Stern also estimated that the net transfers would be approximately "three times" the amount shared in 2010–2011—which was approximately $60 million—and would result in about $15 million being transferred to each "revenue recipient" under the new revenue sharing system, with approximately $180 million in total team revenues being shared during the 2011–2012 NBA season. Fred Whitfield, President of the Charlotte Hornets, acknowledged: "For us, being a small market team, we have the same goals and aspirations of large market teams to compete for a championship, and the new plan gives us a chance. It gives us a chance to put a talented team on the floor and be able to break even or make some money."[69]

The revamped revenue sharing plan effectively requires all NBA teams to contribute an annually fixed percentage (roughly 50%) of the team's total annual local revenue (which includes 50% of revenues generated by jersey patch sponsorships as well as deductions allowed for certain expenses such as arena operating costs) into the league revenue sharing pool.[70] Each team then receives an allocation equal to the league's average team payroll for that season from the revenue pool. As a result, if a team's contribution to the revenue sharing pool is less than the league's average team payroll, that team would be a revenue recipient. Conversely, teams that contribute an amount to the league revenue sharing pool that exceeds the average team salary would be required to fund the revenue given to revenue recipient teams.[71] The NBA revenue sharing plan also contains a series of complex interconnected limits/thresholds, adjustments/formulas, qualifiers and disqualifiers. The following example summarizes one of the many components within the NBA revenue sharing plan:

- *The Revenue Benchmark Threshold*: Each team in the league is responsible for meeting a minimum level of financial performance each NBA season
    - Teams are expected to generate a specific percentage of the league average for annual team revenue (underperforming teams would be penalized by either being required to contribute additional funds to the league revenue sharing pool or being required to forfeit a portion of its revenue sharing payments and as a result receiving a smaller distribution from the league revenue sharing pool);
    - Team revenue expectations are based primarily on each team's market size, which is determined based on the number of television households in each market—teams in a market with more than 2.5 million television households are automatically disqualified from receiving revenue sharing funds;
    - Some teams might be expected to generate less than 75% of the league average for team revenue each season (for example, the Memphis Grizzlies and Oklahoma City Thunder), whereas other teams might be expected to generate more than 125% of the league average for team revenue each season (for example, the Los Angeles Lakers and New York Knicks); and

○ Revenue sharing payments to teams who meet the required revenue benchmark thresholds are subject to additional limitations/adjustments—for example, revenue sharing distributions cannot result in a revenue recipient incurring an adjusted profit above $10 million for an NBA season.

For the 2016–2017 season, ten teams transferred $201 million combined in revenue sharing distributions to 15 other teams. Four NBA teams—the Warriors, Knicks, Lakers and Bulls—accounted for $144 million (72%) of the revenue sharing transfers. The Lakers contributed $49 million to the league revenue sharing pool, and nonetheless still reported $115 million in net income for the 2016–2017 season. On the other end of the spectrum, the Memphis Grizzlies received $32 million from the league revenue sharing pool yet still reported negative net income of $8 million for the 2016–2017 NBA season.[72] Table 3.1 shows which NBA teams reported negative net income for the 2016–2017 season before application of the league's revenue sharing framework. Table 3.1 also lists the NBA teams that reported negative net income after application of the league's revenue sharing plan.

Some NBA teams are thrilled with the NBA revenue sharing model. For example, Cleveland Cavaliers team executive Len Komoroski commented, "The new revenue sharing model clearly helps create a better competitive balance across the league. We think the new model is not only good for the Cavaliers, but good for the entire league."[73] However, not all NBA team owners remain enthused with the NBA revenue sharing system. For example, one NBA team owner recently remarked, "The need for revenue sharing was supposed to be for special circumstances, not permanent subsidies."[74] The NBA revenue sharing plan represents a complex issue that will likely be the subject of continued discussion in the years ahead. One potential partial solution would relate to adding

Table 3.1 NBA teams with reported losses (2016–2017 season)

Negative net income—before revenue sharing	*Negative net income—after revenue sharing*
Milwaukee Bucks	Milwaukee Bucks
Memphis Grizzlies	Memphis Grizzlies
Atlanta Hawks	Atlanta Hawks
Charlotte Hornets	Orlando Magic
Sacramento Kings	Brooklyn Nets
Orlando Magic	Detroit Pistons
Brooklyn Nets	San Antonio Spurs
Indiana Pacers	Washington Wizards
New Orleans Pelicans	Cleveland Cavaliers
Detroit Pistons	
Phoenix Suns	

Data sources: NBA and ESPN.

a new team performance benchmark threshold to the revenue sharing formula, which would require revenue sharing recipients to achieve certain metrics related to a minimum number of team wins each NBA season.[75]

Notes

1 Commissioner Silver is also involved with CBA negotiations between the WNBA and its players. In November 2018, WNBA players exercised their right to opt out of the league's CBA, which as a result ended after the 2019 WNBA season. In an interview with espnW, Silver provided the following candid thoughts: "I feel on the NBA side, we are working very closely with Michele Roberts and her executive committee. It doesn't mean we don't have disagreements, but I think everyone would say that we are truly listening to each other and that there is a sense of real inclusion. To the extent there isn't that in the WNBA for whatever reason—and this is to point fingers at no one—there is an issue that needs to be fixed.... As the players have pointed out, this isn't just about compensation. Of course, that's an important issue for the players, but—listening to what they are saying—it's also about how the league is operated, their working conditions, how we are marketing the league, how we are connecting with their fans." Voepel, M. (2018). Adam Silver Isn't 'Disappointed' That WNBA Players Opted Out of CBA, *available at* www.espn.com.
2 Letter from Adam Silver (NBA commissioner) and Michele Roberts (NBPA executive director) to NBA Players (2018), *available at* www.nba.com. The newly-enhanced mental wellness programs—the product of almost a year of discussions between the league and the players association that began as the sides were negotiating terms for the 2017 CBA—allows players to seek mental health treatment and counseling outside of the framework developed by NBA teams. Existing team physicians and other resources will nonetheless still be available to players. Michele Roberts also commented that, "We don't want players to be discouraged from getting help when they need it because they are concerned that it will get back to the team, or it may affect their play, or it may affect their next contract." *See* Aldridge, D. (2018). NBA, NBPA Taking Steps to Further Address Mental Wellness Issues for Players, *available at* www.nba.com.
3 *See* Shapiro, M. (2019). Report: NBA Finalizes Expanded Mental Health Program, Adds Licensed Psychiatrist, *Sports Illustrated* (explaining that, "The NBA's changes come after a slate of players revealed their battles with mental health both before and during their time in the league").
4 *See* NBA CBA (2017), Article X, Section 1(b).
5 Youngmisuk, O. (2017). Adam Silver: Age Issue 'Needs to be Studied' Outside CBA Negotiations, *available at* www.espn.com (explaining that Commissioner Silver felt that it was essential to "take a new look and a new approach to this issue" of initial age eligibility for the NBA draft).
6 Commission on College Basketball (2018). Report and Recommendations to Address the Issues Facing Collegiate Basketball, at page 3, *available at* www.ncaa.org (emphasizing the recommendation that, "Players with professional earning power should be able to choose a professional path").
7 Commission on College Basketball (2018). Report and Recommendations to Address the Issues Facing Collegiate Basketball, at page 3, *available at* www.ncaa.org (expounding that, "Elite high school players with NBA prospects and no interest in a college degree should not be 'forced' to attend college, often for less than a year").
8 Woike, D. (2019). NBA Proposes Lowering Age of Draft Eligibility with Players Union, *Los Angeles Times*.
9 *See* Youngmisuk, O. (2017). Adam Silver: Age Issue 'Needs to be Studied' Outside CBA Negotiations, *available at* www.espn.com (quoting Commissioner Silver: "The current age minimum is 19 years old, but something Michele and I discussed

directly—and this is different than last time we negotiated a collective bargaining agreement—is that rather than say to you that [you should] talk to us in seven years when we sit back down to negotiate a new collective bargaining agreement, I think she and I both agree that it is the kind of issue that needs to be studied, in essence, outside of the bright lights of collective bargaining"). Nonetheless, once a CBA is negotiated, it is somewhat rare for a league and players association to modify substantive CBA terms because each side typically requests additional (and sometimes unreasonable) benefits/tradeoffs. As a result, oftentimes the league and players association wait until the next formal round of collective bargaining for a new CBA to make system changes even though the system could be improved sooner with a basic side letter agreement between the league and players association.

10 *See* Caron, E. (2019). Report: NBA, Union Resume Talks to Lower Age Limit, End One-and-Done Rule, *Sports Illustrated.*

11 *See* NBA CBA (2017), Article VII, Section 1(a).

12 *See* Bilbao, R. (2019). Orlando Magic Tackle Final Challenge Before Starting $200 Million Downtown Complex, *Orlando Business Journal. See also* Li, R. (2019). Warriors Seek to Build New Hotel, Condos Next to Chase Center Arena, *San Francisco Chronicle.*

13 Arnovtiz, K. (2018). The NBA's Next Big Cash Grab: Taking Over Your Downtown, *available at* www.espn.com (quoting Orlando Magic executive Alex Martins: "This is the next wave that's come along in the past four to six years—expand the portfolio of holdings. When you talk about equity in the project, we have the smallest piece. But it utilizes some of the brand equity of the Orlando Magic, and the Magic ownership owns the land itself").

14 Arnovtiz, K. (2018). The NBA's Next Big Cash Grab: Taking Over Your Downtown, *available at* www.espn.com (quoting Vivek Ranadive, owner of Sacramento Kings: "Real estate is a significant slice of the asset here").

15 Arnovtiz, K. (2018). The NBA's Next Big Cash Grab: Taking Over Your Downtown, *available at* www.espn.com. For a detailed analysis on the private and public funding of sports venues, *see* Long, J.G. (2014). *Public/Private Partnerships for Major League Sports Facilities.* Routledge.

16 Players might want to focus on increasing the types of revenue streams that are included in BRI along with reducing some of the allowed deductions from BRI for expenses and other items by team owners.

17 *See* Lowe, Z. (2018). The NBA Supermax and the Price of Loyalty, *available at* www.espn.com (proposing that supermax contracts do not count against the luxury tax, and that teams who sign a player to a supermax deal receive an additional exception—perhaps a second midlevel exception—so that the team would be able to sign another skilled player to the roster).

18 *See* NBA CBA (2017), Article XXII, Section 13.

19 *See* NBA CBA (2017), Article XXII, Section 13 (emphasizing that, "Pending an agreement between the parties, wearables may not be used in games, and no player data collected from a wearable worn at the request of a team may be made available to the public in any way or used for any commercial purpose").

20 *See* Venook, J. (2017). The Upcoming Privacy Battle Over Wearables in the NBA, *The Atlantic* (explaining that it might be difficult to determine when wearable data is being utilized for strategy as compared with leverage in future contract negotiations). *See also* Aldridge, D. (2016). Nothing Finalized Yet, But Labor Peace Looking More and More Possible in NBA, *available at* www.nba.com. A collective bargaining agreement between a players association and a professional sports league can mitigate concerns about the validity of biometric data, surveillance and privacy issues, confidentiality challenges and the integrity of data security protocols, but might not be able to completely eliminate factors that undermine the autonomy of athletes to consent to biometric monitoring. *See* Karkazis, K. and Fishman, J.R. (2017). Tracking U.S.

Professional Athletes: The Ethics of Biometric Technologies, *American Journal of Bioethics* (explaining that the non-guaranteed nature of NFL player contracts undermine players' autonomy to consent to biometric tracking such as sleep monitoring).

21 Robbins, J. (2018). Adam Silver Says a 'Better System' Can Improve NBA's Competitive Balance, *Orlando Sentinel.*

22 Bulpett, S. (2018). Adam Silver addresses Trying to Curb 'Rich Getting Richer,' *The Boston Herald.*

23 Mahoney, B. (2018). NBA Estimates 40,000 More Travel Miles in Playoff Format Seeding Teams 1 to 16, *available at* www.nba.com.

24 Interview by CJ McCollum (NBA player and aspiring journalist) with Adam Silver (NBA commissioner) (2016), *available at* www.theplayerstribune.com.

25 *See* NBA CBA (2017), Article XX, Section 2.

26 Aschburner, S. (2019). Adam Silver: Shorter Season Something NBA Will 'Continue to Look at,' *available at* www.nba.com (explaining that changing viewership and new forms of competition necessitate that the league consider innovative ways of presenting the game—which could lead to the start of new game-related rules and traditions).

27 Golen, J. (2019). NBA Commissioner Silver Would Consider Shortening Season, Replacing All-Star Game, *available at* www.nba.com.

28 Official Release—NBA Board of Governors Approves Changes to Draft Lottery System (2017), *available at* www.nba.com. The NFL does not have a draft lottery system. Instead, teams are assigned specific draft picks based entirely on each team's prior season record. In October 2019, Commissioner Goodell commented, "The competitiveness of our game is obviously critical. I don't think that is solved with a [draft] lottery. I think that is solved by all the issues we try to deal with on a regular basis through the competition committee and the league in trying to make sure our league is competitive." Fowler, J. (2019). Roger Goodell Says There's No Talk About a Draft Lottery to Combat Tanking, *available at* www.espn.com.

29 Official Release—NBA Agrees on Policy for Resting Healthy Players During Games (2017), *available at* www.nba.com.

30 Official Release—NBA Board of Governors Approves Coach's Challenge and Use of NBA Replay Center to Initiate Instant Replay (2019), *available at* www.nba.com.

31 Under a new experimental G League rule for the 2019–2020 season, one free throw worth one, two or three points will be awarded in the event of any foul that would typically result in one, two or three free throws being shot under standard NBA rules. The experimental free throw rule will not apply during the last two minutes of the fourth quarter or the entirety of any overtime period. Functioning as the research and development arm of the NBA, the G League routinely tests experimental rules and procedures. For example, during the 2019–2020 season, the NBA implemented the "Coach's Challenge," which was first tested in the G League in the 2014–2015 season. *See* Official Release—G League to Experiment with New Free Throw Rule (2019), *available at* www.nba.com.

32 The NBPA has previously challenged the authority of the league to create and impose new rules without consulting with the players association. For example, in October 2012, the NBA adopted an "anti-flopping rule"—flopping was defined as any physical act that appears to have been intended to cause the referees to call a foul on another player. Player fines for flopping were scheduled to range from $5,000 for a second violation/infraction to $30,000 for a fifth violation/infraction; if a player violated the anti-flopping rule six times or more, he would be subject to discipline that is reasonable under the circumstances (including an increased fine and/or suspension). Billy Hunter, then-current NBPA executive director, issued the following response to this rule that was unilaterally implemented by the league without consulting the players association: "The NBA is not permitted to unilaterally impose new economic discipline against the players without first bargaining with the union." *See* Official Release—NBA Announces New Anti-Flopping Rule (2012), *available at* www.nba.com.

33 Golliver, N. (2019). Adam Silver says NBA Must Update Free Agency Rules to Curb Tampering, the *Washington Post.*

34 Official Release—NBA Fines Lakers for Violating Anti-Tampering Rule (2017), *available at* www.nba.com.

35 *See* Official Release—Pelicans' Anthony Davis Fined (2019), *available at* www.nba.com.

36 Golliver, N. (2019). Adam Silver says NBA Must Update Free Agency Rules to Curb Tampering, the *Washington Post.* Commissioner Silver also commented that, "I think the consensus at both our committee meetings and the board meeting was that we need to revisit and reset those rules, that some of the rules we have in place may not make sense." In addition, Commissioner Silver candidly explained, "My job is to enforce a fair set of rules for all our teams and a set of rules that are clear and make sense for everyone. I think right now we are not quite there." Zielonka, A. (2019). Adam Silver Says NBA Must Address Trade Demands, Free Agency 'Balance of Power,' the *Washington Times.*

37 *See* Aschburner, S. (2019). NBA Increases Fines for Tampering, Unauthorized Agreements, *available at* www.nba.com (explaining that the frenzied free agent market during the 2019 offseason "raised red flags about teams' compliance with rules dictating when front-office executives and players' representatives could begin negotiations … the number and enormity of deals that leaked out within minutes of the June 30 [official start to free agency] suggested that contract talks in many cases surely began before the designated period").

38 Golliver, N. (2019). Adam Silver says NBA Must Update Free Agency Rules to Curb Tampering, the *Washington Post.* In September 2019, Commissioner Silver acknowledged, "What we were hearing back from our fans was that to a certain extent, they were losing confidence in our system and at the end of the day, that's part of what we are selling…. There was a sense in fans from many markets that if you weren't violating the rules, you were at a disadvantage in terms of signing players." Buckner, C. (2019). Adam Silver on NBA's Stricter Tampering Rules, the *Washington Post.*

39 Official Release—Free Agent Negotiations Moved up to June 30 at 6 p.m. ET as Part of Agreement Between NBA and NBPA (2019), *available at* www.nba.com (explaining that, "By league rules, teams also will be permitted to communicate with free agents or their representatives beginning at 6 p.m. ET on June 29 solely for the purpose of scheduling a meeting to take place at or after 6 p.m. ET on June 30"). In September 2019, Commissioner Silver was asked about the potential to move free agency prior to the NBA draft in June. Silver responded, "My sense is those conversations will continue. I don't have any expectation that anything is going to happen in the near term." Reynolds, T. (2019). NBA Teams Approve Stiffer Penalties for Tampering, *available at* www.nba.com.

40 *See* NBA CBA (2017), Article XIII (indicating that penalties for circumventing the CBA rules can result in fines of up to $6 million along with the potential forfeiture of first round draft picks). In September 2019, the NBA fined the Milwaukee Bucks $50,000 for "violating league rules governing the timing of discussions regarding future player contracts and permissible commitments to players." Official Release—NBA Fines Bucks for Comments About Offering 'SuperMax' to Giannis Antetokounmpo (2019), *available at* www.nba.com. The fine resulted from the general manager of the Milwaukee Bucks making a public comment during a televised event that the team planned to offer a "supermax" contract extension to Giannis Antetokounmpo during free agency following the 2019–2020 season (that is, in July 2020). Based on rules in the 2017 CBA, teams cannot commit to offer a "supermax" extension prior to the summer following a player's seventh season in the NBA—which, for Giannis, will be following the 2019–2020 NBA season. *See* NBA CBA (2017), Article VII, Section 7(a). *See also* NBA CBA (2017), Article XIII, Section 2 (prohibiting unauthorized agreements).

41 McCann, M. (2019). Understanding Why Salary Cap Circumvention is Dangerous for the NBA, *Sports Illustrated* (explaining that the NBA collective bargaining agreement "forbids teams from compensating players outside of their contract and thus in circumvention of the team's obligations under the salary cap").

42 Official Release—NBA Fines Clippers for Violating Anti-Circumvention Rules, *available at* www.nba.com.

43 McCann, M. (2019). Understanding Why Salary Cap Circumvention is Dangerous for the NBA, *Sports Illustrated* (commenting on the problem of NBA teams paying players outside of the player's contract: "Such a practice gives the team an unfair advantage over its rivals since the team pays a player beyond the reach of a salary cap that restricts all teams. Such a practice also betrays the need for transparency in player transactions. If NBA teams believed that other teams were negotiating secret contracts with players, teams might feel compelled to do the same. This would set off a snowball effect where more and more teams break the rules").

44 In September 2019, NBA player Spencer Dinwiddie expressed his intentions to utilize his player contract as a digital investment vehicle whereby he would sell investors a "tokenized security" that would be backed by the guaranteed payments from his NBA player contract. The NBA prohibited this proposed entrepreneurial concept developed by Dinwiddie, because the 2017 CBA provides that "no player shall assign or otherwise transfer to any third party his right to receive compensation from the team under his uniform player contract." NBA CBA (2017), Article II, Section 13(d).

45 Reynolds, T. (2019). Report: NBA Set to Vote on Raising Tampering Fines, *available at* www.nba.com.

46 *See* Aschburner, S. (2019). NBA Increases Fines for Tampering, Unauthorized Agreements, *available at* www.nba.com (sharing the viewpoint that these tougher potential penalties "only matter if the league's 30 franchises have the will to do what it takes to impose them … and the discipline not to do what triggers them").

47 *See* Bontemps, T. (2019). NBA Board Passes Stricter Tampering Measures, *available at* www.espn.com (explaining that one of the biggest areas of concern for team officials centered around privacy concerns stemming from the league's apparent ability to seize personal communications devices such as iPhones of team general managers). *See also* Reynolds, T. (2019). NBA Teams Approve Stiffer Penalties for Tampering, *available at* www.nba.com. *See also* Reynolds, T. (2019). Report: NBA Set to Vote on Raising Tampering Fines, *available at* www.nba.com. *See also* ESPN News Services (2019). NBA Mulling $10 Million fine for Tampering, Per Memo, *available at* www.espn.com.

48 Press Conference—Commissioner Adam Silver (2019), *available at* www.nba.com.

49 *See* Aschburner, S. (2019). NBA Increases Fines for Tampering, Unauthorized Agreements, *available at* www.nba.com (further quoting Adam Silver: "We think we are dramatically going to increase the likelihood that we are going to catch you. I don't want to suggest there is any perfect system. At some point you are relying, at least in part, on the good faith of partners working together and … that this is a culture in which people want to compete fairly").

50 Spears, M.J. (2019). Michele Roberts Wants to Stop Chatter About Player Power Being a Problem, *available at* www.theundefeated.com (explaining that Michele Roberts believes there is a "double standard" between how star players are viewed when they decide to move on compared with when NBA teams choose to make a major trade).

51 Deb, S. (2019). NBA Begins Investigating Whether Salary Cap Was Violated, the *New York Times*.

52 *See* NBA CBA (2017), Article VII, Section 1(a).

53 Statement of NBA to New York State Senate Standing Committee on Racing, Gaming and Wagering (2018), *available at* www.nba.com.

54 Statement of NBA to New York State Senate Standing Committee on Racing, Gaming and Wagering (2018), *available at* www.nba.com (confirming that the NBA would support the passage of a comprehensive sports betting bill that would serve as a model for a 50-state solution—whether that happens in Congress or on a state-by-state basis). The integrity fee concept has gained little traction, as individual states demonstrated a reluctance to share sports betting income with professional sports leagues. In July 2018, Commissioner Silver commented, "We think the integrity fee is something that we are entitled to, one, because we have the additional costs and also—something that as I've said before, we're not hiding from—that we also think we are due a royalty. And that if the intellectual property that is created by this league—and I know all the leagues support this position, but in the case of the NBA, we will spend roughly $7.5 billion creating NBA basketball this season." Candee, A. (2018). NBA's Adam Silver on Sports Betting: 'The Integrity Fee is Something that We are Entitled to,' *available at* www.legalsportsreport.com.

55 NBA and MLB (2018). Protecting the Integrity of Sports in a Regulated Sports Betting Market," *available at* www.nba.com.

56 *See* Edelman, M. (2018). Explaining the Supreme Court's Recent Sports Betting Decision, *Forbes* (opining that the "Supreme Court appears agnostic on the merits of legalized sports gambling. As the court noted in its ruling, if Congress were to pass a statute to directly ban sports gambling, such a bill would likely survive legal scrutiny"). The Supreme Court case referenced is *Murphy, Governor of New Jersey, et al.* v. *National Collegiate Athletic Association, et al.* (2018), 138 S. Ct. 1461.

57 Official Release—NBA Commissioner Adam Silver's Statement Regarding Supreme Court's Decision to Overturn PASPA (2018), *available at* www.nba.com. Commissioner Silver also stated, "It became clear to me that we would be better off with a regulated framework of sports betting, rather than having it all be illegal and unmonitored. And the intellectual property creators like the NBA, which invest billions of dollars per year creating their product, should share in the proceeds. Legalized sports betting creates an opportunity to be compensated directly by selling our video and data." Vollmer, C. and Gross, D. (2018). NBA Commissioner Adam Silver Has a Game Plan, *available at* www.strategy-business.com.

58 Official Release—Statement from NBPA Executive Director Michele Roberts (2018), *available at* www.nbpa.com. The NFLPA also issued a press release, which indicated that the Supreme Court decision reaffirmed the decision of the NFLPA to collaborate with other players associations on the issues of player safety, integrity of the game, and privacy and publicity rights of players. *See* Official Release—NFLPA Statement on Supreme Court Decision Legalizing Sports Gambling (2018), *available at* www.nflpa.com.

59 Bulpett, S. (2018). Adam Silver Addresses Trying to Curb 'Rich Getting Richer,' the *Boston Herald.*

60 Official Release—MGM Resorts International Becomes Official Gaming Partner of NBA (2018), *available at* www.nba.com (explaining that MGM Resorts and the NBA will also partner on best-in-class practices to protect the integrity of NBA games, including anonymized real-time data sharing). For illustration purposes, if the total value of the three-year collaborative partnership between the NBA and MGM Resorts equaled approximately $25 million, that would result in distributions of slightly more than $400,000 per NBA team over the course of the three-year sponsorship.

61 Official Release—NBA Announces The Stars Group as Authorized Gaming Operator of the League (2018), *available at* www.nba.com (explaining that, "During the partnership, The Stars Group will be promoted across the NBA's digital assets including NBA TV, NBA.com, the NBA App and NBA social media platforms. Additionally, the NBA will be promoted across The Stars Group's gaming platforms including PokerStars which operates the world's most popular online poker sites. The Stars

Group and the NBA will also collaborate on responsible gaming and partner on best-in-class practices to protect the integrity of NBA games").

62   Official Release—NBA and FanDuel Expand Partnership to Include Sports Betting and New Fan Experiences (2018), *available at* www.nba.com (explaining that, "Throughout the partnership FanDuel and the NBA will work together to create new and exciting game formats and collaborate on new experiences in daily fantasy and sports betting to further enhance the fan experience").

63   In October 2019, the NBA also entered into a similar sports betting partnership with William Hill, one of America's leading sports book operators. As part of the partnership agreement, William Hill is permitted to use official NBA betting data and league logos across its mobile platforms and in its sports books throughout the United States. Additionally, William Hill will be promoted across the NBA's digital assets including NBA.com, the NBA app and the NBA's social media platforms. *See* Official Release—NBA and William Hill Announce Sports Betting Partnership (2019), *available at* www.nba.com.

64   Press Release, American Gaming Association—NBA & MLB Could See Combined $1.7 Billion From Legalized Sports Betting (2018), *available at* www.americangaming.org (noting that "legal sports betting will also create substantial opportunities for state and local economies, generating tax revenue, jobs and supporting small businesses across the country"). In late 2019, the NBA slightly modified the deadline for each team announcing its starting lineup prior to the game—previously, teams were required to announce their starting lineup ten minutes prior to tip-off, whereas the new requirement is for teams to announce starting lineups 30 minutes prior to tip-off; however, teams will be able to amend the starting lineups if a player sustains or aggravates an injury during pre-game warmups). Some sports law scholars have commented that this decision might have been in part influenced by sports betting revenue optimization strategy as well as overall integrity concerns.

65   Official Release—NBA Response to ESPN's Tim Donaghy Story/NBA Integrity Initiatives (2019), *available at* www.nba.com.

66   The NBA has not officially publicly released the league's current revenue sharing plan. *See* Coon, L. (2017). NBA Salary CAP FAQ: 2017 Collective Bargaining Agreement, *available at* www.cbafaq.com.

67   Official Release—NBA Board of Governors Ratify 10-Year CBA (2011), *available at* www.nba.com.

68   Aschburner, S. (2011). Revenue Sharing a Vital (Yet Secretive) Component to Talks, *available at* www.nba.com.

69   Lombardo, J. (2012). Inside NBA's Revenue Sharing, *SportsBusiness Journal* (explaining that the revamped league revenue sharing plan is rooted in a philosophy of including locally generated dollars from the big-market, high-revenue teams to be spread among the low-revenue teams).

70   Jersey patch sponsorships sold by individual NBA teams differ from the league's eight-year partnership agreement with Nike that allows the famous Nike "swoosh" to appear on all on-court uniform designs. *See* Townsend, M. and Soshnick, S. (2015). Nike Win's $1 Billion Contract with NBA as Adidas Walks Away, *Bloomberg*.

71   *See* Lombardo, J. (2012). Inside NBA's Revenue Sharing, *SportsBusiness Journal* (explaining that, the revamped league revenue sharing plan, which runs concurrently with the league's new collective bargaining agreement, has drawn its share of criticism from some owners).

72   *See* Windhorst, B. and Lowe, Z. (2017). A Confidential Report Shows Nearly Half the NBA Lost Money Last Season, *available at* www.espn.com (indicating that "the revenue sharing formula is a byzantine maze of calculations based on market size, expected revenue for each team, expense levels and other variables"). For the 2016–2017 NBA season, the Cleveland Cavaliers and the San Antonio Spurs reported positive net income before considering revenue sharing distributions. However, after

making the required revenue sharing payments, each of these two teams reported negative net income for the 2016–2017 NBA season.

73 Reed, T. (2012). Cleveland Cavaliers Will Reap Benefits from Revenue Sharing, *available at* www.cleveland.com.

74 Lombardo, J. (2012). Inside NBA's Revenue Sharing, *SportsBusiness Journal*.

75 Select content within *Chapter 2* and *Chapter 3* has been adapted from a journal article previously written by the author of this book. This excerpted and modified content was originally published in 2015 by the *Jeffrey S. Moorad Sports Law Journal* at Villanova University School of Law. This excerpted and modified content originally authored by Scott Bukstein and published by the *Jeffrey S. Moorad Sports Law Journal* at Villanova University School of Law is properly licensed under "Creative Commons Attribution 2.5 License." The recommended citation for the original journal article is as follows: Bukstein, S. (2015). Preparing for Another Round of Collective Bargaining in the National Basketball Association, *Jeffrey S. Moorad Sports Law Journal*, *available at* https://digitalcommons.law.villanova.edu/mslj/vol.22/iss2/2.

4   Collective bargaining in the NFL
Part 1

Overview of chapter contents

The primary objective of this chapter is to provide a comprehensive overview of collective bargaining within the National Football League (NFL). The first section of this chapter summarizes the current NFL business model at the team and league levels. This initial chapter section also explains how the NFL's current lucrative national media rights agreements, along with recent team profitability and increased franchise valuations, impact the probability of both players and team owners seeking negotiation leverage during future collective bargaining discussions. The next section of this chapter examines the extremely contentious collective bargaining process between NFL team owners and players throughout 2010 and 2011 and also highlights some of the key business issues negotiated in the 2011 NFL collective bargaining agreement. This section includes an analysis of how both the National Football League Players Association (NFLPA) and NFL team owners resorted to the United States legal system in order to boost overall negotiation leverage during the collective bargaining process in 2010 and 2011. The final part of this chapter contains a discussion of select key provisions within the 2011 NFL collective bargaining agreement.

The NFL league and team business model: examining the economics of the NFL

The NFL generated between $9–10 billion in total revenue during the 2012 NFL season. For the 2018 NFL season, total league revenue exceeded $15 billion.[1] During the 2018 season, the league disbursed approximately $8.8 billion in equal allotments to all 32 teams. Each team received more than $274 million for the 2018 NFL season based on the league revenue sharing plan. The salary cap for the 2018 season equaled $177.2 million. For comparison purposes, during the 2012 season, each NFL team received approximately $172 million from the league, and the salary cap equaled $120.6 million. The NFL's revenue sharing plan "has maintained competitiveness across all teams and has helped the league avoid financial disparities faced by other sports that gave teams nearly insurmountable advantages.... All of this contributes to greater parity among teams, competitive games and more teams in the playoff hunt each year—improving the game for fans, players, owners and the league's broadcast partners."[2]

Media rights represent a vital source of NFL league revenue. Table 4.1 provides an overview of current major NFL league media rights agreements.

The NFL forecasted that the combined value of all league media rights deals for the 2020 season would exceed $6.5 billion. As illustrated by Table 4.1, all of the primary NFL leaguewide media rights agreements expire in either 2021 or 2022. With the overall media landscape in the sports industry splintering and shifting away from the broadcast and cable viewership models, league executives are hoping that labor peace/stability would help deliver another financial windfall in the upcoming years with a series of new lucrative media rights agreements.[3] However, some league media rights partners such as AT&T (DirecTV) have expressed reservations about renewing current television deals. For example, in September 2019, AT&T executives indicated that the value of the "Sunday NFL Ticket" rights package has peaked and that a renewal—especially if renewing the agreement comes with a higher price tag—will be hard to justify at a time when consumers are canceling cable connections, including at DirecTV. John Stankey, AT&T chief operating officer, explained, "There is less profitability to support the decision [to renew]. [The NFL contract] becomes less critical to the business over time. I don't think we look at that and say it's a growth product."[4] According to Professor Andrew Zimbalist, "There is an inevitable fragmentation that will hurt [the NFL] … it means that they are not going to get the same rights fees."[5]

Corporate partnerships represent another core source of NFL league and team revenue. Estimated sponsorship spending at the league and team levels eclipsed $1.3 billion for the 2018 NFL season.[6] League sponsors during the 2019 NFL season included companies such as Pepsi, Gatorade, Visa, FedEx, Verizon, Marriott, Microsoft and Ford. Similar to the NBA, the NFL recently entered into collaborative partnership agreements with companies in the casino gaming and sports betting spaces. For instance, in January 2019, Caesars Entertainment became the official casino sponsor of the league. Beginning with the 2019 NFL playoffs, this multi-year sponsorship is focused on Caesars providing unique experiences for NFL fans by using its casino properties, celebrity chefs, premier music artists and a wide range of entertainment elements.[7]

Similar to the NBA, 31 of the 32 teams in the NFL do not report annual financial figures. The Green Bay Packers are the only "fan-owned" team in the league and, therefore, the only team that publicly reports its finances. The annual financial reports from the Green Bay Packers serve as the most detailed public information available on the financial aspects of an NFL team.[8] Table 4.2 provides a summary of Green Bay Packers' revenues and expenses for the team's fiscal years ending March 31, 2016 through March 31, 2019.[9]

Recent transfers of NFL team ownership combined with franchise valuations also reveal the overall financial health of the league. For example, as of September 2019, *Forbes* calculated the average NFL franchise value to equal approximately $2.9 billion. For instance, the value of the Dallas Cowboys equaled $5.5 billion, the

Table 4.1 Primary NFL league media rights deals

Network	Duration of media rights deal	Average annual value	Total value of media rights deal	Deal expiration year
ESPN	8 years	$1.9 billion	$15.2 billion	2021
CBS	9 years	$1 billion	$9 billion	2022
FOX	9 years	$1.1 billion	$9.9 billion	2022
NBC	9 years	$950 million	$8.55 billion	2022
AT&T(DirecTV)	8 years	$1.5 billion	$12 billion	2022

Data sources: NFL and Media Companies.

value of the New England Patriots equaled $4.1 billion and the value of the Tampa Bay Buccaneers equaled $2.2 billion.[10] Individuals continue to pay mammoth amounts of money to purchase NFL teams. In 2018, the Carolina Panthers were purchased for $2.3 billion. In 2014, the Buffalo Bills were sold for $1.4 billion. In 2012, Shahid Khan purchased the Jacksonville Jaguars for $770 million.[11]

The NFL collective bargaining process in 2010 and 2011

The 2006 NFL collective bargaining agreement was initially scheduled to be effective through the 2012 NFL season, which would have resulted in the 2006 CBA expiring in March 2013.[12] However, either the NFLPA or the NFL Management Council could elect to opt out of the 2006 CBA and, as a result, terminate the final two NFL seasons with planned salary caps—the 2010 and 2011 seasons—by providing written notice to the other on or before November 8, 2008.[13] If either side exercised its right to opt out early, the 2010 NFL season would be the final league year of the 2006 CBA. In addition, based on the terms of the 2006 CBA, teams would not be subject to any limits on player compensation expenditures via a salary cap during the 2010 NFL season (i.e., the final league year of the 2006 CBA).[14]

In May 2008, NFL team owners voted unanimously to opt out of the 2006 CBA in order to "continue negotiating a new agreement for the 2011 season and beyond that will work better for both the clubs and the players."[15] The NFL issued a press release that provided the following rationale for the team owners deciding to exercise their collective option to shorten the 2006 CBA by two seasons:

Table 4.2 Green Bay Packers: revenue and expense overview

Season	League (national) revenue	Team (local) revenue	Total revenue	Total expenses	Estimated operating profit
2018–2019	$274.3 million	$203.6 million	$477.9 million	$477.2 million	$700,000
2017–2018	$255.9 million	$199 million	$454.9 million	$420.9 million	$34 million
2016–2017	$244 million	$197.4 million	$441.4 million	$376.1 million	$65.3 million
2015–2016	$222.5 million	$186.2 million	$408.7 million	$333.7 million	$75 million

Data source: Green Bay Packers financial statements.

A collective bargaining agreement has to work for both sides. If the agreement provides inadequate incentives to invest in the future, it will not work for management or labor. And, in the context of a professional sports league, if the agreement does not afford all clubs an opportunity to be competitive, the league can lose its appeal. The NFL earns very substantial revenues. But the clubs are obligated by the CBA to spend substantially more than half their revenues—almost $4.5 billion [during the 2007 NFL season] alone—on player costs. In addition, as we have explained to the union, the clubs must spend significant and growing amounts on stadium construction, operations and improvements to respond to the interests and demands of our fans. The current labor agreement does not adequately recognize the costs of generating the revenues of which the players receive the largest share; nor does the agreement recognize that those costs have increased substantially—and at an ever-increasing rate—in recent years during a difficult economic climate in our country. As a result, under the terms of the current agreement, the clubs' incentive to invest in the game is threatened. There are substantial other elements of the deal that simply are not working. For example, as interpreted by the courts, the current CBA effectively prohibits the clubs from recouping bonuses paid to players who subsequently breach their player contracts or refuse to perform. That is simply irrational and unfair to both fans and players who honor their contracts. Also irrational is that in the current system some rookies are able to secure contracts that pay them more than top proven veterans. Our objective is to fix these problems in a new CBA, one that will provide adequate incentives to grow the game, ensure the unparalleled competitive balance that has sustained our fans' interest, and afford the players fair and increasing compensation and benefits.[16]

Gene Upshaw, then-current executive director of the NFLPA, remarked that the team owners "just don't like what they agreed to in March of 2006." Jeffrey Kessler, an attorney for the NFLPA, allocated responsibility for the early termination opt out decision on internal tension among team owners: "The problem is that the owners could not agree among themselves on how they would share their revenues. The high revenue teams do not want to share money they earn in their markets, and the low revenue teams are unhappy about everything. So, they find a place to agree—they try to get it back from the players."[17] Gene Upshaw tragically passed away due to pancreatic cancer in August 2008. In March 2009, former litigation attorney DeMaurice Smith was elected as executive director of the NFLPA.[18] DeMaurice Smith immediately adopted a more adversarial approach with NFL team owners (and Commissioner Goodell) as compared with the previous consistent "working harmony" between the league and Gene Upshaw.[19] For instance, in March 2009, DeMaurice Smith commented, "There isn't a day where I don't hope for peace. At the same time, there isn't a day we won't prepare for war."[20]

In May 2009, the NFLPA sent Commissioner Goodell a letter to let the league know that the players association looked forward to upcoming negotiations with regard to the collective bargaining agreement.[21] In this letter, the NFLPA also formally requested audited financial statements detailing the profit/loss information for the league and all 32 teams. For example, the NFLPA sought financial data related to operating income from sources such as media rights deals, ticket sales and corporate partnerships along with operating expense information on player costs, team and league administrator salaries, game production expenses, and sales and marketing costs.[22] In June 2009, the NFLPA and NFL engaged in an initial bargaining session during which the league explained that it decided to terminate the CBA two years early due to an inadequate rate of financial return for team owners. The NFLPA once again requested complete financial statements for the league and all teams.

By September 2009, some NFL teams began to ask top-level executives (for example, general managers, coaches and chief operating officers) to accept significant pay decreases in the event of a work stoppage in 2011. The following contract provision examples illustrate how some teams were already starting to prepare financially for a potentially impending work stoppage:

- A team could terminate or suspend an executive's contract with 20 days prior notice;
- A team could reduce an executive's salary by 50% if the lockout continued for more than 90 days; and
- A team could extend the executive's contract for another year at the same terms as 2011 if at least eight NFL games were canceled during the 2011 season.[23]

In August 2010, the NFLPA marketing division notified NFL sponsors that the rights of these corporate partners to use the images (likenesses) of players in advertising would end in March 2011 if a deal on a new CBA was not reached.[24] The following month, in September 2010, Commissioner Goodell acknowledged that time was of the essence with respect to reaching an agreement on a successor CBA. During an interview with ESPN, Goodell said, "This deal is going to be easier to make between now and March [2011]. Once we get to March it just becomes more complicated and more difficult. We really need to work hard in the next several months to get something that works for the players, works for the owners and works for the game."[25] In October 2010, Commissioner Goodell made the following comment to the media regarding the importance of continued collective bargaining progress between the league and the NFLPA: "We have been very clear about the fact that the longer [negotiations go], the harder it gets. We have also made the point that revenue will start decreasing. It probably already has in certain categories. As that revenue decreases, it's less money to be able to negotiate over. So, it will be harder to get a labor agreement at some point."[26]

In November 2010, Bob Batterman (NFL outside labor counsel/attorney), appeared to be optimistic about collective bargaining prospects, as he explained that the NFL and NFLPA "started to make some incremental progress in some of the collateral areas—areas important to the deal but not the core issues."[27]

Also, in November 2010, Jeff Pash (NFL league counsel) boldly remarked, "I know we are going to have an agreement. There is no reason we can't have a deal [by March 4, 2011]. What we need is to have sustained engagement. We need to be meeting regularly. We need to leave meetings not worried about how we are going to characterize meetings ... it has got to be a shared commitment. One side cannot do it alone."[28]

In January 2011, NFLPA public relations and communications executive George Atallah authored an article for ESPN, which provided the following narrative on the perceptions and perspectives of NFL players:

> The players want to play a full NFL season in 2011 and have offered to extend the current deal in an effort to work out a long term deal without an interruption of league operations.... All signs and indicators point to extraordinary success and rapid growth for the business of football. According to the NFL and team owners, however, the "economic model in the NFL doesn't work." What's more, they have prepared for and are openly threatening a lockout if it's not "fixed." What is their proposal to fix it? They've asked the players for more than a $1 billion reduction in the players' portion of revenues in the first year alone of a future CBA. By the way, in a league with no guaranteed contracts, revealed dangers of the game and injury concerns at their peak, they want players to play two extra regular season games.... The players have asked repeatedly for financial transparency and economic information. We have been told publicly and privately that detailed financials are "none of your business." In an era of greater financial transparency, this is confusing. Frankly, it signals that this negotiation is about something much different from figuring out how to work together to secure the future of the game.[29]

The following week, Greg Aiello (NFL public relations executive) authored a response article for ESPN in which he wrote:

> The system does not work as well as it could from the standpoint of the teams. The time has arrived for adjustments that create an opportunity to make the game and league better. The crux of the difference is this: The union accepts the status quo, while the NFL wants to improve and secure the future of the game for the benefit of fans and players. The status quo means no rookie wage scale and the continuation of outrageous sums paid to many unproven rookies instead of shifting significant portions of that money to proven veterans and retired players.... The status quo means no league investment in new stadium development in Los Angeles and other cities, in international games, or in new technology to improve our service to fans in stadiums and at home. Costs must be properly balanced against revenue so that the league and the game can continue to grow. Companies with far more revenue than the NFL have gone bankrupt because they did not properly manage their costs. Our goal is to fix the problem now before it

becomes a crisis. That means negotiating a fair agreement that continues to provide billions to the players while also giving the teams a sustainable business model and improving the quality of everything we do.... The new CBA is about the future of the game and doing what is necessary to improve the quality of the game. That means addressing player safety, retired players, preseason, the way we pay rookies and making sure the league's business model works for the future.[30]

Throughout January 2011, DeMaurice Smith and Commissioner Goodell continued to demonstrate divergent strategic, tactical approaches to collective bargaining discussions. For example, Smith asserted, "Nobody stays strong without fighting. Nobody negotiates their way to strength. Nobody talks their way to a good deal. Nobody sits down and just has miraculous things happen." Conversely, Commissioner Goodell continued to press for more collaborative bargaining sessions: "I think the good thing is that we are talking. These things don't get resolved by making a lot of statements publicly. They get done by negotiating and meeting with one another, understanding one another and having a real serious negotiation and a commitment to getting something done."[31]

In February 2011, the NFL filed an unfair labor practice charge against the NFLPA, alleging that the players association had failed to bargain in good faith as required by the National Labor Relations Act (NLRA). The NFL claimed that the strategy executed by the NFLPA amounted to an unlawful anticipatory refusal to bargain. The NFL alleged that the NFLPA: (1) Refused to schedule collective bargaining sessions; (2) Failed to respond to league contract proposals in a timely and meaningful manner; (3) Insisted on the disclosure of detailed financial data—to which the NFLPA has no legal right—as a condition to further negotiation sessions; and (4) Engaged in additional conduct indicating a lack of intent to reach agreement through good faith collective bargaining with the league. In addition, the NFL's unfair labor practice charge asserted that the NFLPA's negotiation tactics were integral to the players association's "announced strategy to run out the clock and, after the CBA expires on March 3, purport to 'disclaim interest' as the representative of the NFL players, a strategy utilized by the NFLPA in a prior negotiation and one that the NFLPA often has threatened to resort to in this negotiation should it be deemed more advantageous to the players than the collective bargaining process that the NFLPA is obligated by law to follow."[32] The NFL also contended that "the NFLPA's threatened disclaimer as the representative of the players, together with the now-familiar antitrust litigation that is expected to follow, is a ploy and an unlawful subversion of the collective bargaining process ... it is both the reason for and proof of the NFLPA's failure to approach these negotiations with a sincere desire to reach a new agreement at the bargaining table as opposed to the courthouse."[33]

The NFLPA issued the following statement in response to the NFL's unfair labor practice charge: "The players didn't walkout and the players can't lockout. Players want a fair, new and long-term deal. We have offered proposals and solutions on every issue the owners have raised. This claim has absolutely no merit."[34]

Commissioner Goodell then authored a column that appeared in newspapers across the United States. Goodell wrote, "We need an agreement that both sides can live with and obtain what they need, not simply what they want. [The 2006] collective bargaining agreement does not work as it should from the standpoint of the teams. If needed adjustments are made, the NFL will be better for everyone. The first step is making sure a new collective bargaining agreement is more balanced and supports innovation and growth."[35]

Later in February 2011, the NFL and NFLPA agreed to schedule future negotiation sessions under the supervision of the Federal Mediation and Conciliation Service (FMCS). George H. Cohen, FMCS director, thought that the league and its players "engaged in highly-focused, constructive dialogue concerning a host of issues covering both economic and player-related conditions. The tenor of the across-the-table discussions reflected a noteworthy level of mutual respect even in the face of strongly held competing positions ... some progress was made, but very strong differences remain on the all-important core issues that separate" the NFL and the NFLPA.[36] For example, team owners continued to insist on taking approximately 18% of league revenue out of the "total revenues" pool before applying the revenue distribution split between teams and players—permitting this proposed 18% increase in new stadium cost credits for team owners would have reduced the players' salary cap revenue base and resultant share of total revenue—which was 58% of projected total revenues during the 2010 NFL season—by about 10% overall.[37]

A few weeks later, on March 1, 2011, Minnesota federal judge David Doty determined that the NFL violated its obligations under the 2006 CBA to enter into agreements that benefit both the league and its players when the NFL renegotiated a series of media rights deals that would have allowed the NFL to receive approximately $4 billion in guaranteed payments in the event of a lockout. Existing broadcast contracts effectively prevented the NFL from collecting revenue during a lockout in 2011 because the contracts did not require broadcasters to pay rights fees during a work stoppage. For example, the broadcast contract between the league and DirecTV was set to expire at the end of the 2010 NFL season. The existing contract between the league and DirecTV did not contain any work-stoppage guarantee payment provision. As a result, the NFL would receive no revenue if it locked out the players in 2011. However, the renegotiated contract provided that DirecTV would pay a substantial fee if the 2011 NFL season was not canceled, and up to 9% more (at the NFL's discretion) if the 2011 season was canceled. In other words, the NFL would have received substantially more money from DirecTV in 2011 if the league decided to lock out its players. Judge Doty concluded that, "In considering broadcast contract renegotiations, the NFL consistently characterized gaining control over labor as a short-term objective and maximizing revenue as a long-term objective. The NFL used best efforts to advance its CBA negotiating position at the expense of using best efforts to maximize total revenues for the joint benefit of the NFL and the players."[38]

On March 4, 2011, the NFL and NFLPA mutually agreed to postpone the termination date of the 2006 CBA by one week to March 11.[39] After a full day of bargaining sessions on March 9, 2011, NFL attorney Jeff Pash provided the following candid comments:

> There are serious issues; the differences are significant—no one should be misled on that. But we are here, we believe in this process. I've said that many, many times. We believe in collective bargaining. It is an institution that is under attack all over this country. But it is the best means of preserving industrial peace that human beings have ever found. And we believe in it and we want to engage in it. There may be those who don't want to engage in it, who prefer litigation, who prefer other gambles—that is not where we are. We are here to talk, we are here to negotiate, not to file lawsuits.[40]

On March 11, 2011, the NFLPA renounced its status as the exclusive collective bargaining representative of NFL players.[41] In response to this disclaimer of interest by the NFLPA, the NFL issued the following statement:

> The fastest way to a fair agreement is for both the union and the clubs to continue the mediation process. Unfortunately, the players union notified our office that it had "decertified" and walked away from mediation and collective bargaining to initiate the antitrust litigation it has been threatening to file. In an effort to get a fair agreement now, the clubs offered a deal that would have had no adverse financial impact upon veteran players in the early years and would meet the players' financial demands in the latter years. The union left a very good deal on the table.[42]

As soon as the 2006 CBA expired at 11:59 p.m. New York time on March 11, 2011, the NFL and its member teams instituted a lockout of the players. The league issued a statement that provided in relevant part: "The union's abandonment of bargaining has forced the clubs to take action they very much wanted to avoid.... The league has informed the union that it is taking the difficult but necessary step of exercising its right under federal labor law to impose a lockout of the [NFL players]. The clubs are committed to continuing to negotiate until an agreement is reached."[43]

In conjunction with the league announcing the lockout, nine current and prospective NFL players—led by New England Patriots star quarterback Tom Brady, but seeking to represent all players—filed a class action lawsuit against the NFL in Minnesota District Court. Simply put, the NFLPA strategy immediately shifted from negotiation to litigation.[44] The players alleged that the NFL and its 32 independently-operated member teams unlawfully jointly agreed to "a so-called 'lockout' aimed at shutting down the entire free agent marketplace for players no longer under contract, as well as a boycott of rookie players seeking an NFL contract for the first time, and even players currently under NFL contracts, who will not be permitted to enjoy the benefits of those contracts." The lawsuit also claimed that the anticompetitive purpose of the NFL's group boycott was to coerce players "to agree to a new anticompetitive system of player restraints which will, among other things, drastically reduce player compensation levels below those that existed in the past and that would exist in a competitive market."[45]

On March 17, 2011, Commissioner Goodell wrote a letter to all NFL players. In the letter, Commissioner Goodell emphasized his viewpoint that the most recent NFL offer "presented a strong and fair basis for continuing negotiations, allowing the new league year and free agency to begin, and growing our game in the years to come."[46] Key elements of the NFL proposal included:

- A salary cap for the 2011 season that would avoid a negative financial impact on veteran players (salary and benefits would have been set at $141 million per team and, by the 2014 season, salary and benefits would have been set at $161 million per team);
- Free agency for players with four or more accrued seasons, and reduced draft choice compensation for restricted free agents;
- Extensive changes in offseason work requirements that would promote player health and safety, encourage players to continue their education and promote second career opportunities;
- Changes in preseason and regular season practices and schedules that would reduce the number of padded practices, reduce the amount of contact and increase the number of days off for all players;
- Retain the current 16-game regular season format for at least the next two seasons, and further commit not to change to an 18-game regular season without agreement by the NFLPA;
- Expand injury guarantees for players up to $1 million for a second contract year;
- Enhanced retirement benefits for pre-1993 NFL players (more than 2,000 former players would have received an immediate average increase of 60% in pension funds);
- A new entry-level compensation system that would make more than $300 million per draft class available for veterans' pay and player benefits; and
- Significant changes in disciplinary procedures, including a jointly-appointed neutral arbitrator to oversee all drug and steroid appeals.[47]

On March 19, 2011, a group of NFL veteran players sent a letter to Commissioner Goodell, which served as a response to the NFL's proposal two days earlier. The letter aimed to remind team owners that players "were there at the negotiations and know the truth about what happened, which ultimately led the players to renounce the NFLPA's status as the collective bargaining representative of NFL players. The players took this step only as a last resort, and only after two years of trying to reach a reasonable collective bargaining agreement." In the letter, the players also underscored the viewpoint that, "The NFLPA did all it could to reach a fair collective bargaining agreement and made numerous proposals to address the concerns raised by the owners. In response, the owners never justified their demands for a massive giveback, which would have resulted in the worst economic deal for players in major league pro sports."[48] More specifically, the players expressed concerns about the following perceived elements of the league proposal:

- The league proposal established a pegged amount for the salary cap plus benefits regardless of NFL revenues, and the proposal also would have given the owners 100% of all revenues above the unrealistically low revenue projections. The cap system for the past twenty years has always been one in which the players were guaranteed to share in revenue growth as partners, whereas the league proposal would have shifted to a system in which players were told how much they will get, instead of knowing their share will correspondingly grow with league revenues.
  - For example, if NFL revenues grew at 8% each season from 2011 to 2014, then the cap plus benefits with the players' historical share would be $159 million for the 2011 season ($18 million more per team than the league's $141 million proposal) and would grow to $201 million per team for the 2014 season ($40 million more per team than the league's $161 million proposal)
  - In addition, the league proposal would have resulted in a leaguewide giveback by the players of $576 million in 2011, increasing to $1.2 billion in 2014, for a total of more than $3.6 billion during the first four years of the proposed new CBA
  - All of the other revenue distribution elements offered by the league in the proposal—which Commissioner Goodell claimed the players should have been eager to accept—were conditioned on the players agreeing to a rollback of their traditional 50% share of all revenues to what it was in the 1980s, which would have given up the successes the players fought for and won by asserting legal rights in court
  - The compensation proposal went far beyond addressing any problem of rookie "busts," and amounted to severely restricting veteran salaries for all or most of their playing careers, since most players play less than four years in the NFL—the letter from Commissioner Goodell failed to explain that the league proposed to limit compensation long after rookies become veterans (for example, into a player's fourth and fifth years in the NFL);
- The changes in offseason workouts and other benefits to players were conditioned upon the players accepting an economic framework that was unjustified and unfair; and
- The league continued to ask for an 18-game season (offering to delay implementation for only one more year until the 2012 NFL season), even though the players and medical experts warned the league many times that expanding the season would increase the risk of player injury and shorten careers.[49]

On March 21, 2011, the NFL countered the antitrust lawsuit filed by the players with the following arguments and contentions:

[The players] seek an injunction under the Sherman Act prohibiting the NFL's member clubs from imposing a lockout that is unquestionably lawful and permitted by federal labor law. [The players] contend that their union's purported disclaimer of interest in collective bargaining ... converts into an antitrust violation.... The law is not so easily manipulated. One party to a collective bargaining relationship cannot, through its own tactical and unilateral conduct, instantaneously oust federal labor law or extinguish another party's labor law rights.... [The players] allege that the NFL waived its ability to argue that the disclaimer is a sham. That assertion ignores the plain language of the CBA: [the players] could have asserted a waiver only if the purported disclaimer had occurred after CBA expiration. Here, presumably because the CBA would have barred antitrust claims for at least six months if the disclaimer had occurred after the expiration, the union purported to disappear a full eight hours before the expiration.[50]

The 2006 CBA contained the following provisions related to any decertification of (or disclaimer of interest by) the players association: (1) If the NFLPA remained in existence as a players association following the expiration of the term of the 2006 CBA, then NFL players agreed to wait at least six months after expiration of the CBA term to commence any legal action claiming that the NFL was in violation of antitrust laws; and (2) If a decertification or disclaimer of interest were to occur following expiration of the 2006 CBA, players could then file a class action legal complaint after the required six-month waiting period— if this process was followed, the league agreed to waive any legal right to assert any antitrust labor exemption defense based upon any claim that the termination by the NFLPA of its status as a collective bargaining representative of all players amounted to an ineffective sham.[51] NFL players strategically chose to facilitate the disclaimer of interest procedural tool shortly before the expiration of the 2006 CBA in order to avoid the required six-month waiting period for filing an antitrust lawsuit, yet by doing so permitted the league to make the argument that the disclaimer of interest was a sham, that the non-statutory labor exemption still applied and, therefore, prevented antitrust claims by players.[52] As explained by Professor Nathaniel Grow, "The owners hoped that by preventing the players from working—and in the process withholding their salaries—they would gain additional leverage in subsequent negotiations." Similarly, the players "hoped their lawsuit would provide leverage over the owners by not only neutralizing the NFL's lockout—and thereby forcing the owners to continue paying players throughout the course of the labor dispute—but also by introducing the potential threat of treble antitrust damages into the negotiations."[53]

On April 25, 2011, Minnesota District Court judge Susan Nelson determined that the NFL must end its lockout of the players, and at least tentatively resume business operations—pending a future full trial of the case. Judge Nelson failed to find any basis to dispute the validity and effectiveness of the NFLPA's unequivocal disclaimer of any further role as the exclusive representative of players in collective bargaining with the league. In the words of Judge Nelson, "the players took a calculated risk in order to pursue their present antitrust claims. The disclaimer was made in good faith as the players have engaged in no inconsistent conduct.... A court cannot force a union to continue, against its wishes, a relationship that is in its very nature predicated upon voluntariness and consent."[54] Judge Nelson also explained that a lockout is not a substantive term or condition of employment; rather, a lockout is a procedural tool that the courts permit an employer to use to pressure a union back to the bargaining table.

The following day, on April 26, 2011, Commissioner Goodell wrote a column in the *Wall Street Journal* in response to Judge Nelson ordering the end of the league-mandated work stoppage as well as recognizing the right of NFL players to dissolve the players association. Commissioner Goodell expressed the following thoughts in the column:

> Rather than address the challenge of improving the collective bargaining agreement for the benefit of the game, the union-financed lawsuit attacks virtually every aspect of the current system including the draft, the salary cap and free agency rules, which collectively have been responsible for the quality and popularity of the game for nearly two decades. A union victory threatens to overturn the carefully constructed system of competitive balance that makes NFL games and championship races so unpredictable and exciting.... Prior to filing their litigation, players and their representatives publicly praised the current system and argued for extending the status quo. Now they are singing a far different tune, attacking in the courts the very arrangements they said were working just fine.... These outcomes are inevitable under any approach other than a comprehensive collective bargaining agreement. That is especially true of an approach that depends on litigation settlements negotiated by lawyers. But that is what the players' attorneys are fighting for in court. And that is what will be at stake as the NFL appeals Judge Nelson's ruling to the Eighth Circuit Court of Appeals.[55]

Throughout May and June in 2011, both league and player representatives continued to express a sense of cautious optimism concerning the ability to agree to terms on a new CBA despite the ongoing unresolved litigation. For instance, in May 2011, NFL attorney Jeff Pash acknowledged, "Business negotiations can be contentious and they can be heated sometimes but the one thing we know with absolute certainty, this is going to end, it's going to end in an agreement. Once that agreement is forged, we're going to work together as good solid partners for hopefully decades to come. DeMaurice is a real contributor."[56] Commissioner Goodell echoed the mindset of Jeff Pash, as Goodell expressed his view that, "The best and fastest solution to the differences is to negotiate. Let's get together and let's solve those problems in negotiations and with a collective bargaining agreement. We are taking the initiative to make sure that we do everything possible to create that environment and to have those meetings, but frankly, litigation creates delays and creates, unfortunately, an environment where a discussion can only happen in certain forums."[57] In June 2011, DeMaurice Smith was asked if he and Commissioner Goodell remained optimistic. Smith responded, "I think we're both optimistic when we have the right people in the room. We know we are talking about the right issues and that we are working hard to get it done. It is extremely complicated [and] requires a lot of hard work by a lot of people.... We are going to keep working hard and try to make sure we get a deal done."[58]

On July 8, 2011, the Eighth Circuit Court of Appeals—in an opinion authored by judge Kermit Bye—reversed the previous decision made by Judge Nelson because federal courts are not permitted to issue injunctions (for example, requiring the NFL to end its lockout) in cases involving or growing out of a labor dispute. As a result, the league was once again permitted to lock out its players. Judge Bye concluded that the antitrust lawsuit filed by NFL players represented "a controversy concerning terms or conditions of employment." In addition, the federal appeals court made the following findings and conclusions:

> The players seek broad relief that would affect the terms or conditions of employment for the entire industry of professional football. In particular, they urge the court to declare unlawful and to enjoin several features of the relationship between the league and the players, including the limit on compensation that can be paid to rookies, the salary cap, the "franchise player" designation, and the "transition player" designation, all of which the players assert are anticompetitive restrictions that violate Section 1 of the Sherman Act.... The league and the players union were parties to a collective bargaining agreement for almost eighteen years prior to March 2011. They were engaged in collective bargaining over terms and conditions of employment for approximately two years through March 11, 2011. At that point, the parties were involved in a classic "labor dispute" by the players' own definition. Then, on a single day, just hours before the CBA's expiration, the union discontinued collective bargaining and disclaimed its status, and the players filed this action seeking relief concerning industry-wide terms and conditions of employment. Whatever the effect of the union's disclaimer on the league's immunity from antitrust liability, the labor dispute did not suddenly disappear just because the players elected to pursue the dispute through antitrust litigation rather than collective bargaining.[59]

The NFL and all players within the league issued the following joint statement after learning of the Eighth Circuit Court of Appeals ruling: "While we respect the court's decision, today's ruling does not change our mutual recognition that this matter must be resolved through negotiation. We are committed to our current discussions and reaching a fair agreement that will benefit all parties for years to come, and allow for a full 2011 season."[60] The league and players continued to have constructive talks and made substantial progress negotiating a wide range of issues throughout the first three weeks in July 2011. On July 21, 2011, NFL teams approved the terms of a comprehensive settlement of litigation and a new ten-year collective bargaining agreement with the NFLPA. Commissioner Goodell enthusiastically explained, "We are pleased to announce that our clubs have approved the terms of a long-term negotiated agreement with the NFL players. It includes many positive changes that emerged from a spirit of compromise rooted in doing what is best for the game and players. DeMaurice Smith and his team, and the players and owners involved in the negotiations, deserve great credit for their skill and professionalism."[61] Commissioner Goodell and DeMaurice Smith seemed to have learned that the league can thrive in a true collaborative partnership with the NFLPA. The litigation settlement and CBA completion were conditioned on the reformation of a union by the NFLPA and subsequent approval by the players association. During the next few days, a substantial majority of NFL players signed the authorization cards required for recertification of the NFLPA as the exclusive collective bargaining representative of NFL players. On August 4, 2011—after a 132-day lockout—league and NFLPA representatives officially ratified and signed a finalized 2011 CBA.[62]

Summarizing the principal deal terms in the 2011 CBA

The NFL and NFLPA agreed to the following principal deal terms as part of the 2011 CBA:

- *Term of CBA*: The 2011 NFL collective bargaining agreement contains a term of ten NFL seasons, from the 2011 season through the 2020 season (unlike the 2006 CBA, neither the NFL nor the NFLPA have the ability to opt out of the 2011 CBA—subject to a limited early termination option by the NFLPA in the event of widespread collusion among NFL teams).[63]
- *The "All Revenues" (AR) Formula*: Similar to BRI in the NBA collective bargaining agreement, the "All Revenues" system serves as the basis for NFL player compensation. The AR formula consists of three categories ("revenue buckets") of league and team-generated revenues. The following three AR categories are utilized for calculating the salary cap and total player cost amounts:
  1   Projected league media revenues (55% of revenue in this category counts toward the total player cost amount calculation)—during the 2011 NFL season, this AR category included media rights fees paid by FOX (for the NFC afternoon package), CBS (for the AFC afternoon package), ESPN (for the Monday Night Football package), NBC (for the Sunday Night Football package), and DirecTV (for the Sunday Ticket package).
  2   Projected revenues from NFL Ventures (NFL entity that manages league-wide sponsorships, marketing, media rights and sales) and postseason revenues (45% of revenue in this category counts toward the total player cost amount calculation)—this AR category also includes all revenues received by the league arising from NFL playoff games (but not including local postseason revenue earned by teams) as well as revenue generated by: (1) NFL Network (including revenues related to the broadcast, telecast or distribution of live NFL games and the RedZone channel); (2) NFL Digital agreement with Verizon; and (3) NFL Films agreement with ESPN.

3   Projected local (team) revenues (40% of revenue in this category counts toward the total player cost amount calculation)—this AR category includes the following sources of revenue earned by NFL teams: (1) Gate receipts from general tickets and premium seating (for example, luxury boxes/suites) during the preseason, regular season and postseason; (2) Concessions, parking, local advertising/promotions, local sponsorship agreements, most stadium naming rights deals and merchandise sales (at venue and online); and (3) Preseason game television rights and team radio broadcast agreements.[64]

• *Salary Cap Logistics*: The NFL salary cap is calculated prior to each season based on projected annual league and team revenues. The "player cost amount" includes the salary cap amount plus the forecasted amount for player benefits. For example, for the 2011 NFL season, the player cost amount equaled approximately $142.4 million per team (salary cap amount of $120.4 million and player benefits of $22 million per team). As a result, for the 2011 NFL season, the total player cost amount for all 32 teams equaled around $4.56 billion.[65] For comparison purposes, for the 2019 NFL season the salary cap equaled $188.2 million. In addition, the NFL and NFLPA also projected $40 million per team in player benefit costs. As a result, for the 2019 season, the total player cost amount for all 32 teams equaled around $7.3 billion.[66] The 2011 CBA also guarantees that players receive a minimum percentage of the total AR amount each season. The players share must equal at least 47% of projected AR but no more than 48.5% of projected AR (before application of the team stadium credit allowance). The 2011 CBA contains a stadium credit allowance, whereby NFL teams are permitted to deduct a specific percentage of costs associated with the construction or renovation of a stadium. Each season the aggregate stadium credit sum for all 32 teams cannot exceed 1.5% of the total AR amount. These stadium credits for team owner investments are not permitted to reduce the total player cost amount below a specific threshold—47% of AR for the 2012 to 2014 NFL seasons, and 46% of AR for the 2017 to 2020 NFL seasons.[67]

    ○   As part of the 2011 CBA, NFL teams made a leaguewide commitment to cumulative annual team spending on player salaries and benefits. For instance, teams were required to collectively spend at least 99% of the salary cap threshold during the 2011 and 2012 NFL seasons. For each of the two successive four-season time periods from 2013 to 2020, teams are jointly required to spend at least 95% of the salary cap. For example, if the salary cap thresholds from the 2017 to 2020 league years equaled $168 million, $177 million, $188 million and $200 million, the guaranteed leaguewide cash spending over that four-year period would need to equal at least $22.3 billion (95% of $733 million total salary cap amounts over the four-year period multiplied by 32 NFL teams). In addition, teams are individually required to spend a minimum amount on player salaries. For each of the two four-season periods from 2013 to 2020, teams are individually required to spend at least 89% of the salary cap. For illustration purposes, if the salary cap thresholds from the 2017 to 2020 league years once again equaled $168 million, $177 million, $188 million and $200 million, the minimum individual team cash spending over that four-year period would need to equal at least $652 million (89% of $733 million total salary cap amounts over the four-year period). Any shortfalls related to these minimum leaguewide and team spending requirements at the end of each four-year period (i.e., after the 2016 and 2020 league years) are required to be paid directly to players who were on the team's roster during one or more of the applicable seasons.[68]

- *Rookie Contracts*: The 2011 CBA includes a set of nuanced guidelines related to contracts for rookies (new NFL players).
  - *Total and Year One Rookie Compensation Pools*: The "total rookie compensation pool" refers to the leaguewide limit on the total aggregate amount that each team is permitted to spend on rookie contracts for both drafted and undrafted players over the entire term of those contracts. For example, a rookie drafted in the second round who signs a four-year contract with a salary of $1 million in year one, $1.1 million in year two, $1.2 million in year three and $1.3 million in year four, would have $4.6 million count against the total rookie compensation pool for that team. For the 2011 NFL season, the total rookie compensation pool limit equaled $874.5 million. The "year one rookie compensation pool" for the first year of rookie contracts signed following the 2011 NFL draft equaled $159 million. The total rookie compensation pool and the year one rookie compensation pool both increase or decrease in conjunction with the salary cap each year after the 2011 NFL season, up to a maximum of 5% plus half of any salary cap increase over the baseline 5%. For example, if the salary cap increases by 11% from one season to the next, then each of these two rookie compensation pools would correspondingly increase by 8% (5% baseline increase plus half of the additional 6% salary cap increase to 11% overall).[69]
  - *Rookie Contract Length and Compensation*: All rookie contracts are required to include a fixed and unalterable contract length. All first round draft picks receive a four-year contract with a team option for a fifth year. All players drafted in rounds two through seven receive a four-year contract (but with no team option for a fifth year). All undrafted players receive a three-year contract.[70] For the 2011 NFL season, the minimum rookie salary equaled $375,000. For the 2020 NFL season, the minimum rookie salary equaled $510,000.[71] Also, rookie contracts can include annual salary increases of up to 25% of the player's first year rookie salary (subject to limited exceptions). For illustration purposes, if a player drafted in the second round signs a four-year contract that includes a base salary of $500,000 and a

$400,000 signing bonus, that player's year one rookie salary would equal $600,000 because signing bonuses are prorated on a straight line basis over the life of a contract for player compensation and salary cap calculation purposes. Accordingly, the player's maximum annual base salary increase during his four-year rookie contract may not exceed $150,000 (25% of $600,000) from one season to the next.[72]

○ *Rookie Proven Performance Escalator*: Rookies drafted in rounds three through seven are eligible to earn a "proven performance" salary escalator if the player achieves at least one of two qualifiers: (1) Participates in a minimum of 35% of his team's offensive or defensive plays in any two of the three previous regular seasons; or (2) Participates in a "cumulative average" of at least 35% of his team's offensive or defensive plays over the three previous regular seasons. For instance, if a player participates in 600 of the team's 1,000 offensive plays in his first NFL season, 290 of the team's plays during his second season and 310 of the team's plays during his third season for a total of 1,200 plays out of a possible 3,000 plays, the cumulative average would equal 40% and, as a result, the player would qualify for the proven performance escalator—which, during the 2011 season, would have escalated the player's fourth-year salary to $1.2 million (equivalent to the qualifying offer amount for restricted free agents).[73]

○ *Performance Incentives for Rookies Drafted in First Two Rounds*: Rookie contracts for players selected in the first two rounds may contain performance incentives based upon achievement of specified playtime percentage metrics of at least 35% of the team's total regular season plays in the first year of the player's rookie contract, or at least 45% of the team's total regular season plays in any subsequent year of a rookie contract. Performance incentives for rookies are not permitted to be based on the achievement of any other statistic, honor or award.[74]

○ *Fifth-Year Team Option*: Each team is permitted to extend a player's initial four-year rookie contract for a fifth year at a pre-established amount calculated as follows: (1) For players drafted 1–10, the average salary of the top ten highest paid players at the player's position; and (2) For players drafted 11–32, the average salary of the 3rd through 25th highest paid players at the player's position. For example, a quarterback who was drafted with the 1st pick in the 2011 NFL draft could earn $22 million over the first four years of his contract plus a fifth-year option salary of $14.3 million (assuming a 5% salary cap growth rate) for a total of $36.3 million in compensation during his first five years in the league.[75]

○ *Rookie Contract Renegotiations*: A rookie contract for a drafted player may not be renegotiated (or amended) in any way until after the final regular season game of the player's third contract year. A rookie contract for an undrafted player may not be renegotiated (or amended) in any way until after the final regular season game of the player's second contract year.[76]

- *Veteran Contracts and Free Agency*: For the 2011 NFL season, the minimum salary for veteran players with five years of NFL experience equaled $685,000, and $910,000 for veteran players with at least ten seasons of NFL experience. For the 2020 season, the minimum salary for veteran players with five years of NFL experience equaled $820,000, and $1,045,000 for veteran players with at least ten seasons of NFL experience.[77] NFL players become eligible for free agency after playing three NFL seasons. For the 2019 season, players with three accrued seasons who received a qualifying offer (a salary tender predetermined by the CBA) became restricted free agents when their contracts expired at the conclusion of the 2018 league year on March 13, 2019. For example, if a team wanted to make a specific player a restricted free agent in order to secure a right of first refusal to match any offer form another team—and also wanted to receive draft pick compensation equivalent to the same round in which the player was originally drafted—the team would be required to offer the player a one-year salary of at least $2,025,000 for the 2019 NFL season. If that team wanted to receive a first round draft pick as compensation for another team signing the restricted free agent, the team would need to tender the player a qualifying offer of at least $4,407,000 for the 2019 season. A player becomes an unrestricted free agent after playing in the NFL for four seasons. Unrestricted free agents are permitted to sign with any team. The player's prior team does not receive any draft pick compensation if the player decides to sign with another team.[78]
- *Additional Notable Provisions*: The 2011 CBA consists of 316 total pages, and certainly contains many other important (and intriguing) elements.
  - *Minicamps*: Each league year, a team may hold a maximum of one mandatory minicamp for veteran players. If a team hires a new head coach after the end of the prior regular season, that team may hold one additional voluntary minicamp for veteran players. Any mandatory minicamp for veteran players counts as one of the nine weeks of the team's official offseason workout program. There is no limitation on the number of minicamps a team may hold for rookie players during the seven weeks of the team's Rookie Football Development Program.[79]
  - *Offseason Workouts*: For the 2019 NFL season, teams were required to pay each player a minimum of $235 for each workout or classroom instruction session in which the player participated as part of the team's voluntary offseason workout program.[80]
  - *Practice Rules—Reducing the Number of Padded Practices*: During the regular season, padded practices at which all players are required to wear helmets and shoulder pads must be limited to a total of 14 practices—11 of which must be held during the first 11 weeks of the regular season, and three of which must be held during the remaining six weeks of the regular season. The team may choose the days of the week on which practices are held. Each team may hold two padded practices in the same week during one week of the regular season, provided that

such week falls within the first 11 weeks of the regular season. Teams participating in the postseason may hold one padded practice per week, on a day of the team's choosing, commencing with the week following the team's last regular season game.[81]

- *Number of Regular Season Games*: The league and/or teams may increase the number of regular season games per team above the standard 16 regular season games only with the approval of the NFLPA, which approval may be withheld at the NFLPA's sole discretion.[82]

- *Practice Squad Players*: For the 2020 NFL season, the minimum salary for practice squad players equaled $8,400 per week. Each team is permitted to have eight players on the practice squad. Practice squad players on a team that wins the Super Bowl will be entitled to a ring similar in appearance to the one provided to players on the active/inactive list; however, the team may provide any practice squad player with a commemorative ring of lesser value.[83]

- *Reimbursement for Meals*: Players get reimbursed for meals not provided by teams on travel days. During the 2020 NFL season, reimbursement amounts were $31 for breakfast, $41 for lunch and $59 for dinner.[84]

- *Pro Bowl Game*: For the 2020 season, players who participate on the losing team in the NFL Pro Bowl receive $37,000, and players who participate on the winning team receive $74,000.[85]

- *Player Fines*: For the 2020 season, players could be fined up to $2,745 for throwing the football into the stands or damaging team-provided equipment, $14,650 for missing team transportation or losing a playbook or scouting report and $38,785 for being ejected from a game.[86]

- *Tuition Assistance Plan*: The NFL Player Tuition Assistance Plan provides up to $20,000 per league year as reimbursement for tuition, fees and books to any player who earns an average of "C" or better per semester at an eligible educational institution.[87]

- *Retired Player Benefits*: In August 2011, the NFL established the "Legacy Benefit," which planned to provide more than $620 million over the term of the 2011 CBA to players who were in the NFL prior to 1993. The 2011 CBA also established and revamped other funds, benefits and insurance programs for retired players such as the disability fund, long term care insurance plan, former player life improvement plan and the neurocognitive disability benefit. NFL players also receive five years of medical and dental insurance benefits after retirement, but only if players are credited with at least three seasons as a player in the league.[88]

- *Revenue Circumvention*: In the event that a team or anyone acting on its behalf fails to materially report or materially misreports team revenue in a manner designed to serve the purpose of defeating or circumventing the intention of the league and its players related to AR and non-AR revenue classifications, the NFLPA and/or the NFL would have the right to initiate a formal proceeding before a system arbitrator.

If the system arbitrator concludes that a team engaged in revenue circumvention, the arbitrator is permitted to impose a significant fine payable to the NFL for donation to charitable funds (for example, up to $5 million for the 2011 NFL season).[89]

Notes

1 Commissioner Goodell has previously stated that the NFL aspires to surpass $25 billion in total revenue by the 2027 season.
2 National Football League—Impact of Television (2014), *available at* www.nfl.com (explaining that other professional sports leagues "have modified their revenue sharing since 2000 to adopt systems more like the NFL's").
3 *See* Draper, K. and Belson, K. (2019). NFL Begins Moves to Avoid Another Labor War, the *New York Times* (explaining that digital streaming companies have not shown an appetite to pay the billions of dollars necessary to win an exclusive package of games, and the NFL has resisted selling exclusive rights to one digital platform). It is worthwhile to note that, during the 2019 NFL season, Amazon spent about $65 million for digital rights to 11 "Thursday Night Football" games. Twitter and Verizon have also previously purchased rights to digitally stream select NFL games. *See also* Carter, D.M. (2011). *Money Games: Profiting from the Convergence of Sports and Entertainment.* Stanford University Press, at page 28 (providing the following historical example of the exponential growth of NFL media rights deals: "In 1970, networks would pay $50 million to broadcast the NFL, and by 1985 the going rate was $450 million ... [in 2010], the NFL averaged approximately $4 billion per year in broadcast rights fees"). *See also* Bodenheimer, G. (2015). *Every Town is a Sports Town.* Grand Central Publishing, at page 59 (explaining that, "In 1987, it was unprecedented for the NFL to put their games on cable television. Not only was this their first cable contract, but the NFL had never before played games on Sunday nights.... [The ESPN] package consisted of eight games in the second half of the regular season over each of the next three years.... In return, ESPN agreed to pay the National Football League $153 million—an extraordinary amount at the time").
4 Flint, J. (2019). DirecTV Rethinks NFL Sunday Ticket Deal Amid Cord-Cutting, *Wall Street Journal.*
5 *See* Boudway, I. and Novy-Williams, E. (2018). The NFL's Very Profitable Existential Crisis, *Bloomberg Businessweek.*
6 *See* IEG Research (2019). NFL Sponsorship Revenues Reach $1.39 Billion for 2018–19 Season, *available at* www.sponsorship.com.
7 *See* Official Release—NFL Selects Caesars Entertainment as First Casino Sponsor (2019), *available at* www.nfl.com. Caesars Entertainment agreed to pay the NFL approximately $25–30 million per year based on the terms of the three-year sponsorship agreement.
8 *See* Ryman, R. (2018). Packers Set New Records with 2017 Revenue, Expenses, *The Green Bay Press-Gazette. See also* Zimbalist, A. (2006). *The Bottom Line: Observations and Arguments on the Sports Business.* Temple University Press, at page 176 (explaining that, "In the NBA and the NFL, where an explicit salary cap restricts the payroll, the players have every reason to be concerned that team revenue is correctly identified").
9 Green Bay Packers executive Mark Murphy explained that 2018–2019 "was a unique year." Murphy emphasized that the team remained in a "strong, stable financial position" because 2018–2019 included "atypical expenses" such as increased expenditures on free agent signings, coaching staff changes, costs associated with the "Packers 100 Seasons" celebration and $40 million in liability due to the leaguewide

concussion settlement (as compared with $27 million the prior fiscal year). As of March 31, 2019, the Packers had approximately $390 million in the team's reserve fund. *See* Ryman, R. (2019). Green Bay Packers Report Record Revenue, Record Expenses, *The Green Bay Press-Gazette* (explaining that the Packers also contributed $5 million to the Packers Foundation).

10 *See* Forbes—Sports Money: 2019 NFL Valuations (2019), *available at* www.forbes. com. *See also* Winfree, J. (2012). The Economic Structure of the NFL, in *The Economics of the National Football League* (Edited by Quinn, K.G.), at pages 34–35 (explaining that franchise values in the NFL are difficult to calculate because financial data is not readily available for most teams, and individual teams are evolving into one foundational piece of broader entertainment and real estate investment portfolios).

11 *See* Battista, J. (2018). Carolina Panthers Finalize Terms to Sell Franchise to David Tepper, *available at* www.nfl.com. *See also* Zimbalist, A. (2006). *The Bottom Line: Observations and Arguments on the Sports Business*, at page 37 (writing that, "Owners get substantial intangible returns in the form of business and political connections, related-party transaction benefits, perquisites [access privileges], ego gratification, enhanced influence, and fun ... owners have also realized appreciable capital gains when they have sold their teams").

12 *See* NFL CBA (2006), Article LVIII, Section 2.

13 *See* NFL CBA (2006), Article LVIII, Section 3 (indicating that the CBA provided both the players and the league an option to shorten the agreement by one or two years). The NFL Management Council is responsible for handling labor negotiations (collective bargaining) on behalf of the NFL member teams. The NFL Management Council is comprised of team owners. Both the NFL Management Council and the NFLPA review the terms of any contract negotiated between a team and player before the deal becomes official. *See* Fitzgerald, J. and Natarajan, V. (2016). *Crunching Numbers: An Inside Look at the Salary Cap and Negotiating Player Contracts*, at page 15. As an aside, in 1993, the NFL became the second professional sports league in the United States to agree to institute a team salary cap after years of acrimonious dealings between the league and the NFLPA. The salary cap system was first implemented during the 1994 NFL season. *See* Kaplan, R.A. (2004). The NBA Luxury Tax Model: A Misguided Regulatory Regime, *Columbia Law Review*, at page 1625. The salary cap was initially designed as an accounting system that would be applied to NFL players. Each team was allotted an equal budget that could be spent, in a given season, on players. One of the novel features of the salary cap was the introduction of a special bonus—the signing bonus—that would be allocated over the course of a contract, despite being paid at the beginning of the contract. *See* Fitzgerald, J. and Natarajan, V. (2016). *Crunching Numbers: An Inside Look at the Salary Cap and Negotiating Player Contracts*, at pages 5–6.

14 *See* NFL CBA (2006), Article LVIII, Section 3. *See also* NFL CBA (2006), Article XVI, Section 1 (explaining that the NFL would still have the college draft in the league year immediately following the expiration or termination of the CBA—as a result, the 2006 CBA rules relating to the NFL draft continued through April 2011). The 2006 CBA provided that the final league year would be an "uncapped year" (salary cap would not be in effect). Stated differently, the final "capped year" under the 2006 CBA refers the league year immediately prior to the final league year. *See* NFL CBA (2006), Article I, Sections 3, 4. This "uncapped year" provision was likely designed as a "poison pill" that would encourage both the league and its players to agree to terms on a new CBA prior to the final league year of the then-current CBA. Perhaps one of the most demanding challenges a team's salary cap manager and player agent face when negotiating a contract toward the end of a CBA term is the application of the 30% rule. For example, if a player is under contract in a final league year (i.e., 2020 NFL season)—and the player's contract extends beyond that season—the player is not permitted to earn a salary increase for the season following

the final league year (2021 NFL season) of more than 30% of his salary in the final league year (2020 NFL season). *See* NFL CBA (2011), Article 13, Section 7.

15 Official Release—NFL Owners Opt Out of CBA (2008), *available at* www.nfl.com (explaining that, "The 2008 and 2009 seasons will be played with a salary cap. If there is no new agreement before the 2010 season, that season will be played without a salary cap under rules that also limit the free agency rights of the players. If not extended, the agreement would expire at the end of the 2010 league year. We are resolved to do our best to achieve a fair agreement that will allow labor peace to continue through and beyond the 2011 season").

16 Official Release—NFL Owners Opt Out of CBA (2008), *available at* www.nfl.com. *See also* Staudohar, P.D. (2012). The Football Lockout of 2011, *Monthly Labor Review*, at page 29 (writing that, "Initially the owners were pleased with the [2006 CBA], which was negotiated during a period of national economic prosperity and generous public funding for stadium construction").

17 Munson, L. (2008) Storm Clouds Gather and Lockout Looms Large in NFL Labor Strife, *available at* www.espn.com. *See* Lydakis, M. and Zapata, A. (2012). Tackling the Issues: The History of the National Football League's 2011 Collective Bargaining Agreement and What it Means for the Future of the Sport, *Willamette Sports Law Journal*, at page 17 (observing that "every few years professional sports leagues experience work stoppages, reminding fans that these organizations are in fact businesses concerned with profit margins and bottom lines"). For a different perspective, *see* Nieh, H. (2017). A Less Perfect Union: Why Injury Risk Prevents NFL Players from Driving as Hard a Bargain as MLB Players in CBA and Contract Negotiation, *Harvard Journal of Sports & Entertainment Law*, at page 225 (expressing the viewpoint that, "Due to the more collectivist nature of the NFL's revenue sharing system, NFL team owners have largely identical economic interests and incentives").

18 In September 2017, DeMaurice Smith was re-elected as executive director of the NFLPA.

19 *See* Staudohar, P.D. (2012). The Football Lockout of 2011, *Monthly Labor Review*, at page 31 (noting that, "When new leadership takes over, it is not unusual for collective bargaining relationships to be strained"). *See also* Deubert, C., Wong, G.M., and Howe, J. (2012). All Four Quarters: A Retrospective and Analysis of the 2011 Collective Bargaining Process and Agreement in the National Football League, *UCLA Entertainment Law Review*, at page 15 (explaining that, "Smith, who had no prior experience in football or labor negotiations, had to quickly meet his constituents, learn the 2006 CBA, and begin negotiating a new CBA"). *See also* Quinn, K.G. (2012). Getting to the 2011–2020 National Football League Collective Bargaining Agreement, *International Journal of Sport Finance*, at page 149 (explaining that the negotiations between the NFL and NFLPA in 2010 and 2011 "were complicated by personality issues that had not been part of league labor relations for three decades"). *See also* Redding, M.J. (2009). Third and Long: The Issues Facing the NFL Collective Bargaining Agreement Negotiations and the Effects of an Uncapped Year, *Marquette Sports Law Review*, at page 97 (anticipating that the negotiation process in 2010 and 2011 could be hindered based on the lack of familiarity of Goodell and Smith in working with each other). *See also* Levine, J.F., Gunn, I.P., and Moorman, A.M. (2019). Peterson, Brady, and Elliot: Analyzing 'the Trilogy' in Light of the NFL Commissioner's Discipline Authority, *Journal of Legal Aspects of Sport*, at page 227 (explaining that Goodell's use of an adversarial approach starkly differed from his predecessor Paul Tagliabue, which increased bitterness between the league and the players association). Although Commissioner Goodell and DeMaurice Smith handled the overall direction of collective bargaining discussions throughout 2010 and 2011, the primary negotiators were Jeff Pash (NFL general counsel) and George Atallah (NFLPA public relations and communications executive). *See* Staudohar, P.D. (2012). The Football Lockout of 2011, *Monthly Labor Review*, at page 34

(noting that, "The negotiations between the NFL and NFLPA were conducted in the new age of email, Twitter, and text messaging ... [which] made keeping everyone informed easier").

20 Battista, J. (2009). New Head of NFL Union Gets to Work Right Away, the *New York Times* (further quoting DeMaurice Smith: "I hope our discussions with the owners are both early and fruitful. It's my sincere hope we can come to an agreement extremely quickly so everybody knows this game can continue").

21 The NFLPA constitution contains guidelines on player involvement in the collective bargaining process. For example, Article 6.01 of the NFLPA constitution requires that, "In advance of collective bargaining negotiations, each player representative shall meet with the members from his club to ascertain the provisions that such members wish to be incorporated in the NFLPA collective bargaining agreement."

22 *See* Letter from NFLPA to Roger Goodell (2009), *available at* www.nflpa.com. The letter also indicated that the NFLPA would approach the negotiations "with an open mind to finding the right balance between those who play this game and the entire membership of owners, coaches, workers and fans who benefit from and enjoy this game."

23 *See* Mullen, L. (2009). NFL Labor Fears Affect Deals for Execs, Coaches, *Sports-Business Journal*. *See also* Mullen, L. (2009). NFL Rejects Players' 'Lock In' Idea for Future Talks, *SportsBusiness Journal* (explaining that the NFLPA proposed to the NFL that both groups "hunker down in a hotel room for four or five days of negotiations in order to avoid a lockout"). *See also* Muret, D. (2011). Stadiums Review Options for Events, *SportsBusiness Journal* (explaining that a few teams began to adjust their business model to pursue stadium concerts to offset the potential loss of gameday income from a future lockout).

24 *See* Letter from NFLPA to NFL Sponsors (2010), *available at* www.nflpa.com. *See also* Mullen, L. and Kaplan, D. (2010). NFL Players Alert Sponsors to Post-CBA Plan, *SportsBusiness Journal* (explaining that, based on the sponsorship agreement between the NFL and NFLPA that was signed in 2001, the NFL paid an annual sponsorship fee to the NFLPA—for example, in 2009, the NFL paid the NFLPA a $25.1 million sponsorship fee).

25 Interview by ESPN with Roger Goodell (NFL commissioner) (2010), *ESPN Radio* (further quoting Goodell: "When you have a loss of revenues, there is less money for us to negotiate over. That is always a harder situation for anyone to negotiate in. We think that opportunity is now between here and March [2011]").

26 Official Release—Commissioner Goodell on CBA Negotiations (2010), *available at* www.nfl.com.

27 Official Release—Batterman Cites Some Progress; Wants New CBA to Avoid Lockout (2010), *available at* www.nfl.com. A few months later, in January 2011, Bob Batterman provided the following perspective on whether NFL teams owners wanted to lock out the players: "No employer in its right mind wants to shut down its business. There is damage when there is either a strike or a lockout. It is not in the employer's interest to shut down the business. It is in the employer's interest to get a deal which gets this industry straightened out for the next generation for the good of the fans, for the good of the players, and yes indeed, the good of the owners. Nobody is looking for a lockout." Official Release—Transcript of Bob Batterman Interview (2011), *available at* www.nfl.com.

28 Official Release—Jeff Pash: 'We Are Going to Have a Deal' (2010), *available at* www.nfl.com. A few months later, in January 2011, Jeff Pash provided the following perspective on the collective bargaining process: "We need to see a parallel commitment by our negotiating partner. One side can't do it on its own. I've said before the owners have the bite in their teeth—they want an agreement. The notion that NFL owners are looking to shut down the NFL is nonsensical. But they can't make an agreement themselves. They have to have a negotiating partner who is willing to work as hard at it as they are and who is seriously interested in compromise and the

hard work that goes into collective bargaining. It is not a glamorous process." Official Release—Commissioner Goodell and Jeff Pash Transcript from League Meeting (2011), *available at* www.nfl.com.

29 Atallah, G. (2011). Players' Case for Football in 2011, *available at* www.espn.com (writing that, "It's a shame that, nearly 1,000 days after the NFL owners opted out of the CBA, they can't guarantee NFL games next year. It's a shame heading into exciting playoffs with great games ahead that this unresolved issue continues to steal headlines. It's a shame that the owners are threatening to prevent players from playing football. It's a shame that the unanswered question remains: Why is this deal so bad? The NFL players have asked me to share a simple request on their behalf: Open the books and let us play"). NFLPA executive George Atallah also insisted that, "The NFL wants to artificially inflate the percentage of incremental revenue going to players by excluding revenues that never go to players. League officials have been selling a lockout to owners based on misleading and incomplete financial information. They excluded the cost credits to be able to tell owners that player costs are rising faster than all revenues. That is not true." Associated Press—League, Players Disagree on Interpretation of Revenue Figures (2011), *available at* www.nfl.com.

30 Aiello, G. (2011). The NFL's Case for a New CBA, *available at* www.espn.com (writing that, "The union has said its 'internal deadline' for reaching an agreement has passed. Does that mean the union has abandoned negotiations in favor of decertification and litigation? We hope not. Rather than litigating and firing misguided salvos about the 'shame' of the situation, it would be far more productive and much more in keeping with the interests of teams and fans if the union returned to the bargaining table and made a good faith effort to reach an agreement before March 4. After that, it is going to become much more difficult").

31 Official Release—Commissioner Goodell Opposes Union Leader's Approach (2011), *available at* www.nfl.com. Commissioner Goodell acknowledged that it would take a "sustained and disciplined commitment and around-the-clock talks" to reach terms on a new agreement before the scheduled expiration of the 2006 CBA on March 4, 2011.

32 NFL Unfair Labor Practice Charge Against NFLPA (February 2011), filed with National Labor Relations Board (accusing the NFLPA of engaging in unlawful "surface bargaining and an anticipatory refusal to bargain").

33 NFL Unfair Labor Practice Charge Against NFLPA (February 2011), filed with National Labor Relations Board (alleging that the "NFLPA's statements and conduct over the course of the last 20 months plainly establish that it does not intend to engage in good faith collective bargaining with the NFL after the CBA expires").

34 Kaplan, D. (2011). NFL Files Unfair Labor Practice Charge with NLRB Against NFLPA, *SportsBusiness Journal*.

35 Official Release—Commissioner Goodell: 'We Need an Agreement Both Sides Can Live With' (2011), *available at* www.nfl.com.

36 Official Release—Statement by FMCS Director George H. Cohen on NFL-NFLPA Talks (2011), *available at* www.nfl.com. *See* Grow, N. (2013). Decertifying Players Unions: Lessons from the NFL and NBA Lockouts of 2011, *Vanderbilt Journal of Entertainment and Technology Law*, at page 489 (explaining that, "Given the owners had never alleged any financial hardship under the [2006] agreement but instead simply appeared to be seeking an even more lucrative deal, the NFL players rejected the owners' demands during preliminary negotiations"). *See also* Staudohar, P.D. (2012). The Football Lockout of 2011, *Monthly Labor Review*, at page 32 (expounding that, "At some point in a work stoppage, negotiators have to decide whether to continue to fight or whether to engage in appreciable compromises toward reaching an agreement").

37 Based on the terms of the 2006 CBA, the league was permitted to deduct 5% of "total revenues" for expenses such as youth football programming costs and funding operations for NFL Europe and NFL Charities. In addition, team owners were also permitted

to deduct 1.8% of total revenues in order to account for private investments by team owners in stadium construction and renovation. *See* NFL CBA (2006), Article XXIV, Section 1. *See also* Vrooman, J. (2012). The Economic Structure of the NFL, in *The Economics of the National Football League* (Edited by Quinn, K.G.), at page 9. Springer Publishing (writing that, "The underlying cause of the profit squeeze of NFL owners is the polarizing dynamic of unshared venue revenue available to owners in new venues"). *See also* Staudohar, P.D. (2012). The Football Lockout of 2011, *Monthly Labor Review*, at page 31 (explaining that team owners believed that investing in infrastructure such as new stadiums would increase revenues, which would benefit all teams and subsequently all players in the league). *See also* Quinn, K.G. (2012). Getting to the 2011–2020 National Football League Collective Bargaining Agreement, *International Journal of Sport Finance*, at page 148 (noting that the central issue during CBA negotiations related to how to share revenues between team owners and players). *See also* Redding, M.J. (2009). Third and Long: The Issues Facing the NFL Collective Bargaining Agreement Negotiations and the Effects of an Uncapped Year, *Marquette Sports Law Review*, at page 106 (opining that, "The conflict between the [team owners] and the NFLPA regarding the split of the NFL's total revenues likely will be the primary issues of the CBA negotiations"). *See also* Deubert, C., Wong, G.M., and Howe, J. (2012). All Four Quarters: A Retrospective and Analysis of the 2011 Collective Bargaining Process and Agreement in the National Football League, *UCLA Entertainment Law Review*, at page 5 (explaining that, with no evidence that the teams were in any type of financial distress, the players did not agree that fundamental changes were needed to the current revenue distribution model between team owners and players under the 2006 CBA).

38 *White* v. *National Football League* (Minnesota District Court, 2011), 766 F. Supp. 2d 941, at page 954 (finding that the NFL undertook contract renegotiations to advance its own interests and harm the interests of the players). *See* Staudohar, P.D. (2012). The Football Lockout of 2011, *Monthly Labor Review*, at page 31 (explaining that Judge Doty determined that the league's acceptance of below-market fees in order to bankroll a lockout was improper). *See also* Deubert, C., Wong, G.M., and Howe, J. (2012). All Four Quarters: A Retrospective and Analysis of the 2011 Collective Bargaining Process and Agreement in the National Football League, *UCLA Entertainment Law Review*, at page 19 (emphasizing that Jude Doty's ruling appeared to provide leverage to the NFLPA by eliminating substantial revenues the teams would have otherwise received during a lockout). *See also* NFL Unfair Labor Practice Charge Against NFLPA (February 2011), filed with National Labor Relations Board (alleging that the NFLPA conditioned future bargaining sessions on the league agreeing to a non-mandatory subject of collective bargaining—namely, extension of federal court oversight of the collective bargaining relationship between the league and its players). In 1993, the NFL and NFLPA agreed that certain disputes arising under the NFL collective bargaining agreement would first go to a private judge called a special master. That decision could then be appealed by the NFL or NFLPA to Minnesota federal judge David Doty. It is important to note that a final ruling was never made in this media rights case. All claims were dismissed as part of the NFL and players eventually agreeing to the 2011 CBA in August 2011. As part of the 2011 CBA, the league and its players agreed to end what was viewed as "player-friendly" federal court oversight of certain CBA related disputes.

39 In early March 2011, President Obama commented, "You've got owners, most of whom are worth close to $1 billion. You've got players who are making millions of dollars. My working assumption at a time when people are having to cut back, compromise and worry about making the mortgage and paying for their kids' college education is that the two parties should be able to work it out without the President of the United States intervening." Official Release—President Obama on NFL Labor Negotiations (2011), *available at* www.nfl.com.

40 Official Release—Transcript of Executive Vice President Jeff Pash (2011), *available at* www.nfl.com.
41 *See* Siler, R. (2013). The Lesson of the 2011 NFL and NBA Lockouts: Why Courts Should Not Immediately Recognize Players' Union Disclaimers of Representation, *Washington Law Review*, at page 282 (explaining that disclaimer of interest is a less demanding and more immediate process as compared with formal decertification, albeit a process with less certainty in litigation).
42 Official Release—NFLPA, NFLA Release Statements About Labor Situation (2011), *available at* www.nfl.com (indicating that, "The NFL clubs remain committed to collective bargaining and the federal mediation process until an agreement is reached. The NFL calls on the [NFLPA] to return to negotiations immediately. NFL players, clubs, and fans want an agreement. The only place it can be reached is at the bargaining table").
43 Official Release—NFL Statement on 'Decertification,' Litigation and Lockout (2011), *available at* www.nfl.com (stating that, "At a time when thousands of employees are fighting for their collective bargaining rights, this union has chosen to abandon collective bargaining in favor of a sham 'decertification' and antitrust litigation. This litigation maneuver is built on the indisputably false premise that the NFLPA has stopped being a union and will merely delay the process of reaching an agreement"). As explained on the official NFLPA website, during the lockout players were barred from using team facilities and contacting team coaches; many players organized their own workout programs. The 2011 NFL lockout was the first lockout in the NFL since 1987—a lockout that lasted 24 days and resulted in a 15-game regular season for all NFL teams.
44 *See* Brandt, A. (2016). The CBA at Halfway, Part II, *Sports Illustrated* (explaining that the NFLPA had little success at the bargaining table and, therefore, attempted to increase negotiation leverage by resorting to litigation).
45 *See Tom Brady et al.* v. *National Football League et al.*, Class Action Complaint, United States District Court, District of Minnesota (March 2011), at pages 2–3 (arguing that the NFL "cannot defend [the league's] violations of the federal antitrust laws by hiding behind the non-statutory labor exemption to the antitrust laws. That exemption only conceivably applies as long as a collective bargaining relationship exists between the NFL Defendants and the players"). *See also* Epstein, T. (2011). NFL Players' Decertification: Hail Mary or a Smart Play?, *Chicago Daily Law Bulletin*, at page 1 (explaining that, "By decertifying, the players are attempting to unilaterally disqualify the NFL from that exemption thereby subjecting legitimate bargaining tactics, such as a lockout, to antitrust scrutiny. In sum, without the protections afforded by collective bargaining, the NFL may be exposed to liability under the Sherman Act").
46 Letter from Roger Goodell (NFL commissioner) to NFL Players (2011), *available at* www.nfl.com (indicating that the league was "prepared to negotiate a full agreement that would incorporate these features and other progressive changes that would benefit players, clubs, and fans. Only through collective bargaining will we reach that kind of agreement").
47 Letter from Roger Goodell (NFL commissioner) to NFL Players (2011), *available at* www.nfl.com (encouraging the NFLPA to return to the bargaining table in order to reach agreement on a new CBA). An "accrued season" requires six or more regular season games at "full pay status" (that is, player is on the active/inactive or injured reserve list). *See* NFL CBA (2011), Article 8, Section 1. In September 2014, the NFL and NFLPA reached agreement on a wide-ranging series of improvements concerning policies and programs on substance abuse and performance enhancing substances. Key protocols and policies related to performance enhancing substances and substances of abuse include: (1) Implementation of testing for human growth hormone (HGH) through serum (blood) analysis commencing with the 2014 NFL season;

(2) Appeals of positive tests in both the substance abuse and performance enhancing drug programs (including HGH) will be heard by third-party arbitrators jointly selected, appointed and retained by the NFL and NFLPA—a first violation will result in suspension without pay of up to six games depending on the nature of the violation; and (3) Players who test positive for banned stimulants in the offseason will no longer be suspended—instead, the player will be referred to the league's substance abuse intervention program. *See* Official Release—Joint NFL-NFLPA Statement on Wide-Ranging Changes to Drug Programs (2014), *available at* www.nfl.com. In recent years, professional sports leagues such as the NFL started to consider whether players should be allowed to use marijuana for medicinal and/or recreational purposes. For example, the NBA no longer tests players for marijuana use during the off-season, as the primary potential issue from a competition standpoint relates to players being blazed/high from marijuana use during actual games. In October 2018, NFLPA executive director DeMaurice Smith expressed his viewpoint that use of marijuana should be addressed "more in a treatment and less punitive measure." For a detailed discussion of the potential ability of marijuana to manage pain caused by injuries sustained by NFL players, *see* Nguyen, A.B.Y. (2019). The Alternative to Opioids: Marijuana's Ability to Manage Pain Caused by Injuries Sustained in the National Football League, *Texas Review of Entertainment and Sports Law*. Relatedly, in May 2019, the league and its players launched two interconnected initiatives to provide additional resources for pain management (including research on alternatives to opioids such as cannabinoids), player mental and behavioral health as well as to promote overall wellness for NFL players. *See* Hagemann, A. (2019). NFL, NFLPA Joint Agreements Address Player Health, *available at* www.nfl.com.

48 Letter from NFL Players to Roger Goodell (NFL commissioner) (2011), *available at* www.espn.com.

49 *See* Letter from NFL Players to Roger Goodell (NFL commissioner) (2011), *available at* www.espn.com. The players believed that the league "had ample time over the last two years to make a proposal that would be fair to both sides" but failed to do so—the NFL "had no intention to make a good faith effort to resolve these issues in collective bargaining and the owners were determined to carry out the lockout strategy." The NFLPA "thus had no choice except to conclude that it was in the best interests of all NFL players to renounce collective bargaining so the players could pursue their antitrust rights to stop the lockout." As a result, the NFLPA no longer had "the authority to collectively bargain on behalf of NFL players, and are supporting the players who are asserting their antitrust rights in the *Brady* litigation." It is common for veteran professional athletes to "coalesce with management to bargain away the rights of future generations of disenfranchised rookies and forgotten former players." Vrooman, J. (2012). The Economic Structure of the NFL, in *The Economics of the National Football League* (Edited by Quinn, K.G.), at page 8.

50 *Tom Brady et al.* v. *National Football League et al.*, Memorandum of Law of the National Football League, United States District Court, District of Minnesota (March 2011), *available at* www.nfl.com (arguing that, "The non-statutory labor exemption continues to apply until a point sufficiently distant in time and in circumstances from the collective bargaining process that a rule permitting antitrust intervention would not significantly interfere with that process").

51 *See* NFL CBA (2006), Article LVII, Sections 1–3. In response to the counter-claims by the league in this case, the players responded with the somewhat uncompelling argument that, even though NFL players announced an intention to end the NFLPA's status as the exclusive collective bargaining representative of all players approximately eight hours before expiration of the 2006 CBA, the disclaimer of interest was not meant to become effective until after official expiration of the 2006 CBA.

52 *See* Grow, N. (2013). Decertifying Players Unions: Lessons from the NFL and NBA Lockouts of 2011, *Vanderbilt Journal of Entertainment and Technology Law*, at page

489 (explaining that, "The players dissolved the NFLPA so quickly in no small part due to a provision in the previous CBA requiring them to either disband the union prior to the expiration of the agreement or else wait at least six months to file an anti-trust lawsuit against the league").

53 Grow, N. (2013). Decertifying Players Unions: Lessons from the NFL and NBA Lock-outs of 2011, *Vanderbilt Journal of Entertainment and Technology Law*, at page 490 (reiterating that the lawsuit filed by the players was ultimately a battle for bargaining leverage between the players and team owners). On March 24, 2011, Commissioner Goodell emphatically commented, "Litigation is not going to solve this problem. It is clearly going to be solved through labor negotiations. The faster we can back to medi-ation, the faster we will get an agreement." Official Release—We Agree on This—Let's Collectively Bargain and Negotiate a New Deal (2011), *available at* www.nfl.com.

54 *Tom Brady et al.* v. *National Football League et al.*, Court Opinion and Order, United States District Court, District of Minnesota (April 2011), at page 49 (finding that the NFLPA's unequivocal disclaimer was valid and effective, and concluding there was no need to defer any issue to the NLRB. Because the disclaimer was valid and effective, the Norris-LaGuardia Act's prohibition against injunctive relief should not preclude granting the players' motion for a preliminary injunction against the league lockout).

55 Goodell, R. (2011). Football's Future if the Players Win, *Wall Street Journal* (writing that, "In an environment where they are essentially independent contractors, many players would likely lose significant benefits and other protections previously pro-vided on a collective basis as part of the union-negotiated collective bargaining agree-ment"). Goodell emphasized that the NFL and NFLPA must work together to find a partnership and relationship via the collective bargaining process that will "allow everyone to flourish." *See* Official Release—Goodell: It's About Creating Something Better Together (2011), *available at* www.nfl.com.

56 Official Release—Jeff Pash on DeMaurice Smith: 'A Very Skilled Leader' (2011), *available at* www.nfl.com.

57 Official Release—Commissioner Goodell: Let's Find Solutions (2011), *available at* www.nfl.com.

58 Official Release—Post-Meeting Comments from Commissioner Goodell and DeMaurice Smith (2011), *available at* www.nfl.com.

59 *Tom Brady et al.* v. *National Football League et al.* (Eighth Circuit Court of Appeals, July 2011), 644 F.3d 661, at pages 670, 673 (explaining that the Norris-LaGuardia Act restricts the power of federal courts to issue injunctions in cases "involving or growing out of a labor dispute," and concluding that Section 4(a) of the Norris-LaGuardia Act "deprives a federal court of power to issue an injunction prohibiting a party to a labor dispute from implementing a lockout of its employees"). *See also* Siler, R. (2013). The Lesson of the 2011 NFL and NBA Lockouts: Why Courts Should Not Immediately Recognize Players' Union Disclaimers of Representation, *Washington Law Review*, at page 283 (noting that the Eighth Circuit Court of Appeals offered no opinion on the merits of the players' antitrust claims or the effectiveness of the disclaimer of representation; rather, the Eighth Circuit narrowly held that the Norris-LaGuardia Act prevented a court from enjoining/preventing the league imposed lockout that evolved from a labor dispute). It is also important to note that, during oral arguments in June 2011, Judge Bye cautioned attorneys for the NFL and players that the court could reach a decision that neither the league nor the players would like; Judge Bye further added, with a smile, the court "wouldn't be all that hurt if you go out and settle the case" on your own. *See* McCann, M.A. (2011). What We Learned from NFL Hearing, *Sports Illustrated* (explaining that, "Both sides know that a prolonged lockout—particularly one that leads to a cancellation of games—could cause the league irreparable harm, be it in the form of current fans who tune out … or television networks that no longer offer as much money to broadcast NFL games. Both sides would be worse off if the pie of wealth they are fighting over

shrinks because of their fighting. Judge Bye's remarks clearly admonish the owners and players to think about these consequences").

60 Official Release—NFL-NFLPA Joint Statement on Eighth Circuit Court Ruling (2011), *available at* www.nfl.com.

61 Official Release—NFL Clubs Approve Comprehensive Agreement (2011), *available at* www.nfl.com. *See also* Staudohar, P.D. (2012). The Football Lockout of 2011, *Monthly Labor Review* (explaining that the 132-day lockout in 2011 was not the result of the owners' inability to pay, but rather was due to the owners' unwillingness to pay).

62 As explained on the official NFLPA website, the NFLPA stood by its promise to make player health and safety non-negotiable. From the perspective of the NFLPA, the 2011 CBA ensures players receive quality care before, during and after their NFL playing careers. The CBA also takes an aggressive approach to player/patient medical rights and the accountability of the NFL's healthcare providers. Greater protections for active players came in a wide range of changes to on-the-field and off-the-field regulations—for example, longer periods between rigorous practices and seasons will provide players' bodies with greater time for necessary recovery and repair. Citing significant health and safety concerns, the NFLPA refused to agree to the NFL's desire to increase the regular season from 16 to 18 games. *See* National Football Players Association—History (www.nflpa.com). In the view of Professor Gabe Feldman, although the players "lost" these labor battles, both the NFLPA and the NBPA took unique measures to neutralize the offensive lockouts by dissolving their unions and challenging the lockouts as antitrust violations. *See* Feldman, G. (2012). *Brady* v. *NFL* and *Anthony* v. *NBA*: The Shifting Dynamics in Labor-Management Relations in Professionals Sports, *Tulane Law Review*, at page 846. *See also* Nieh, H. (2017). A Less Perfect Union: Why Injury Risk Prevents NFL Players from Driving as Hard a Bargain as MLB Players in CBA and Contract Negotiation, *Harvard Journal of Sports & Entertainment Law*, at page 227 (expressing the viewpoint that NFL players lack negotiation leverage during the collective bargaining process in part as a result of higher injury risk and shorter playing careers as compared with athletes in other professional sports leagues).

63 The 2011 CBA is effective from August 4, 2011 until the last day of the 2020 league year (season), except for the CBA provisions in Article 6 relating to the NFL draft in 2021, which will remain in effect for the year immediately following the expiration or termination of the CBA. *See* NFL CBA (2011), Article 69. For illustration purposes, the NFLPA would be permitted to terminate the CBA if 14 or more teams engage in collusive conduct by agreeing not to negotiate with a specific player (for example, Colin Kaepernick). *See* NFL CBA (2011), Article 17, Sections 1, 16.

64 The 2011 CBA defines "All Revenues" as "the aggregate revenues received or to be received on an accrual basis, for or with respect to a League Year during the term of this Agreement, by the NFL and all NFL Clubs (and their designees), from all sources, whether known or unknown, derived from, relating to or arising out of the perfor-mance of players in NFL football games." NFL CBA (2011), Article 12, Section 1. The AR formula also includes 50% of any new line of business project (for example, the NFL deciding to add another International Series game in London). In addition, each season 47.5% of a "joint contribution amount" is subtracted when determining the final AR amount. For instance, during the 2012 NFL season, the joint contribution amount equaled $55 million, of which $22 million was dedicated to healthcare and other benefits for retired players, $11 million was dedicated to medical research, and $22 million was dedicated to NFL-affiliated charities. The 2011 CBA also contains a list of revenue categories that are excluded from the AR calculation. For example, the following items are excluded from AR: (1) Revenues generated from stadium events unrelated to NFL football (concerts and soccer matches); (2) Revenue from "Personal Seat Licenses" (initial fee that provides the purchaser with the right to acquire or

retain season tickets) and "Premium Seat Revenues" (periodic charge in excess of ticket price that is required for purchaser to acquire or retain tickets) to the extent that proceeds are unequivocally dedicated to stadium construction or stadium renovation projects; (3) Certain naming rights and cornerstone sponsorship proceeds that are used for stadium construction or renovation (waiver from the general requirement of sharing gross receipts must be approved by the league); (4) Proceeds from the sale of an NFL team; (5) Revenue sharing among NFL teams; (6) Sales of interests in real estate by team owners; and (7) Network television revenue to the extent that such revenue results in an increase in AR and is used to fund the construction or renovation of one or more stadiums. The 2011 CBA includes additional examples of revenues received by the NFL and/or NFL teams that are not derived from and do not relate to or arise out of the performance of players in NFL football games—and, as a result, are not factored into the overall AR calculation. It is important to note that, in 2002, the Dallas Cowboys opted out of the NFL leaguewide merchandise licensing deal. As a result, the Cowboys manufacture, market and distribute merchandise at the team level yet are still required to make an annual royalty payment to the league because merchandise distributed by the Cowboys includes NFL league trademarks/logos—in 2011, the royalty payment from the Cowboys to the league equaled approximately $80 million. *See* NFL CBA (2011), Article 12, Sections 1–6.

65 *See* NFL CBA (2011), Article 12, Section 6(b).

66 *See* Gordon, G. (2019). NFL Salary Cap for 2019 Season Set at $188.2 Million, *available at* www.nfl.com (indicating that some teams such as the Minnesota Vikings and Philadelphia Eagles had less than $5 million in effective salary cap space for the 2019 season, as compared with teams such as the Indianapolis Colts and New York Jets that had more than $90 million in effective salary cap space). The salary cap for the 2019 NFL season ($188.2 million) represents the highest permitted team payroll amount in the history of the league. The NFL first instituted the salary cap system during the 1994 season—the salary cap for the 1994 NFL season equaled $34.6 million. Also, the salary cap for the 2000 NFL season equaled $62.2 million, and the salary cap for the 2005 NFL season equaled $85.5 million. *See* Official Release—Year-by-Year Salary Cap (2010), *available at* www.nfl.com.

67 *See* NFL CBA (2011), Article 12, Sections 4–7. Throughout the term of the 2011 CBA (from the 2011 NFL season through the 2020 NFL season), the cumulative overall average players share of AR during the upcoming season combined with all prior seasons must equal at least 47% of AR (this baseline metric is known as the "guaranteed player cost percentage"). The 2006 CBA projected that, for the 2010 NFL season, players would receive 58% of "Total Revenues" (formula that preceded the "All Revenues" framework in the 2011 CBA). However, as discussed earlier in this chapter, team owners were allowed to claim substantial cost credits and make numerous expense deductions before players received their revenue distribution share each season. As a result of these team owner credits and deductions, the true players share most seasons under the 2006 CBA equaled closer to 50% of AR. *See* NFL CBA (2006), Article XXIV, Section 4. The 2011 CBA limits allowable expense deductions to "reasonable and customary direct costs and initial investments" by NFL Ventures in any new lines of business. The 2011 CBA also contains a credit carveout for team owner costs related to the construction or renovation of stadiums, which investments are designed to result in future increases to the total AR amount; however, these stadium credits for team owners are not permitted to reduce the total player cost amount below a specific threshold (47% of AR for the 2012 to 2014 NFL seasons, and 46% of AR for the 2017 to 2020 NFL seasons). Beginning with the 2012 NFL season, the league would make an annual "true up" payment if actual AR drastically exceeds projected AR and, therefore, the true up payment is necessary to get the players share to the minimum threshold level. *See* NFL CBA (2011), Article 12, Sections 1, 4–6. *See also* Deubert, C., Wong, G.M., and Howe, J. (2012). All Four Quarters: A Retrospective

and Analysis of the 2011 Collective Bargaining Process and Agreement in the National Football League, *UCLA Entertainment Law Review*, at page 47 (emphasizing that, under the 2011 CBA, "players are receiving a more definite piece of a larger pie").

68 *See* NFL CBA (2011), Article 12, Sections 8–9. As explained on the NFLPA website, the minimum team cash spending requirement prevents teams that have historically underspent on their rosters to invest more heavily in player contracts. The new formula is simple: as the owners make more money, players make more money through guaranteed minimum spending in cash. Unlike the "soft" salary cap system in the NBA that contains various exceptions, the 2011 NFL collective bargaining agreement contains a "hard" salary cap. In general, no team is permitted to have a total team salary the exceeds the salary cap. *See* NFL CBA (2011), Article 13, Section 2. However, the 2011 CBA also contains specific provisions that provide teams with a small amount of salary cap relief when signing veteran players with at least four seasons of NFL experience to a minimum one-year contract. For example, during the 2012 NFL season, a "qualifying player" was required to receive a minimum salary of $700,000; however, only $540,000 counted against his team's salary cap (the $160,000 difference counted as a player benefit). In addition, teams are permitted to "carry over" cap room/space from one season to the next. For example, the Cleveland Browns carried over more than $50 million in unused cap room from the 2018 league year to the 2019 league year. As of September 2019, NFL teams reported cumulative salary cap carryover of more than $330 million. *See* NFL CBA (2011), Article 27. *See also* NFL CBA (2011), Article 13, Section 6. *See also* Deubert, C., Wong, G.M., and Howe, J. (2012). All Four Quarters: A Retrospective and Analysis of the 2011 Collective Bargaining Process and Agreement in the National Football League, *UCLA Entertainment Law Review*, at page 48 (explaining that players are not interested in how teams structure contracts and allocate salaries for salary cap purposes, but instead are concerned with ensuring that all players actually receive a certain percentage of total available money).

69 *See* NFL CBA (2011), Article 7, Section 2. For comparison purposes, the total rookie compensation pool for the 2019 NFL season equaled approximately $1.3 billion. Overall, the 2011 CBA limits "creative contract structures designed to increase player compensation." Deubert, C., Wong, G.M., and Howe, J. (2012). All Four Quarters: A Retrospective and Analysis of the 2011 Collective Bargaining Process and Agreement in the National Football League, UCLA Entertainment Law Review, at pages 54–55, 60–61 (explaining that the "total rookie compensation pool" system within the 2011 CBA removes nearly all of the flexibility that teams and sports agents previously used to inflate rookie compensation). Based on the total rookie compensation pool and year one rookie compensation pool figures, the league determines what has become known as the "slotted salary" (or "year one formula allotment") for each player drafted in the NFL. Each draft pick is slotted a salary cap figure and total contract value that is a percentage of the overall pool numbers, which would prevent an agent from negotiating a higher salary for the 22nd pick in the draft as compared with the 12th pick in the same draft. *See* NFL CBA (2011), Article 7, Section 1(g). Prior to the 2011 NFL season, teams and agents used to negotiate (and sometimes argue about) total contract value, performance escalators, guarantees, one-time incentives and free agency qualifiers. The 2011 CBA "stripped agents and incoming rookies from this [negotiation flexibility] and saw the rookie wage scale give less money to rookies with the intent of having more money set aside for veterans and retired players." Fitzgerald, J. and Natarajan, V. (2016). *Crunching Numbers: An Inside Look at the Salary Cap and Negotiating Player Contracts*, at pages 73, 82. The standard NFL athlete representation agreement sets the default fee for sports agents at 1.5% of the total compensation received by the player. Agents and players are permitted, but not required, to adjust the sports agent fee below 1.5% or up to a 3% of player salary threshold limit. *See* NFLPA Regulations Governing Contract Advisors—Appendix D (2016), *available at* www.nflpa.com.

70 *See* NFL CBA (2011), Article 7, Section 3(a).
71 *See* NFL CBA (2011), Article 26. NFL players are expected to propose an increase to minimum salary amounts for both rookies and veteran players during the next round of collective bargaining with the league.
72 *See* NFL CBA (2011), Article 7, Section 3(e). *See also* NFL CBA (2011), Article 7, Section 3(g).
73 *See* NFL CBA (2011), Article 7, Section 4. *See also* NFL CBA (2011), Article 9, Section 2(b).
74 *See* NFL CBA (2011), Article 7, Section 6.
75 *See* NFL CBA (2011), Article 7, Section 7 (clarifying that a player's fifth-year option salary will not be considered "rookie salary" and will not count against the total rookie compensation pool). The overall new rookie compensation model was anticipated to result in approximately $175 million of salary cost reductions based on overall lower salaries for rookies. *See* Keefer, Q.A.W. (2016). The 2011 NFL Collective Bargaining Agreement and Drafted Player Compensation, *International Journal of Sport Finance*, at pages 221, 230 (concluding that the new rookie wage scale in the 2011 CBA increased overall initial compensation distributed to players selected in the first two rounds of the draft; however, the 25% annual increase limit on compensation growth ultimately resulted in a large negative effect on drafted player compensation—for example, second year salaries for first round draft picks tend to be much lower under the 2011 CBA as compared with the 2006 CBA). *See also* Quinn, K.G. (2012). Getting to the 2011–2020 National Football League Collective Bargaining Agreement, *International Journal of Sport Finance*, at page 149 (explaining that both the league and the players association were in favor of diverting some rookie pay to veteran players).
76 *See* NFL CBA (2011), Article 7, Section 3(k).
77 *See* NFL CBA (2011), Article 26.
78 *See* NFL CBA (2011), Article 9, Sections 1–2. *See also* 2019 NFL Free Agency FAQ, *available at* www.nfl.com.
79 *See* NFL CBA (2011), Article 22.
80 *See* NFL CBA (2011), Article 21.
81 *See* NFL CBA (2011), Article 24.
82 *See* NFL CBA (2011), Article 31.
83 *See* NFL CBA (2011), Article 33. *See also* NFL CBA (2011), Article 51, Section 14.
84 *See* NFL CBA (2011), Article 34.
85 *See* NFL CBA (2011), Article 38.
86 *See* NFL CBA (2011), Article 42.
87 *See* NFL CBA (2011), Article 56.
88 *See* NFL CBA (2011), Articles 57, 58, 59, 61, 62, 64 and 65. *See also* National Football League Players Association Benefits Book (2019), *available at* www.nflpa.com (reminding NFL players to keep in mind that a player must be considered a 'vested player'—three or more 'credited seasons'—to receive retirement benefits). NFL players earn one "credited season" for each season during which the player receives full pay status for a minimum of three regular season games. *See* NFL CBA (2011), Article 26, Section 2. In 2013, the NFLPA launched The Trust, which is designed to provide an "ecosystem of support for former players, with an emphasis on overall health and successful transition from professional football." The primary pillars of the wellness plan for former players include: (1) Brain and body health; (2) Career transition and development; (3) Education and entrepreneurship; and (4) Financial literacy. *See* Official Release—NFLPA Announces The Trust (2013), *available at* www.nflpa.com.
89 For each season after the 2011 league year, the maximum fine is adjusted by the same percentage as the change in projected AR for that league year as compared to the projected AR for the prior season (up to a maximum fine increase of 10% per league year). *See* NFL CBA (2011), Article 14, Section 7.

5   Collective bargaining in the NFL
Part 2

Overview of chapter contents

This chapter highlights some of the core challenges and opportunities concerning league and team governance/operations that have surfaced within the NFL in recent years. The chapter also dissects the ongoing discussions and negotiations between the league and the NFLPA related to reaching an agreement on a new CBA—the current 2011 CBA is scheduled to expire after the 2020 NFL season.

Preparing for another round of collective bargaining after expiration of the 2011 CBA

The 2011 CBA runs through the 2020 NFL season. NFL players and league representatives will once again need to negotiate (collectively bargain) in order to compromise and create consensus on numerous issues before a new CBA is finalized. The NFLPA will almost certainly attempt to increase the revenue share for players from the current 47% of AR average guaranteed floor amount to something closer to 49–50% of AR. Additional key economic and system issues include the role and authority of Commissioner Goodell pertaining to player discipline, league support of player social activism, restrictions on player mobility, guaranteed contracts and the number of regular season games.

The role and authority of the league commissioner: penalizing player misconduct

Professional sports leagues have historically developed personal conduct policies for players, coaches and other team and league personnel in order to preserve the "integrity of the game." For example, the 2008 NFL Personal Conduct Policy emphasized that all persons associated with the NFL were required to avoid "conduct detrimental to the integrity of and public confidence in the National Football League."[1] Before finalizing the 2008 Personal Conduct Policy, Commissioner Goodell reached out to Gene Upshaw (then-current NFLPA executive director) in order to get Upshaw's advice and input on preliminary versions of the revamped Personal Conduct Policy. Commissioner Goodell also consulted with then-current NFL players before the league implemented the 2008 policy, which granted the commissioner extensive authority to discipline players for non-criminal off-the-field conduct that undermined or put at risk the integrity and reputation of the NFL, member teams or players.[2]

By July 2009, DeMaurice Smith commented that, during the next round of collective bargaining with league representatives, NFL players intended to raise the issue of what players perceived to be overly broad commissioner authority to discipline players for off-the-field misconduct. For example, as explained by Professor Richard Karcher, collectively bargained limitations on a commissioner's disciplinary authority could take a variety of forms, including the following:

- Defining the types of misconduct (which might distinguish between on-field and off-field behavior) subject to disciplinary action by the commissioner;
- Outlining the level and extent of disciplinary action that may be imposed by the commissioner under specific circumstances; and
- Providing the right of appeal to a neutral arbitrator or panel of neutral arbitrators.[3]

Also, in July 2009, Commissioner Goodell acknowledged that his power to discipline players has "long been a subject of negotiations." Commissioner Goodell expressed the following viewpoint with respect to his decision-making approach involving the 2008 Personal Conduct Policy: "I believe I have been responsible with my authority. It's important to have somebody who can make the best decisions on behalf of the league and the game. I do that with a great deal of consideration of everyone involved in the league."[4]

As previously discussed in *Chapter 4*, the NFLPA decided to focus on other business and system issues during the collective bargaining process in 2010 and 2011. As a result, the players did not prioritize reducing the authority of the league commissioner to discipline players for misconduct. Article 46 of the 2011 CBA provides Commissioner Goodell with discretion to discipline players for "for conduct detrimental to the integrity of, or public confidence in, the game of professional football."[5] If a player decides to appeal a suspension and/or fine issued by Commissioner Goodell, then Commissioner Goodell is required to consult with DeMaurice Smith before appointing one or more designees to serve as hearing officers. Commissioner Goodell is allowed to appoint himself as the hearing officer for the appeal ("non-injury grievance") hearing.[6] Stated differently, Article 46 allows the commissioner to oversee appeals through the NFL's version of arbitration. As the arbitrator (presiding officer of an appeal hearing), Goodell reviews the decision making of the person who originally punished the player. In other words, "Goodell reviews Goodell, meaning an 'appeal' is not so much an appeal as we understand the word in law but rather merely a request for reconsideration."[7]

Legal scholars such as Professor Richard Karcher believe that, until the NFL collective bargaining agreement provides players with the right to appeal commissioner discipline to an independent/neutral arbitrator, decisions made by the commissioner "will continue to be challenged in court over the disciplinary procedures utilized as well as the commissioner's ability to be fair and impartial, which only serves to intensify the media's coverage of the player's misconduct and the league's handling of the issue."[8] Historically, NFL players have been unable to secure through litigation what the players failed to achieve through collective bargaining, which highlights the need for the NFLPA to focus on collective bargaining as opposed to litigation in order to secure gains related to limitations on the authority of the league commissioner to impose discipline for player misconduct.[9]

In 2014, the NFL developed and implemented a new Personal Conduct Policy, which was not the byproduct of collective bargaining with the NFLPA. During collective bargaining sessions in 2010 and 2011, the league (and its commissioner) retained the ability to modify and strengthen existing policies related to player discipline, including the 2008 Personal Conduct Policy; consulting with the NFLPA with respect to revisions to the existing player conduct guidelines remained optional but not required.[10] In August 2014, the NFLPA did not seem to be extremely enthused when the league informed the players association of increased penalties for domestic violence. The NFLPA released the following official statement: "We were informed today of the NFL's decision to increase penalties on domestic violence offenders under the Personal Conduct Policy for all NFL employees. As we do in all disciplinary matters, if we believe that players' due process rights are infringed upon during the course of discipline, we will assert and defend our members' rights."[11]

In December 2014, the NFL officially announced a comprehensive revamped 2014 Personal Conduct Policy, which applies to all NFL personnel (team owners, coaches, players, other team employees, game officials and league office employees). According to the NFL league office, the 2014 Personal Conduct Policy was developed after discussions with more than 150 experts from across the country—including domestic violence and sexual assault experts, advocates and survivors, law enforcement officials, academic experts, business leaders, current and former players and the NFLPA.[12] Commissioner Goodell commented: "With considerable assistance from the many people and organizations we consulted, NFL ownership has endorsed an enhanced policy that is significantly more robust, thorough and formal. We now have a layered evaluation process to take into account a diversity of expert views. This will better enable us to make appropriate decisions and ensure accountability for everyone involved in the process."[13]

The 2014 Personal Conduct Policy explains that, "Conduct by anyone in the league that is illegal, violent, dangerous or irresponsible puts innocent victims at risk, damages the reputation of others in the game and undercuts public respect and support for the NFL. We must endeavor at all times to be people of high character; we must show respect for others inside and outside our workplace; and we must strive to conduct ourselves in ways that favorably reflect on ourselves, our teams, the communities we represent and the NFL."[14] The 2014 Personal Conduct Policy established a clear series of steps to be taken when there is an incident that requires review. The 2014 Personal Conduct Policy included the following measures and guidelines:

- A baseline suspension of six games without pay for violations involving assault, battery, domestic violence, dating violence, child abuse, other forms of family violence or sexual assault, with consideration given to possible mitigating or aggravating circumstances;
- A more extensive list of prohibited conduct (including conduct that poses a genuine danger to the safety and well-being of another person, and conduct that undermines or puts at risk the integrity of the NFL, NFL clubs or NFL personnel);
- Additional NFL-funded counseling and services for victims, families and violators;
- Specific criteria for paid leave for an individual formally charged with a crime of violence, including domestic violence, sexual assault and child abuse;
- An expert group of outside advisors to review and evaluate potential violations and consult on other elements of the conduct policy;
- Appeals of any disciplinary decision will be processed based on Article 46 of the 2011 CBA for players, and the commissioner may name a panel that consists of independent experts to recommend a decision on the appeal; and
- The appointment by Commissioner Goodell of a new league Conduct Committee comprised of team owners that will review the policy at least annually and recommend appropriate changes with advice from outside experts.[15]

On the same day the NFL released the new 2014 Personal Conduct Policy, the NFLPA issued the following statement: "Our union [was not] offered the professional courtesy of seeing the NFL's new Personal Conduct Policy before it hit the presses. Their unilateral decision and conduct today is the only thing that has been consistent over the past few months."[16] Another consistent reality throughout 2014 related to players and the NFLPA appealing/challenging disciplinary penalties issued by Commissioner Goodell concerning player misconduct. The following two case studies involving Ray Rice and Adrian Peterson demonstrate the expansive scope of—as well as the limits to—commissioner authority to discipline players for misconduct.

The Ray Rice situation

In February 2014, then-current NFL player Ray Rice punched his then-fiancée, Janay Palmer, in the elevator of a New Jersey hotel and casino.[17] Janay hit her head on the rail in the elevator and fell unconscious to the floor. A surveillance camera inside the elevator captured Ray Rice dragging Janay Palmer unconscious out of the elevator. In March 2014, Rice was subsequently charged with criminal assault for evidencing indifference to the value of human life. In May 2014, Ray Rice pleaded not guilty and applied for the New Jersey Pretrial Intervention

Program, which provides alternatives to the traditional criminal justice process of ordinary prosecution. The criminal proceeding involving Rice ended with a court ordered pre-trial intervention, an agreement that the case would be dismissed after one year if Rice satisfactorily completed an anger management course, attended counseling and committed no further crimes.[18]

In June 2014, Ray Rice met with Commissioner Goodell to discuss the incident and potential discipline under the then-existing 2008 Personal Conduct Policy. At the meeting, Rice confirmed that he hit Janay in the elevator.[19] In July 2014, Commissioner Goodell suspended Rice for two games without pay with an additional fine equivalent to one week of Rice's salary. When asked to justify what appeared to be a light punishment for such a serious situation involving player misconduct, Commissioner Goodell responded, "We have a very firm policy that domestic violence is not acceptable in the NFL, and there are consequences for that.... We have to remain consistent. We can't just make up the discipline. It has to be consistent with other cases, and it was in this matter."[20] By August 2014, Commissioner Goodell acknowledged that he "didn't get it right" with respect to the decision to suspend Rice for only two games. In a letter to NFL team owners, Goodell explained that he was revising the 2008 Personal Conduct Policy in order to establish a minimum six game suspension for any player misconduct involving domestic violence.[21]

On September 8, 2014, TMZ (a media company) released a video that allowed members of the public to see the actual footage of Ray Rice striking Janay Palmer at the Atlantic City hotel/casino in February 2014. That same day, the Baltimore Ravens terminated Rice's player contract.[22] The following day, the owner of the Ravens sent a letter to team fans, which acknowledged that the team let fans down and did not do all the team should have done in terms of pursuing an independent investigation more vigorously.[23] Also, on September 8, 2014, Commissioner Goodell modified his initial discipline of Rice. Goodell decided to suspend Rice indefinitely.[24] Both the Ravens and Commissioner Goodell declared that neither the team nor the league office viewed the graphic video of Ray Rice punching his then-fiancée before TMZ released the video.[25] Commissioner Goodell justified this increased penalty—from a two-game suspension to an indefinite suspension—solely on the basis that the horrific video released by TMZ was new evidence that showed a "starkly different sequence of events" of what happened in the elevator than what Rice described during the June 2014 meeting.[26] On September 10, 2014, Commissioner Goodell wrote a letter to executives at all NFL teams in which he confirmed that "when the new video evidence became available, [the league] acted promptly and imposed an indefinite suspension."[27]

On September 16, 2014, the NFLPA filed an appeal of the indefinite suspension of Ray Rice by the NFL. The NFLPA indicated that the appeal was based on supporting facts that reveal a lack of a fair and impartial process, including the role of the office of the commissioner of the NFL. The NFLPA requested that a neutral and jointly selected arbitrator hear this case as the commissioner and his staff will be essential witnesses in the proceeding and thus cannot serve as impartial arbitrators.[28] Commissioner Goodell agreed to appoint a neutral arbitrator, Judge Barbara Jones, to hear and decide the appeal filed by the NFLPA on behalf of Ray Rice.[29] The NFLPA issued another statement following the appointment of Judge Jones to preside over the appeal:

> The NFLPA thanks Judge Barbara Jones for presiding over a fair and thorough hearing. This is the first time in the history of our league that a disciplinary hearing has been conducted pursuant to a joint agreement on a neutral arbitrator. We commend NFL owners and officials for the wisdom of this decision, which enhances the credibility and integrity of our business. The collectively bargained rights of all players must be vehemently preserved and we take that obligation seriously. This appeal, presided over by a neutral arbitrator, which included a presentation of all the relevant facts, witness testimony to the truth and cross examination, is the due process that every athlete deserves.[30]

On November 28, 2014, Judge Jones issued her decision, which included the following central findings and conclusions:

> If this were a matter where the first discipline imposed was an indefinite suspension, an arbitrator would be hard pressed to find that the commissioner had abused his discretion. But that is not the case before me. Rather, based on what I believe was Rice's accurate description of the assault of his then fiancée, the commissioner determined, consistent with past punishment, that Rice was to be suspended for two games and fined the pay for an additional game.... Under Article 46, the commissioner is entitled to great deference in the review of his decisions, but review for abuse of discretion is not a rubber stamp approval. An abuse of discretion can be found where the decision maker has acted in an "arbitrary or capricious manner." ... Because Rice did not mislead the commissioner and because there were no new facts on which the commissioner could base his increased suspension, I find that the imposition of the indefinite suspension was arbitrary. I therefore vacate the second penalty [indefinite suspension] imposed on Rice.[31]

Immediately following the release of Judge Jones' decision, the NFLPA issued another statement in which the players association declared that, "This decision is a victory for a disciplinary process that is fair and transparent. This union will always stand up and fight for the due process rights of our players. While we take no pleasure in seeing a decision that confirms what we have been saying about the commissioner's office acting arbitrarily, we hope that this will bring the NFL owners to the collective bargaining table to fix a broken process."[32]

In January 2015, Robert S. Mueller III released an in-depth report based on his independent investigation of the entire situation involving Ray Rice. The report set forth a series of recommendations as to how the NFL could further strengthen the rigor of its internal investigations—the recommendations included:

- *Expand the NFL Security Department*: The NFL committed, in connection with its new 2014 Personal Conduct Policy, to employ a Special Counsel for Investigations and Conduct. The league should also consider adding other experienced personnel to the Security Department to assist in supervising the 32 league-affiliated security representatives (investigations require persistence and follow through, and there must be sufficient supervision to manage and drive investigations run by team representatives).

- *Establish a Specialized Investigative Team*: The NFL should establish (or have on retainer) a specialized investigative team—comprised of experienced domestic violence and sexual assault investigators and victim/witness advocates—to handle or otherwise assist with the league's domestic violence and sexual assault cases.

- *Adopt Investigative Guidelines*: The NFL Security Department should create written guidelines for conducting investigations. In drafting the guidelines, the Security Department should consider providing the following: (1) A specific statement that investigators must focus on the underlying player conduct, including regularly updating the league on what is known and what is not known about that conduct; (2) A specific set of guidelines for investigations when there has been no arrest and, therefore, little risk of interference with law enforcement; (3) Directions on obtaining relevant records and contacting relevant individuals and authorities in instances in which law enforcement is involved; and (4) Expectations in terms of the timing and thoroughness of the resulting work product.[33]

In March 2015, Ray Rice settled a wrongful termination claim filed by the NFLPA on his behalf against the Ravens. The team allegedly agreed to pay Ray Rice approximately $1.6 million in the confidential settlement.

The Adrian Peterson situation

In May 2014, NFL player Adrian Peterson disciplined his four-year-old son after the child pushed another one of Adrian Peterson's sons off a motorbike video game. Adrian Peterson utilized a switch (thin tree branch) to discipline his child, which resulted in bruises and lacerations on the boy's back, legs and arms. On September 11, 2014, a grand jury in Texas indicted Adrian Peterson on a charge of felony reckless or negligent injury of a child.[34] On September 17, 2014, the NFL and NFLPA agreed that Adrian Peterson would be placed on the "Commissioner's Exempt List" until the criminal charges were formally adjudicated/resolved. This administrative suspension resulted in Peterson being deemed ineligible to play in games yet he would still be paid based on the terms of his player contract.[35] On November 4, 2014, Adrian Peterson pleaded "no contest" to (i.e., accepted punishment for) a reduced misdemeanor charge of reckless assault of a child. The court placed Adrian Peterson on community supervision for two years, at the conclusion of which the criminal charge would be removed from his record.[36]

Adrian Peterson was also assessed a fine of $4,000 and was required to complete 80 hours of community service.

On November 6, 2014, the NFL advised Peterson that "the matter warrants review for potential disciplinary action under the Personal Conduct Policy."[37] On this same day, the NFLPA released another statement. The statement explained that the players association worked with the NFL, the Minnesota Vikings and Adrian Peterson's representatives on a mutual agreement pending the final adjudication of his criminal case. Because the legal matter had been resolved, the NFLPA believed that Adrian Peterson deserved "to be treated in a manner that is consistent with similar cases under our collective bargaining agreement.... [The NFLPA] will pursue any and all remedies if those rights are breached."[38]

On November 18, 2014, the NFL announced that Adrian Peterson would be suspended without pay for at least the remainder of the 2014 NFL season, and would not be considered for reinstatement to the NFL before April 15, 2015. Commissioner Goodell determined that Peterson's conduct was detrimental to the league. In addition, Commissioner Goodell expressed concerns that Peterson did not fully appreciate the seriousness of his conduct and, therefore, might be prone to engage in similar conduct in the future.[39] On the same day, the NFLPA issued the following statement related to the suspension of Adrian Peterson:

> The decision by the NFL to suspend Adrian Peterson is another example of the credibility gap that exists between the agreements they make and the actions they take. Since Adrian's legal matter was adjudicated, the NFL has ignored their obligations and attempted to impose a new and arbitrary disciplinary proceeding. The facts are that Adrian has asked for a meeting with Roger Goodell, the discipline imposed is inconsistent and an NFL executive told Adrian that his time on the commissioner's list would be considered as time served. The NFLPA will appeal this suspension and will demand that a neutral arbitrator oversee the appeal. We call on the NFL Management Council to show our players and our sponsors leadership by committing to collective bargaining so a fair Personal Conduct Policy can be implemented as quickly as possible.[40]

One day later, on November 19, 2014, the NFLPA sent a letter to Commissioner Goodell appealing the indefinite suspension of Adrian Peterson.[41] Similar to the Ray Rice situation, Commissioner Goodell recused himself from the appeals process and assigned a neutral arbitrator to oversee the discipline appeals process. On December 12, 2014, arbitrator Harold Henderson sustained/upheld Commissioner Goodell's decision to indefinitely suspend Adrian Peterson:

> The commissioner has considerable discretion in assessing discipline. If he should determine that the current level of discipline imposed for certain types of conduct has not been effective in deterring such conduct, it is within his authority to increase discipline in such cases. He is not forever

bound to historical precedent.... I conclude that the player has not demonstrated that the process and procedures surrounding his discipline were not fair and consistent; he was afforded all the protections and rights to which he is entitled, and I find no basis to vacate or reduce the discipline.[42]

On December 15, 2014, the NFLPA filed a federal lawsuit requesting that the court vacate the arbitration award issued by Harold Henderson. The NFLPA legal complaint alleged that the arbitration award should be set aside because: (1) The decision is contrary to the essence of the 2011 NFL collective bargaining agreement; (2) The decision defies fundamental principles of notice, fairness and consistency; and (3) The decision was rendered by an evidently partial arbitrator who exceeded the scope of his authority.[43] In February 2015, the District Court of Minnesota issued a decision, which overturned Harold Henderson's arbitration award. Judge David Doty noted that, in August 2014, the league increased the sanctions for domestic violence and sexual assault incidents. Doty determined that the NFLPA submitted to Henderson "the pure legal issue" of whether the "new policy" (automatic minimum six game suspension) could be applied retroactively to the Adrian Peterson matter (which took place in May 2014). As a result, Judge Doty concluded that, "Henderson strayed beyond the issues submitted by the NFLPA and in doing so exceeded his authority.... Nothing in the record supports a finding that the NFLPA asked Henderson to determine whether the discipline imposed was consistent with the previous policy."[44]

On February 26, 2015, immediately following the issuance of this court decision, the NFLPA released the following statement: "This is a victory for the rule of law, due process and fairness. Our collective bargaining agreement has rules for implementation of the personal conduct policy and when those rules are violated, our union always stands up to protect our players' rights. This is yet another example why neutral arbitration is good for our players, good for the owners and good for our game."[45] That same day, the NFL formally appealed Judge Doty's decision. In the view of the NFL, "Judge Doty's order did not contain any determinations concerning the fairness of the appeals process under the CBA, including the commissioner's longstanding authority to appoint a designee to act as hearing officer. Even so, we believe strongly that Judge Doty's order is incorrect and fundamentally at odds with well-established legal precedent governing the district court's role in reviewing arbitration decisions."[46] Despite the ongoing legal controversy, on April 16, 2015, Commissioner Goodell officially reinstated Adrian Peterson—which meant that Peterson was once again permitted to practice as well as play in NFL games.[47]

In December 2015, the NFLPA sent a letter to NFL team owners and player agents. The letter contained a proposal regarding neutral arbitration of commissioner discipline along with recommended protocols for league investigations into alleged violations of the 2014 Personal Conduct Policy. For example, the letter proposed that all player appeals of discipline for conduct detrimental to the integrity of the game should be heard by a panel of three arbitrators comprised of attorneys who have special expertise in the business of football, and any discipline imposed may only be affirmed, reduced or vacated by the panel of neutral arbitrators (i.e., the penalty initially issued by Commissioner Goodell may not be increased).[48] Somewhat expectedly, the NFLPA did not receive any substantive feedback from the NFL in response to this proposal.

In August 2016, the Eighth Circuit Court of Appeals reversed Judge Doty's decision and determined that so long as the arbitrator (in this case, Harold Henderson) is even arguably construing or applying the 2011 CBA and acting within the scope of his authority, the arbitral decision must stand. Judge Colloton provided the following rationale for the court's decision:

> Allowing the commissioner or the commissioner's designee to hear challenges to the commissioner's decisions may present an actual or apparent conflict of interest for the arbitrator. But the parties bargained for this procedure, and the [NFLPA] consented to it. It was foreseeable that arbitration under the [2011 CBA] sometimes would involve challenges to the credibility of testimony from Goodell or other league employees. When parties to a contract elect to resolve disputes through arbitration, a grievant can ask for no more impartiality than inheres in the method they have chosen.... The players association does not identify any structural unfairness in the Article 46 arbitration process for which it bargained. The player association's fundamental fairness argument is little more than a recapitulation of its retroactivity argument against the merits of the arbitrator's decision. We have never suggested that when an award draws its essence from the collective bargaining agreement, a dissatisfied party nonetheless may achieve vacatur of the arbitrator's decision by showing that the result is "fundamentally unfair".... We conclude that the parties bargained to be bound by the decision of the arbitrator, and the arbitrator acted within his authority, so we reverse the district court's judgment vacating the arbitration decision.[49]

If the NFLPA wants to secure additional procedural and substantive protections for its players during the overall discipline process, the players association will need to negotiate changes to the 2011 CBA—which, as confirmed by Judge Barbara Jones as well as the Eighth Circuit Court of Appeals—currently provides Commissioner Goodell with significant autonomy and flexibility with respect to penalizing players for misconduct.[50]

Player social activism and the NFL national anthem policy

During the 2016 and 2017 NFL seasons, some players decided to sit or kneel during the pre-game playing of the national anthem to protest racial inequality, police brutality and other social justice issues. In October 2017, league executives and NFLPA representatives met "to discuss the important issue of social activism by NFL players."[51] Also, in October 2017, NFL veteran player Russell Okung wrote a letter to all players in which he emphasized the importance of players communicating, collaborating and uniting. In his sincere letter, Okung wrote:

The NFLPA, for better or worse, is limited in its capacity to "unify" our interests. Unlike a traditional labor union, the foundational nature of our relationship to each other is defined by fierce competition and learned opposition. The system is designed to keep us divided and to stifle our attempts to collaborate—we're made to see each other as the enemy. Indeed, the system celebrates when it puts us at odds with one another. As a competitor who loves the game, I can appreciate this aspect of the league to a certain extent. But the current controversy is obviously about much more than football. Rather than our collective voice prevailing in a way that spans the league, you are seeing individual teams respond separately to the protest in 32 different ways. It's telling that these decisions are being made at the team level and not being driven by the interests of the players collectively. Some teams are standing and locking arms. Some are staying in the locker room. And some are now being banned from protesting altogether. Owners have the ability to quickly and efficiently communicate, collaborate and align their objectives to serve the broader interests of the shield. By and large, they are carrying out a strategy to this end, regardless of how it impacts us as players and regardless of how much it reflects our actual will. While I don't have all the answers as to how to ensure we are not robbed of this moment, I am convinced that we will never make progress if we do not find a way to come together and take action that represents the will of the players. What we have is strength in numbers. But our strength is currently not being leveraged because we have no means of direct communication that is not—in some way, shape or form—controlled, monitored or manipulated by outside forces.[52]

In December 2017, the NFL expanded its social justice program that supports and shines a light on the actions players take every day that unquestionably have a positive impact in local communities. The NFL's social justice efforts focus on reducing barriers to opportunity, and prioritizes making improvements in three key areas: (1) Education and economic advancement; (2) Community-police relations; and (3) Criminal justice reform. Additional programs focus on reducing poverty, promoting racial equality and supporting workforce development.[53] In May 2018, the NFL and the Players Coalition—an organization founded by NFL players that aspires to make an impact on social justice and racial equality issues—finalized a partnership that dedicated close to $90 million for efforts and programs combating social inequality.[54]

Also, in May 2018, the NFL announced a policy for the 2018 season that required all team and league personnel on the field to stand and show respect for the American flag during the customary pre-game playing of the national anthem. Commissioner Goodell issued the following statement on behalf of the league:

The efforts by many of our players sparked awareness and action around issues of social justice that must be addressed. The platform that we have created together is certainly unique in professional sports and quite likely in

American business. We are honored to work with our players to drive progress. It was unfortunate that on-field protests created a false perception among many that thousands of NFL players were unpatriotic. This is not and was never the case. This season, all league and team personnel shall stand and show respect for the flag and the anthem. Personnel who choose not to stand for the anthem may stay in the locker room until after the anthem has been performed.[55]

In response to the league's issuance of the new national anthem policy, the NFLPA released the following statement:

The NFL chose to not consult the union in the development of this new "policy." NFL players have shown their patriotism through their social activism, their community service, in support of our military and law enforcement and yes, through their protests to raise awareness about the issues they care about. The vote by NFL club CEOs today contradicts the statements made to our player leadership by Commissioner Goodell and the chairman of the NFL's Management Council John Mara about the principles, values and patriotism of our league. Our union will review the new "policy" and challenge any aspect of it that is inconsistent with the collective bargaining agreement.[56]

In July 2018, the NFLPA filed a non-injury grievance on behalf of all NFL players challenging the league's national anthem policy.[57] The NFLPA claimed that the new policy—which was imposed by the league without consultation with the NFLPA—was inconsistent with the 2011 CBA and infringed on player rights.[58] Throughout much of July 2018, the league and the NFLPA worked together to create a resolution. A joint statement from the league and its players reiterated, "The NFL and NFLPA reflect the great values of America, which are repeatedly demonstrated by the many players doing extraordinary work in communities across our country to promote equality, fairness and justice. Our shared focus will remain on finding a solution to the anthem issue through mutual, good faith commitments, outside of litigation."[59] After a series of productive meetings between league executives and player representatives, the NFL eventually agreed to suspend the policy (and the NFLPA agreed to withdraw its grievance). In October 2018, Commissioner Goodell reiterated that, "The focus of both the NFLPA and the NFL, the clubs and our players has been to focus on the effort of the players on the issues they have raised and how [they] can make their communities better. They are incredibly passionate about that. They have brought these issues greater awareness and they are working in their communities to try to make them better. They are working on issues, such as criminal justice reform."[60]

In January 2019, the NFL launched the "Inspire Change" platform, which was developed to showcase the collaborative efforts of players, team owners and the league to create positive change in communities across the United States. The Inspire Change initiative intends to function as a comprehensive platform for social change by combining the synergistic impact of community activation, grassroots funding and digital/social media integration.[61] In August 2019, the NFL and Roc Nation—the entertainment company founded by musical artist and entrepreneur Shawn "Jay-Z" Carter—announced a multiyear collaborative partnership designed to improve the NFL's live game experiences and to amplify the league's social justice efforts. As part of the collaboration, Roc Nation will advise the NFL on the selection of musical artists for events such as the Super Bowl. Another meaningful component of the partnership will be to "nurture and strengthen community through football and music, including through the NFL's Inspire Change initiative."[62]

Restrictions on player mobility: the franchise and transition player designations

The NFL's franchise player and transition player designations allow a team to "tag" one player each season who would otherwise be a restricted or unrestricted free agent.[63] This gives the team either exclusive negotiation rights (for franchise players) or the right of first refusal to match an offer sheet that the player signs with another team (for transition players).[64] Franchise tags are a form of ultra-restricted free agency that enable a team to prevent a player who is considered too valuable for the team to risk losing in an open free agent market from signing a contract elsewhere. Each "tag" is for a one-year contract, which significantly restricts the ability of that player to change teams and sign a long-term contract that could provide greater financial security.

These franchise and transition player rules have been embedded into the NFL collective bargaining agreement since 1993. The rationale for the NFLPA agreeing to these player mobility restrictions was that NFL players collectively embraced that one "right of refusal player" per team via the franchise and transition player system was more tolerable than numerous "tags" per team—which was the reality before the 1993 CBA included the league's first free agency system. As a result, NFL players accepted the compromise back in 1993 likely without understanding the long-term ramifications of having this provision in the 2011 CBA.

The NFL's designations require teams to make a specific type of one-year tender offer to the player whom they wish to label as its franchise or transition player. The one-year tender offer salary amount is initially calculated based on either the average value of the top-five or top-ten player salaries at the designated player's relevant position, depending on whether the player is labeled a franchise or transition player.[65] The franchise and transition average values are calculated the same way for every player at the player's position. Thus, there is not an independent calculation of the fair market value for a particular player based on statistics or production—it is assumed to be the average of the annual salaries of the top-five or top-ten highest-paid players at that specific position. A team can only use one of each type of tag per year, and a team may use a franchise tag on the same player for up to three consecutive years.[66]

There are two types of franchise players, which are classified based on the type of required tender that the team offers the player. The first category of franchise player—exclusive franchise tender—is offered the highest-value one-year tender, which equals the greater of: (1) The average salary of the five largest salaries for players at the franchise player's position (average salary determined for both the five prior seasons and upcoming season); or (b) 120% of the player's prior year salary. The franchise player given this type of "exclusive franchise tender" designation is prevented from negotiating with any other team.[67] The second category of franchise player—nonexclusive franchise tender—is offered a lower-value one-year tender, which is typically the average of the five largest prior year salaries for the five players at the franchise player's position (average based on prior five years of salary data). The franchise player given this "nonexclusive franchise tender" designation can negotiate with another team. However, the prior team retains a right of first refusal and would also receive two first round draft selections if the prior team does not match an offer sheet, thereby allowing the player to sign with a new team.[68] If a player is designated as a transition player, the player is permitted to sign a contract with a new team, but his prior team retains a right of first refusal. However, the prior team would not receive any draft choice compensation if the team declines to exercise its rights of first refusal.[69]

The time period for NFL teams to designate franchise players begins on the twenty-second day preceding the first day of the new league year and ends at 4:00 p.m. New York time on the eighth day preceding the first day of the new league year—this time period occurs during the same two weeks each year after the conclusion of the Super Bowl in February.[70] Even after a team designates a player as a franchise player, the team can negotiate with that player on a multi-year contract. The deadline for agreeing to a multi-year contract is July 22 each year, and if no multi-year deal is agreed upon, the player must sign the one-year designation and cannot negotiate for an extension or new contract again until the conclusion of the team's last regular season game that upcoming season.[71]

The franchise and transition player system in the NFL arguably discourages a team from signing a player to a long-term contract, since team owners can always fall back on "franchising" the player the following season.[72] Renowned NBA and NFL player agent Mark Bartelstein said, "With the franchise tag in football, the players always prefer to get long-term deals [because] you only have so many years to do this and the security and long-term money is what players prefer."[73] NFL team owners have previously utilized the threat of attaching the franchise tag in order to convince a player to agree to a longer-term contract at lower annual salaries than the player might have commanded from a new team in a true open market. Some players have historically agreed to sign multi-year contracts or extensions with their prior team because of the risk of the franchise tag being applied and the corresponding uncertainty of having only one season of guaranteed salary (combined with the possibility of suffering a career-ending injury). For example, prior to the 2019 NFL season, six players were designated as non-exclusive franchise players.[74] NFL players unquestionably would prefer modifying CBA rules that limit free agency (and overall player mobility). The NFLPA will likely prioritize attempting to convince the league to overhaul—and perhaps even eliminate—the franchise and transition player designation system during the next round of collective bargaining. NFL team owners will probably not easily concede on this issue, and instead will perhaps even insist on further expanding the current franchise and transition player designation system in order to provide teams with increased leverage to retain key players.[75] If team owners express reluctance to modify the franchise and transition player designation framework, the NFLPA could perhaps push to eliminate the fifth-year team option for former first-round draft picks so that these players can become free agents after four years in the NFL instead of the current requirement of five years.[76]

Relatedly, NFL players and the league might also decide to collectively address the issues of players "holding out" by refusing to report to training camp and/or play in preseason and regular season games. For example, prior to the 2019 NFL season, Los Angeles Chargers running back Melvin Gordon was entering his fifth year in the NFL (and the final year of his rookie contract—the fifth-year team option). Melvin Gordon's base salary for the 2019 NFL season equaled $5.6 million. Gordon felt he should be paid much more money and sought to renegotiate his contract with the Chargers. Melvin Gordon did not participate in training camp, any of the four preseason games or the first three games of the regular season. Gordon forfeited approximately $330,000 for each of the three regular season games he refused to play in. The Chargers were also permitted to fine Gordon for missing preseason training camp and preseason games. For instance, the 2011 CBA explains that, after a team has exercised its fifth-year option, any unexcused late reporting to or absence from preseason training camp by a player in the fifth league year of his contract (the option year) will subject the player to a fine of $30,000 per day, plus one week's regular season salary for each preseason game missed.[77]

Professor Charles Grantham believes "the rookie scale undervalues the talent of incoming players … [and] is an attempt to control the costs at entry."[78] The league and the NFLPA could establish specific criteria that would provide players like Melvin Gordon—who significantly outperform statistical expectations during their first few seasons in the league—with additional performance-based incentive compensation in addition to the limited performance escalators permitted by the 2011 CBA. The league and the NFLPA could also agree to adjust the qualifying offer amount for the fifth-year team option based in part on performance (similar to the NBA "starter criteria" model for qualifying offers) and/or grant players the ability to renegotiate and extend their rookie contract after accruing two seasons as a player in the league (instead of the three accrued seasons required under the 2011 CBA). Team owners might also push to drastically increase allowable fines if players decide to "hold out" and miss preseason training camp and/or actual games in order to further deter future contract holdouts by indispensable players. The league is apparently very conscientious of and concerned about the recent proliferation of players pushing back against their rookie contract situations.[79]

Guaranteed player contracts

The standard NFL player contract provides that each NFL player "understands that he is competing with other players for a position" on the team's roster. In addition, the standard player contract explains that a team is permitted to terminate a player's contract if at any time and in the sole judgment of the team, a player's "skill or performance has been unsatisfactory as compared with that of other players competing for positions" on the team's roster.[80] Stated differently, subject to limited exceptions and negotiated guarantees, NFL teams are permitted to terminate a player's contract without any requirement to pay the player his expected salary for the remainder of the season if the team merely (and subjectively) determines that the skill or performance of the player has been unsatisfactory.

Compensation in NFL contracts can be guaranteed for three purposes: skill, salary cap and/or injury. Compensation in a player contract can be guaranteed for one, two, all or none of the three guarantees. If money in a player contract is protected for skill, salary cap and injury, that money is fully guaranteed at signing and will be paid to the player. If money is only guaranteed for one or two of the three protections, then the player's contract is technically only partially guaranteed.

- *Skill Guarantee*: If a player contract is terminated because, in the team's opinion, he does not have the requisite skill (due to a loss or lack of skills comparable to others on the team at his position or prospects attempting to earn a position on the team), the player will be entitled to any money that is protected by a skill guarantee.
- *Salary Cap Guarantee:* If a player contract is terminated so that a team can get under the salary cap, sign a free agent or re-sign one of its current players, the player is entitled to any money that is protected by a salary cap guarantee.
- *Injury Guarantee:* If a player is released but is currently unable to perform football duties (i.e., player does not pass a physical exam) as a result of team activities, the player is entitled to any money in his contract protected against injury. An injury-only guarantee is the most common in terms of negotiated partially guaranteed money.[81]

The salary of players on rookie contracts may be guaranteed for skill, salary cap related contract terminations and/or football related injuries. However, teams are not required to provide these salary guarantees to players who sign rookie contracts.[82] Based on terms within the 2011 CBA, a player's salary can only be guaranteed for one or all of these categories if the player's entire rookie salary (excluding performance incentives) was similarly guaranteed for the same type(s) of contract termination in the immediately preceding year of the contract. For illustration purposes, if a rookie drafted in the second round signs a four-year contract with a rookie salary of $1 million in year one, $1.25 million in year two, $1.5 million in year three and $1.75 million in year four, no portion of his fourth-year rookie salary may be guaranteed for skill and injury unless the player's full rookie salary for year two and year three were also previously guaranteed for skill and injury.[83]

Certain specific types of NFL contracts are automatically guaranteed for skill, salary cap related contract terminations and/or football related injuries. For example, a player's entire base salary will be guaranteed if a team exercises its fifth-year option following the first four years of a rookie's contract (and the player is on the team's roster at the start of his fifth league year).[84] In addition, if a player subject to a franchise or transition player designation accepts the required tender offer from a team, that player's contract will be fully guaranteed if the contract is terminated because of perceived lack of comparative skill, as a result of a football-related injury or due to the team's decision to create room for salary cap purposes.[85]

The 2011 CBA also provides limited injury protection for players with multiple years on their contracts. For example, for the 2020 NFL season, a player on a multi-year contract who suffers a severe football injury would be eligible to receive up to $1.2 million for the season immediately following his injury and up to $500,000 for the second successive season following his injury.[86]

Number of regular season games

In May 2011, Commissioner Goodell spoke with approximately 7,000 Carolina Panthers season ticket members. During that conversation, Commissioner Goodell commented on the league's then-current proposal to reduce the number of preseason games from four to two, and to correspondingly increase the number of regular season games from 16 to 18:

> The 18-and-2 format … improves the quality of what we are doing as a league, which I think is always important to your fans and to your customers. It also improves the value…. But if we do that, it's important that we do it the right way and we do it with the proper consideration to player health and safety. We have made some steps, we have made some proposals on how to do that in the offseason and the training camp, and even in the regular season. And I think if we do that, we will do it with the players and we will do it in a responsible way.[87]

In July 2019, the NFL once again proposed an 18-game regular season to the NFLPA. The owners proposed capping players' participation to only 16 of the 18 regular season games in an attempt to address NFLPA concerns about player safety. An NFLPA analysis concluded that two additional games could add as much as $2.5 billion in annual revenue at the team and league levels from increased ticket and corporate partnership revenue along with additional media rights income. Nonetheless, the NFLPA rejected the league proposal.[88] DeMaurice Smith commented, "I don't see an 18-game schedule—under any circumstance—being in the best interest of our players."[89]

Once team owners realized that the 18-game proposal faced bleak prospects of gaining traction with league players, team executives such as Mark Murphy of the Green Bay Packers suggested creative concepts such as expanding the regular season by one week and utilizing the additional game for international or neutral site games in order to increase overall fan engagement. By September 2019, the NFL pivoted to a proposal that would expand the regular season to 17 games. Mark Murphy acknowledged, "Our preseason is not very good. I would be very concerned about the health and safety aspects of adding two regular season games. I also think there is a possibility of expanding the playoffs."[90]

Expect the league and its players to continue the conversation about reducing the number of preseason games and potentially adding one additional regular season game (or extending the playoffs by adding two or more additional teams). The ultimate compromise will need to balance potential increased revenue from additional regular season or playoff games with genuine concerns about player health and safety.

Player health and safety will certainly represent another focal point during future collective bargaining sessions involving league and player representatives. In 2016, the NFL finally acknowledged a link between playing football and the degenerative brain disease known as chronic traumatic encephalopathy (CTE). Throughout 2016 and 2017, the NFL pledged more than $200 million in support for independent medical research and engineering advancements in neuroscience in order to develop protocols that further support player health and safety. In 2018, the league launched an "Injury Reduction Plan" that aimed to reduce the incidence of concussions. One element of the Injury Reduction Plan requires football helmets worn by NFL players to undergo extensive annual laboratory testing by biomechanical engineers appointed by the NFL and the NFLPA to evaluate which helmets best reduce head impact severity. Another central aspect of the Injury Reduction Plan involves developing new league rules that emphasize player safety. Since 2002, the NFL has made approximately 50 rules changes intended to eliminate potentially dangerous playing tactics, reduce the risk of injuries, improve practice methods, better educate players and team personnel on concussions and strengthen the league's medical protocols.[91] According to the official NFL website, the league continues to make advances, on and off the field, in an effort to protect its players by championing new developments in engineering, biomechanics, advanced sensors and material science that mitigate forces and better prevent against injuries in sports. The league also supports independent research to advance progress in the prevention, diagnosis and treatment of head injuries. The NFL "Play Smart Play Safe" initiative consists of the following four core pillars: (1) "Protecting Players"—evolution of rules related to the concussion protocol and limits on padded practices to ensure player safety; (2) "Advanced Technology"—championing new developments in engineering, biomechanics and material science designed to better protect players from injuries; (3) "Medical Research"—supporting preeminent experts and institutions to advance progress in the prevention, diagnosis and treatment of head injuries; and (4) "Sharing Progress"—sharing applicable learnings across all levels of football—and to other sports and society at large.[92]

Concluding thoughts on collective bargaining in the NFL

In August 2017, NFLPA executive director DeMaurice Smith emphatically pronounced that he believed "the likelihood of either a strike or a lockout in 2021 is almost a virtual certainty."[93] Despite this somewhat dire forecast, the NFL and NFLPA seem to have approached the next round of collective bargaining with more collaborative and less combative mindsets.[94] For instance, in July 2019, the NFL and NFLPA engaged in bargaining sessions that were mutually considered "productive, constructive and beneficial for both sides."[95] Similarly, in October 2019, several league and players association representatives huddled in Jacksonville to continue collective bargaining discussions. When asked about a timeline or deadline for agreeing to a new CBA, Commissioner Goodell responded, "You don't have timelines in CBA negotiations. We've had a lot of discussions over several months."[96]

During the first few months of the 2019 NFL season, DeMaurice Smith visited with players on every NFL team in order to learn about players' concerns related to working conditions, insurance coverage (workers' compensation) and other aspects of player compensation/benefits. In addition, DeMaurice Smith provided detailed guidelines and recommendations on how players should prepare for a potential lockout after the 2020 NFL season. In fact, the cover slide for the presentation that DeMaurice Smith delivered to each team contained the following message: "Work Stoppage is Coming. #StayReady."[97] Similarly, in October 2019, Dana Shuler (NFLPA senior director of player affairs) emphasized that "it is critically important at this juncture that [NFL players] focus on a potential work stoppage in 2021 … and that [players] are preparing aggressively for that to occur."[98]

Brian McCarthy (an NFL spokesperson) explained that the 2011 CBA has "produced growth in player compensation, improvements to player health and safety, state-of-the-art stadium and training facilities, and additional retirement benefits." McCarthy also emphasized that the primary goal of the league is to timely finalize a "new labor agreement with the NFLPA that extends our partnership and ensures ongoing investments in the game."[99]

Hopefully, the NFLPA and NFL continue to appreciate the importance and impact of continued labor stability, as players and team owners continue collective bargaining discussions in the months ahead in order to agree to terms on what would be known as the 2021 NFL collective bargaining agreement.

Notes

1 National Football League Personal Conduct Policy (2008), *available at* www.nfl. com. The 2008 Personal Conduct Policy also contained the following content: "For many years, it has been well understood that rules promoting lawful, ethical, and

responsible conduct serve the interests of the league, its players, and fans. Illegal or irresponsible conduct does more than simply tarnish the offender. It puts innocent people at risk, sullies the reputation of others involved in the game, and undermines public respect and support for the NFL."

2 National Football League Personal Conduct Policy (2008), *available at* www.nfl.com. *See also* Withers, B.P. (2010). The Integrity of the Game: Professional Athletes and Domestic Violence, *Harvard Journal of Sports & Entertainment Law*, at page 169.

3 Karcher, R.T. (2018). Commissioner's Power to Discipline Players, in *The Oxford Handbook of American Sports Law*, at page 71 (opining that exactly where these lines should be drawn is for the players association and league to decide). *See also* Wilson, M.R. (2010). Why So Stern?: The Growing Power of the NBA Commissioner, *DePaul Journal of Sports Law and Contemporary Problems*, at page 48 (expressing the viewpoint that, "Because the players unions negotiate on behalf of the athletes, the relative strength of a league's players union often determines the extent of the limits on commissioner authority under the CBA").

4 *See* ESPN News Services (2009). Goodell's Authority to be Part of Talks, *available at* www.espn.com (quoting NFLPA executive director DeMaurice Smith: "If you imagined a world where our court systems were not public and people meted out justice and all you heard was what the result was, well, they might even get the decision right—but there would be a sense that it wasn't fair because you couldn't see why things were. I think that same underlying philosophy is true here").

5 NFL CBA (2011), Article 46, Section 1(a). Article 8.13 of the NFL constitution and bylaws also permits the league commissioner to suspend and/or fine players and other team and league personnel for "conduct detrimental to the welfare of the league or professional football."

6 *See* NFL CBA (2011), Article 46, Section 2. *See also* NFL CBA (2011), Article 43 (detailing the non-injury grievance requirements, protocols and processes).

7 McCann, M.A. (2018). *Introduction*, in *The Oxford Handbook of American Sports Law*, at page 12. *See* Einhorn, E. (2016). Between the Hash Marks: The Absolute Power the NFL's Collective Bargaining Agreement Grants Its Commissioner, *Brooklyn Law Review*, at pages 402, 420 (reiterating that, "While many criticize Goodell for abusing his power as commissioner, it is the language of the CBA that grants Goodell the authority to arbitrate appeals of his own disciplinary decisions for detrimental player conduct.... Nothing in the CBA stops the commissioner from serving as an arbitrator when his own conduct is being challenged"). *See also* Levine, J.F., Gunn, I.P., and Moorman, A.M. (2019). Peterson, Brady, and Elliot: Analyzing 'the Trilogy' in Light of the NFL Commissioner's Discipline Authority, *Journal of Legal Aspects of Sport*, at page 229 (noting that the somewhat undefined procedures in Article 46 of the 2011 CBA provide the commissioner with broad power).

8 Karcher, R.T. (2018). *Commissioner's Power to Discipline Players*, in *The Oxford Handbook of American Sports Law* at page 79. *See* Einhorn, E. (2016). Between the Hash Marks: The Absolute Power the NFL's Collective Bargaining Agreement Grants Its Commissioner, *Brooklyn Law Review*, at page 428 (explaining that, "Removing Goodell from the arbitration process, and replacing him with an impartial arbitrator for lesser punishments and a special committee for harsher punishments, will enhance players' due process rights under federal law and prevent player grievances from requiring further litigation in federal court"). *See also* Cole, J. (2015). Dropping the Ball: How the Commissioner's Exercise of His 'Best Interests' Authority is Failing the NFL and What Can Be Done About It, *Texas Review of Entertainment & Sports Law*, at page 43 (proposing an "independent adjudicatory committee" system whereby the NFL commissioner would take on a prosecutorial role and leave disciplinary decision-making authority to an independent committee of former judges). *See also* Reece, J. (2010). Throwing the Red Flag on the Commissioner: How Independent Arbitrators Can Fit into the NFL's Off-Field Discipline Procedures

Under the NFL Collective Bargaining Agreement, *Valparaiso University Law Review*, at page 412 (proposing a new impartial grievance procedure that would allow the NFL commissioner to maintain authority to discipline in the best interests of the NFL while players would receive a meaningful right of appeal to an impartial arbitrator rather than "the empty right to ask the commissioner to reconsider the punishment he already granted").

9 *See* Levine, J.F., Gunn, I.P., and Moorman, A.M. (2019). Peterson, Brady, and Elliot: Analyzing 'the Trilogy' in Light of the NFL Commissioner's Discipline Authority, *Journal of Legal Aspects of Sport*, at pages 223, 248 (emphasizing the importance of the NFLPA adjusting its strategy in order to focus on negotiating player discipline rules during the next round of collective bargaining with the league, and writing that "the NFLPA should eschew its litigious strategy of attempting to substitute judges for arbitrators in favor of improving the CBA with specific proposals negotiated at the bargaining table").

10 *See* Official Release—NFL Teams Unanimously Endorse Comprehensive New Conduct Policy (2014), *available at* www.nfl.com (explaining that all NFL personal conduct policies are issued based on the commissioner's authority under Article 8 of the NFL constitution and bylaws).

11 Official Release—Statement from NFL Players Association on Update to Personal Conduct Policy (2014), *available at* www.nflpa.com.

12 *See* Official Release—NFL Owners Endorse New Personal Conduct Policy (2014), *available at* www.nfl.com.

13 Official Release—NFL Owners Endorse New Personal Conduct Policy (2014), *available at* www.nfl.com. *See also* Letter from Roger Goodell (NFL commissioner) to NFL Team Executives—Personal Conduct Policy (2014) (reiterating that the "goal is to have a layered evaluation and discipline process with a number of clear steps, defined procedures, and substantive expertise").

14 NFL Personal Conduct Policy (2014), *available at* www.nfl.com (noting that the NFL "has increased education regarding respect and appropriate behavior, has provided resources for all employees to assist them in conforming their behavior to the standards expected of them, and has made clear that the league's goal is to prevent violations of the Personal Conduct Policy. In order to uphold our high standards, when violations of this Personal Conduct Policy do occur, appropriate disciplinary action must follow").

15 NFL Personal Conduct Policy (2014), *available at* www.nfl.com. *See* Official Release—The New NFL Personal Conduct Policy (2014), *available at* www.nfl.com (explaining that the policy establishes clear standards of behavior for all NFL personnel. Teams are obligated to promptly report any potential violation of the policy that comes to their attention and must fully cooperate with any related law enforcement and NFL investigations. When a potential violation occurs, the NFL will make available evaluation and counseling services for the player or employee, as well as resources to assist victims and families. The NFL will follow a fair and predictable process for investigating the incident and ultimately taking disciplinary action if a violation has occurred).

16 Official Release—NFLPA Statement on NFL's Policy Announcement (2014), *available at* www.nflpa.com.

17 Ray Rice and Janay Palmer were married on March 28, 2014. Ray Rice was a running back on the Baltimore Ravens. Approximately one week after the incident, the general manager of the Baltimore Ravens stated that the team would allow the league to take its position before the team made any decisions related to player discipline.

18 *See* Decision by Barbara S. Jones—*In Re the Matter of Ray Rice* (2014), *available at* www.nfl.com. *See also* Mueller, R.S. III (2015), Report to the National Football League of an Independent Investigation into the Ray Rice Incident, *available at* www.nfl.com.

19 *See* Decision by Barbara S. Jones—*In Re the Matter of Ray Rice* (2014), *available at* www.nfl.com (finding that, "The NFL knew of the indictment and the results of the criminal proceeding. They had seen the video of Rice's conduct outside the elevator. They had gathered comparator cases of disciplines given for previous violations of the Personal Conduct Policy based on acts of domestic violence. They believed that there was a second video from a camera inside the elevator. Various sources, including NFL security, had reported its existence. Rice had received this video in discovery during his criminal case, but it had not been aired publicly, as had the first video. The NFL never asked Rice for the second video").

20 Rosenthal, G. (2014). Roger Goodell Defends Ray Rice Suspension, *available at* www.nfl.com (further quoting Commissioner Goodell: "Ray has been accountable for his actions. He recognizes he made a horrible mistake that is unacceptable by his standards, by our standards, and he's got to work to re-establish himself. The criminal justice system, as you know, put him in a diversionary program with no discipline, and we felt it was appropriate to have discipline and to continue counseling programs and to continue our educational work"). Adolpho Birch, NFL senior vice president of labor policy and government affairs, provided the following rationale for Commissioner Goodell deciding to suspend Ray Rice for only two games: "The commissioner's authority in this case doesn't provide for a particular ceiling on what he could do. However, we are bound in large part by precedent in prior cases, decisions that have been heard on appeal in the past, and notions of fairness and appropriateness. You have to [look] at what would happen relative to other leagues, other organizations, other entities, and determine whether or not you think the action that the commissioner took was appropriate, but the reality is that we have to make decisions that are fair and consistent with both the prior case law and the prior precedent, but also the message that we need to send as a league to ensure that people understand the standards of conduct expected of them." Decision by Barbara S. Jones—*In Re the Matter of Ray Rice* (2014), *available at* www.nfl.com, at page 6.

21 *See* Letter from Roger Goodell (NFL commissioner) to NFL Team Owners—Ray Rice Matter (2014), *available at* www.nfl.com. *See also* Decision by Barbara S. Jones—*In Re the Matter of Ray Rice* (2014), *available at* www.nfl.com (explaining that, after announcing this increased penalty under the conduct policy, the commissioner called Rice to assure him that the new policy would not affect him—that it was forward looking and his penalty would not be increased). During a press conference on September 19, 2014, Goodell similarly acknowledged, "I got it wrong on a number of levels—from the process that I led to the decision that I reached…. We can use the NFL to help create change not only in our league but in society with respect to domestic violence and sexual assault"). Official Release—NFL Commissioner Roger Goodell Press Conference Opening Statement (2014), *available at* www.nfl.com.

22 Section 11 of the standard NFL player contract provides that, "Player understands that he is competing with other players for a position on Club's roster within the applicable player limits. If at any time, in the sole judgment of Club, Player's skill or performance has been unsatisfactory as compared with that of other players competing for positions on Club's roster, or if Player has engaged in personal conduct reasonably judged by Club to adversely affect or reflect on Club, then Club may terminate this contract." NFL CBA (2011), Appendix A, Section 11, *available at* www.nfl.com.

23 Letter from Stephen Bisciotti (owner of Baltimore Ravens) to Ravens Stakeholders (2014), *available at* www.baltimoreravens.com (also writing: "Because of his positive contributions on and off the field over the last six years, Ray had earned every benefit of the doubt from our organization. We took everything we knew and decided to support Ray Rice until we could not").

24 The 2011 NFL collective bargaining agreement denotes that, "Player recognizes the detriment to the League and professional football that would result from impairment of public confidence in the honest and orderly conduct of NFL games or the integrity and

good character of NFL players. Player therefore acknowledges his awareness that if he … is guilty of any other form of conduct reasonably judged by the League Commissioner to be detrimental to the League or professional football, the Commissioner will have the right, but only after giving Player the opportunity for a hearing at which he may be represented by counsel of his choice, to fine Player in a reasonable amount; to suspend Player for a period certain or indefinitely; and/or to terminate this contract." NFL CBA (2011), Appendix A, Section 15, *available at* www.nfl.com. Importantly, the NFL CBA clarifies that, "The Commissioner and a Club will not both discipline a player for the same act or conduct. The Commissioner's disciplinary action will preclude or supersede disciplinary action by any Club for the same act or conduct." NFL CBA (2011), Article 46, Section 4, *available at* www.nfl.com. The NBA collective bargaining agreement contains a slightly different approach related to team and league/ commissioner discipline for the same act or conduct. The 2017 NBA collective bargaining agreement explains that, "The NBA and a Team shall not discipline a player for the same act or conduct. The NBA's disciplinary action will preclude or supersede disciplinary action by any Team for the same act or conduct…. The same act or conduct by a player may result in both a termination of the player's Uniform Player Contract by his Team and the suspension of the player by the NBA if the egregious nature of the act or conduct is so lacking in justification as to warrant such double penalty." NBA CBA (2017), Article VI, Section 10, *available at* www.nba.com.

25 Commissioner Goodell asserted that, "None of the law enforcement entities we approached was permitted to provide any video or other investigatory material to us…. We did not ask the Atlantic City casino directly for the video." Letter from Roger Goodell (NFL commissioner) to NFL Team Executives—Ray Rice Matter (2014), *available at* www.nfl.com. On September 10, 2014, the NFL hired Robert S. Mueller III to conduct an independent inquiry into two questions: (1) Whether anyone at the NFL had received or seen the in-elevator video prior to its public release on September 8, 2014; and (2) What other evidence was obtained by, provided to, or available to the NFL in the course of its investigation.

26 Decision by Barbara S. Jones—*In Re the Matter of Ray Rice* (2014), *available at* www.nfl.com, at page 7.

27 Letter from Roger Goodell (NFL commissioner) to NFL Team Executives (2014)— Ray Rice Matter, *available at* www.nfl.com (writing that, "I believe that we took a significant step forward with the enhanced policies on domestic violence and sexual assault that were announced last month. I also know that we will be judged on our actions going forward. I am confident that those actions will demonstrate our commitment to address this issue seriously and effectively, and will reflect well on the NFL, all member clubs, and everyone who is a part of our league").

28 Official Release—NFLPA Statement on Appeal of Ray Rice Suspension (2014), *available at* www.nflpa.com (indicating that the action was taken by the players association to protect the due process rights of all players).

29 Official Release—Hearing Officer in Ray Rice Appeal Announced (2014), *available at* www.nflpa.com (clarifying that, "Under the collective bargaining agreement, Commissioner Goodell is obligated to consult with NFLPA executive director DeMaurice Smith before appointing an appeal officer. The NFL and NFLPA collaborated on the selection and the union agreed to the appointment of Judge Jones").

30 Official Release—NFLPA Statement on Ray Rice Hearing (2014), *available at* www. nflpa.com.

31 Decision by Barbara S. Jones—*In Re the Matter of Ray Rice* (2014), *available at* www.nfl.com, at pages 15–17. *See also* Parlow, M.J. (2010). Professional Sports League Commissioners' Authority and Collective Bargaining, *Texas Review of Entertainment and Sports Law*, at page 189 (explaining that arbitrators have been far more likely than courts to reduce commissioner-imposed punishment of players). Courts have consistently determined that when a dispute is resolved in accordance with a

CBA, judicial review of an arbitration hearing (including discipline appeal hearings with league commissioners) is "very limited" and generally restricted to instances where the arbitration award was procured by corruption, fraud or undue means, or where the arbitrator was impartial, refused to hear material evidence, or exceeded his or her power as granted by the CBA. *See* Ehrlich, S.C. (2018). A More Perfect (NFL Players) Union: Secret 'Side Deals,' the NFLPA, and the Duty of Fair Representation, *Ohio Northern University Law Review*, at page 34 (examining a potential breach by the NFLPA of its "duty of fair representation" based on alleged side deals entered into between the NFLPA and the NFL aimed at modifying certain elements of collectively bargained drug testing policies without going through the proper channels to modify these policies).

32 Official Release—NFL Players Association Statement on Ray Rice Ruling (2014), *available at* www.nflpa.com.

33 *See* Mueller, R.S. III (2015). Report to the National Football League of an Independent Investigation into the Ray Rice Incident, *available at* www.nfl.com, at pages 61–65 (also noting that the NFL "long operated on the principle that, when potential misconduct resulted in a criminal investigation, it should defer to the criminal justice system both as to the investigation of the facts and the imposition of discipline … it is not always possible to draw precise factual conclusions from outcomes in a criminal case").

34 When asked about the charges, Adrian Peterson explained, "No one can understand the hurt that I feel for my son and for the harm I caused him. My goal is always to teach my son right from wrong and that's what I tried to do that day." Terlep, S. (2014). Adrian Peterson: 'I Am Not a Child Abuser,' *Wall Street Journal*. Relatedly, when asked by the media what message he thought he and the Minnesota Vikings were sending to abuse victims by initially deciding to let Peterson remain on the active team roster while the legal process played out, Vikings general manager Rick Spielman responded, "I understand that this is a very difficult thing to handle, but we also feel strongly as an organization that this is disciplining a child … we feel very strongly that that is the court's decision to make, but we also understand the seriousness of abusing children as well." Farrar, D. (2014). As Vikings Clear Peterson to Play, More Child Abuse Allegations Surface, *Sports Illustrated*.

35 *See* Official Release—NFLPA Statement on Adrian Peterson: Commissioner's Exempt List (2014), *available at* www.nflpa.com (explaining that, "Adrian Peterson made a decision to take a voluntary leave with pay to take care of his personal and legal issues. The NFLPA and NFL worked with Adrian and the Minnesota Vikings to resolve this unique situation. We support this decision and hope the best for him and his family").

36 *See National Football League Players Association* v. *National Football League* (Minnesota District Court, 2015), 88 F. Supp. 3d 1084.

37 *See National Football League Players Association* v. *National Football League* (Minnesota District Court, 2015), 88 F. Supp. 3d 1084 (explaining that the NFL requested that Peterson provide certain information regarding the criminal case, and notified Peterson that he would have the opportunity to participate in a hearing before the commissioner imposed any discipline).

38 Official Release—NFLPA Statement on Adrian Peterson: Legal Matter Resolved (2014), *available at* www.nflpa.com. The NFLPA released yet another statement on November 10, 2014, which provided: "The NFLPA has filed an expedited, non-injury grievance to remove Adrian Peterson from the Commissioner's Exempt list based on explicit language in a signed agreement dated September 18, 2014. We asked the NFL to honor the terms of that agreement last week and as of now, they have failed to respond or comply. It is our obligation to protect all players' rights, and we will pursue any and all breaches of any contract between a player and his team or the NFL." Official Release—NFLPA Statement on Adrian Peterson Grievance (2014), *available at* www.nflpa.com.

39 *See* Official Release—Adrian Peterson Suspended Without Pay for At Least the Remainder of 2014 Season, *available at* www.nfl.com (explaining that Peterson would also be required to participate in a multi-faceted counseling and therapy program). Based on the 2008 NFL Personal Conduct Policy, "Discipline may take the form of fines, suspension, or banishment from the league and may include a probationary period and conditions that must be satisfied prior to or following reinstatement. The specifics of the disciplinary response will be based on the nature of the incident, the actual or threatened risk to the participant and others, any prior or additional misconduct (whether or not criminal charges were filed), and other relevant factors." National Football League Personal Conduct Policy (2008), *available at* www.nfl.com. Remember that the incident involving Adrian Peterson disciplining his son took place in May 2014, whereas the NFL increased sanctions for domestic violence incidents (i.e., baseline six-game suspension) in August 2014. It is also important to note that several Minnesota Vikings team sponsors decided to suspend or decided not to renew corporate partnership agreements with the organization based on the situation involving Adrian Peterson.

40 Official Release—NFLPA Statement on Adrian Peterson Suspension (2014), *available at* www.nflpa.com.

41 *See* Letter from NFLPA to Roger Goodell (NFL commissioner)—Notice of Appeal of Article 46 Discipline (Adrian Peterson) (2014), *available at* www.nflpa.com (alleging that the actions of the NFL league office "in the disciplinary 'process' applied to Mr. Peterson included attempts to impose new disciplinary processes and procedures in violation of the CBA and in complete disregard of proper and fair procedures consistent with custom and practice under the CBA").

42 Decision by Harold Henderson—*In Re the Matter of Adrian Peterson* (2014), *available at* www.nfl.com (explaining that the Ray Rice situation differed from the Adrian Peterson matter in that the Ray Rice arbitrator decision turned on a second, later discipline more severe than the first, whereas in the Adrian Peterson situation there was only one decision by the commissioner related to player discipline). *See also* Official Release—NFLPA Statement on Ruling in Adrian Peterson Appeal (2014), *available at* www.nflpa.com (explaining that, "The NFLPA expected this outcome, given the hearing officer's relationship and financial ties to the NFL. The decision itself ignores the facts, the evidence and the collective bargaining agreement. This decision also represents the NFL's repeated failure to adhere to due process and confirms its inconsistent treatment of players").

43 *National Football League Players Association* v. *National Football League and National Football League Management Council*, Petition to Vacate Arbitration Award, United States District Court, District of Minnesota (2014) (claiming that Commissioner Goodell lacked authority under the 2011 CBA to apply the new guidelines concerning increased suspensions for domestic violence to punish conduct that had occurred before the new guidelines were announced).

44 *National Football League Players Association* v. *National Football League and National Football League Management Council*, Court Order, United States District Court, District of Minnesota (2014), at pages 14–15 (also finding that, "Henderson's conclusion that the new policy is consistent with the previous policy is contradicted by the commissioner's own statements in which he acknowledged that the new policy included 'changes' to the policy").

45 Official Release—NFLPA Statement on Federal District Court's Decision to Vacate NFL's Arbitration Decision on Adrian Peterson (2015), *available at* www.nflpa.com.

46 Official Release—NFL Statement on Adrian Peterson (2015), *available at* www.nfl.com (indicating that Adrian Peterson would return to the Commissioner's Exempt List pending further court proceedings by appeals officer Harold Henderson or a determination by the Eighth Circuit Court of Appeals).

47 Letter from Roger Goodell (NFL commissioner) to Adrian Peterson (2015) (emphasizing that Peterson's continuing participation in the NFL expressly depends on his avoidance of any further conduct that violates NFL policies).

48 *See* Letter from DeMaurice Smith (NFLPA executive director) to NFL Team Executives and Player Agents (2015), *available at* www.nflpa.com (also proposing that, on appeal, the burden of proof should be on the NFL Management Council and the standard of review should be "just cause," including without limitation, notice and fair and consistent treatment; the arbitration panel should also follow applicable legal standards, including arbitral precedents to the extent relevant, along with the law of the shop (past industry practices)).

49 *National Football League Players Association* v. *National Football League and National Football League Management Council*, Court Order, Eighth Circuit Court of Appeals (2016) (reasoning that the NFL commissioner is not forever bound to historical precedent if prior discipline under the 2008 Personal Conduct Policy provided insufficient deterrence). *See also* Levine, J.F., Gunn, I.P., and Moorman, A.M. (2019). Peterson, Brady, and Elliot: Analyzing 'the Trilogy' in Light of the NFL Commissioner's Discipline Authority, *Journal of Legal Aspects of Sport*, at page 235 (explaining that, "Because the court refused to examine the merits of the actual dispute, this holding did not disturb the commissioner's immense scope of disciplinary authority, given the language in the CBA bargained for" by the league and the NFLPA).

50 *See* Crawford, K. (2019). NFL 3–0 in Federal Appellate Court Challenges to Player Suspensions: A Pattern of 'Substantial Deference' to the NFL, *Jeffrey S. Moorad Sports Law Journal*, at page 78 (explaining that, "Under the current CBA between the NFL and the NFLPA, the players are essentially powerless to overcome the unfairness of the league's dispute resolution process"). *See also* Golen, J. and Zola, W.K. (2018). The Evolution of the Power of the Commissioner in Professional Sports, in *The Oxford Handbook of American Sports Law*, at page 41 (explaining that, with the rise of players associations, the commissioner "took an active role in labor negotiations and his job was exposed to be less as a guardian of the game and more of a hireling representing the interest of the owners who hired him"). As explained on the official NFL website, "As the league's chief executive, the commissioner has a great deal of influence. But he still must answer to the owners, who by executive committee vote have the power to remove him." As explained by Professor Andrew Brandt (former NFL team executive and current sports law scholar), "Owners are in a position of strength on this issue and, if we have learned anything about this group, they are relentless negotiators. There could certainly be tweaks made in the commissioner power area—adding a union representative to the disciplinary process would be a reasonable one—but those tweaks would likely come with a price." Brandt, A. (2016). The CBA at Halfway, Part I, *Sports Illustrated*. In the words of an NFL team owner, "The players are not going to get something for nothing" when it comes to requesting a reduction in the power and authority of Commissioner Goodell to discipline players and also oversee the appeals process. *See* Belson, K. (2019). NFL Labor Talks Likely to Hinge on 18 Game Proposal, the *New York Times*.

51 Official Release—Joint NFL-NFL Players Association Statement (2017), *available at* www.nflpa.com. In October 2017, the NFLPA released a statement on players' constitutional rights, which provided in relevant part: "NFL players are union members and part of the labor movement that has woven the fabric of America for generations. Our men and their families are also conscientious Americans who continue to be forces for good through our communities and some have decided to use their platform to peacefully raise awareness to issues that deserve attention. It is a source of enormous pride that some of the best conversations about these issues have taken place in our locker rooms in a respectful, civil and thoughtful way that should serve as a model for how all of us can communicate with each other." Official Release—NFLPA Statement on Players' Constitutional Rights (2017), *available at* www.nflpa.com.

52 Okung, R. (2017). An Open Letter to All NFL Players: Let's Get Organized, *The Players Tribune*.

53 NFL Social Justice Initiative (2017), *available at* www.nfl.com (explaining that, "The NFL supports a player-led platform to engage with team owners, public officials, law enforcement, academic institutions, community partners and others to identify meaningful ways to strengthen local communities and the greater society").

54 *See* Knoblauch, A. (2018). NFL, Players Coalition Finalize Social Justice Partnership, *available at* www.nfl.com (explaining that, "The initiative comes in response to player demonstrations during the national anthem before games" during the 2017 NFL season).

55 Official Release—Statement from NFL Commissioner Roger Goodell on Anthem Policy (2018), *available at* www.nfl.com (explaining that, "The national anthem policy reflects the NFL's ongoing commitment to local communities and our country—one that is extraordinary in its scope, resources and alignment with our players. We are dedicated to continuing our collaboration with players to advance the goals of justice and fairness in all corners of our society"). Based on the policy, Commissioner Goodell was authorized to impose appropriate discipline on league personnel who refused to stand and show respect for the flag and the anthem.

56 Official Release—NFLPA Statement on New Anthem Policy (2018), *available at* www.nflpa.com.

57 Colin Kaepernick, who last played for an NFL team in 2016, filed a separate grievance through the NFLPA against the league in October 2017. Kaepernick alleged collusion by NFL teams that denied him a prospective future opportunity with any team after he took a knee during the national anthem in 2016 to raise awareness of racial inequality and social injustices. Kaepernick eventually settled his grievance with the league in February 2019. *See* Teope, H. (2019) NFL, Kaepernick, Reid to Resolve Pending Grievances, *available at* www.nfl.com.

58 Official Release—NFLPA Files Grievance Challenging NFL's New Anthem Policy (2018), *available at* www.nflpa.com.

59 Official Release—Joint Statement on Anthem Policy (2018), *available at* www.nflpa. com (describing the meetings and discussions as constructive related to "very serious social justice issues that have been the basis of some players' protests").

60 Official Release—NFL Commissioner Roger Goodell News Conference (2018), *available at* www.nfl.com.

61 Official Release—NFL Announces Launch of 'Inspire Change' (2019), *available at* www.nfl.com.

62 Official Release—Jay-Z's Roc Nation Entering Partnership with NFL (2019), *available at* www.nfl.com.

63 *See* NFL CBA (2011), Article 10, Section 1.

64 *See* NFL CBA (2011), Article 9, Sections 1–2 (defining an "unrestricted free agent" as a player with four or more accrued seasons and is thus completely free to negotiate and sign a player contract with any team without the prior team having any first refusal rights; and defining a "restricted free agent" as a player with at least three accrued seasons but less than four accrued seasons and is thus completely free to negotiate and sign a player contract with any team but with the prior team being able to receive a right of first refusal and/or draft choice compensation by tendering the player a qualifying offer).

65 *See* NFL CBA (2011), Article 10, Sections 2(a), 4(a). The required tender amount would be calculated at 120% of the player's prior year salary only if that amount exceeds the applicable player average calculation.

66 *See* NFL CBA (2011), Article 10, Section 2(b).

67 *See* NFL CBA (2011), Article 10, Section 2(a)(ii).

68 *See* NFL CBA (2011), Article 10, Section 2(a)(i). *See also* Borsack, D. (2019). Exploration of the NFL Franchise Tag Functioning as a Non-Compete Clause,

Cardozo Arts & Entertainment Law Journal, at page 124 (explaining that the franchise tag system used to be utilized as a tool for teams to ensure a signature player would remain on their team, but the system has recently morphed into a tool for teams to reduce a player's negotiating power while also ensuring that the team does not lose a star player without receiving draft pick compensation from another team).

69 *See* NFL CBA (2011), Article 10, Sections 3, 4.

70 "League Year" is defined as "the period from March [_] of one year through and including March [_] of the following year, or such other one-year period to which the NFL and the NFLPA may agree." NFL CBA (2011), Article 1.

71 *See* NFL CBA (2011), Article 10, Sections 14, 15.

72 *See* Ochab, C. (2007). Don't Franchise Me! The NFL's Emerging Dilemma, *Illinois Business Law Journal*.

73 Bartelstein also commented that, "Contracts, like anything in life, are a product of the market. So, if people want you enough, whether it's a big signing bonus or a long-term contract, that's what you're going to get. That's the way it should work: supply and demand." Berger, K. (2010). Should NBA Adopt NFL-Like Player Movement Rules? Good Question, *available at* www.cbssports.com.

74 For comparison purposes, during the 2014 NFL season, six players were tagged—two were transition tags while the other four were non-exclusive franchise tags. In 2013, eight NFL teams used franchise or transitions tags—a considerable drop off from the record 21 players who received the franchise or transition tag designation for the 2012 NFL season. It is also worthwhile to note that an argument can be made that the fact that both the NBA and NFL employ a salary cap but not a salary arbitration system implies that salary arbitration and the salary cap are mutually exclusive. If properly designed, both systems together can foster competitive balance and maintain economic stability for all teams. Although the NFL does not have a salary arbitration system, the league's franchise and transition player designations provide a CBA formulated mechanism that attempts to calculate a player's fair value for one season without having to appeal to a third-party arbitrator to determine what a player should be paid for that season. *See* Bukstein, S. (2012). A New Solution for Salary Disputes: Implementing Salary Arbitration in the National Basketball Association, *Marquette Sports Law Review*.

75 Gramling, G. (2018). Chiefs Show How to Close Out Games in 2018, Steelers Get What They Deserve in Le'Veon Saga, Aaron Rodgers Is 10 Days Away from Saying 'Relax,' *Sports Illustrated* (expressing the viewpoint that the "franchise tag is now a contradictory loophole that allows front offices to claim a certain player is so valuable that they can't possibly afford to lose him, but also isn't valuable enough to give a market-value deal"). Many players will prefer to sign lucrative long-term contracts that protect against injury rather than receive the one-year franchise or transition tag.

76 *See* Bukstein, S. and Eisenberg, J. (2015). Implementing a Franchise Player Designation System in the NBA, *Harvard Journal of Sports and Entertainment Law*.

77 *See* NFL CBA (2011), Article 7, Section 7(g).

78 Belson, K. (2019). NFL Draft Day and Labor Talks Share a Focus: Rookie Contracts, the *New York Times* (explaining that the fifth-year team option has created an unintended dynamic whereby a talented player such as Dak Prescott does almost as well—if not better—financially if he is not drafted in the first round because he becomes one year closer to a second contract because a team is not permitted to exercise a fifth-year option on his contract).

79 *See* Graziano, D. (2019). How NFL Players are Taking Control, and What the League Could Do Next, *available at* www.espn.com.

80 *See* NFL CBA (2011), Appendix A, Section 11. *See also* NFL CBA (2011), Exhibit H. The standard player contract also provides NFL teams with the ability to terminate a player's contract if the player fails to "maintain himself in excellent physical condition" as determined via an evaluation by a team physician. *See* NFL CBA (2011), Appendix A, Section 8.

81 *See* Holzman-Escareno, A. (2019). 2019 NFL Free Agency Glossary, *available at* www.nfl.com. Veteran NFL players with at least four years of playing experience are also eligible for termination pay. For illustration purposes, a player who is terminated from a contract that was signed after the beginning of the regular season in which he is terminated would be eligible to receive termination pay equal to the greater of the unpaid balance of the initial 25% of such player's base salary (prorated based on the number of weeks left in the regular season when the player signed his contract), or one week's salary up to a maximum of the minimum required base salary of a player with ten or more credited seasons (i.e., $1.03 million for the 2019 NFL season). However, an otherwise qualified player will not be entitled to termination pay if a team can demonstrate that, after receipt of a written warning from his team, the player failed to exhibit the level of good faith effort which can be reasonably expected from NFL players on that team. *See* NFL CBA (2011), Article 30. In addition, NFL players are also entitled to severance pay (for example, $22,500 for each season from 2017 through 2020). *See* NFL CBA (2011), Article 60, Section 2.

82 *See* Graziano, D. (2019), 2021 CBA Negotiations: The Nine Biggest Looming Issues, *available at* www.espn.com (clarifying that nothing in the NFL's collective bargaining agreement prohibits fully guaranteed deals, just as nothing in the CBAs for the NBA or MLB requires guaranteed contracts).

83 *See* NFL CBA (2011), Article 7, Section 3(h) (explaining that a team would be permitted to guarantee a player's fourth year rookie salary for injury only if the team also previously guaranteed the second and third years of the player's contract just for injury, or for injury, skill and salary cap related termination).

84 *See* NFL CBA (2011), Article 7, Section 7(e).

85 *See* NFL CBA (2011), Article 10, Sections, 2–4.

86 *See* NFL CBA (2011), Article 45. In September 2019, the New England Patriots released wide receiver Antonio Brown amid allegations of sexual assault and another inappropriate conduct. The Patriots signed Antonio Brown after the start of the 2019 NFL regular season, and he only played in one game for the Patriots before he was cut from the team. The league issued the following statement: "Our office is presently investigating multiple allegations, some of which are the subject of pending litigation. We have as yet made no findings regarding these issues. The investigation is ongoing and will be pursued vigorously and expeditiously…. Upon the conclusion of the investigation, he may also be subject to discipline if the investigation finds that he has violated the law or league policies." Official Release—NFL Statement on the Status of Antonio Brown (2019), *available at* www.nfl.com. Antonio Brown's contract with the Patriots contained a $1 million base salary along with a $9 million signing bonus ($5 million of which was scheduled to be paid a few days after he was released from the Patriots). His contract also included various roster bonuses and performance incentives. Brown and the NFLPA contended that the Patriots must pay Brown all of the $9 million signing bonus in accordance with key language in the CBA. The NFLPA was likely concerned about the precedent of a team being able to deny guaranteed/earned payments to a player who has not been charged with a crime, who was not suspended or exempted by the league and who was not first fined or suspended by the team. To counter, the Patriots insisted that the team was relieved of the obligation to pay as a result of Brown's personal conduct that violated provisions in his player contract. The dispute between Brown and the Patriots involves somewhat conflicting and arguably ambiguous terms from the CBA and his player contract. *See* McCann, M.A. (2019). How Antonio Brown's Likely Labor Grievance Against the Patriots Will Play Out, *Sports Illustrated*. For instance, the NFL collective bargaining agreement indicates that any base salary "already earned may never be forfeited by player." NFL CBA (2011), Article 4, Section 9. Teams are only authorized to obtain a forfeiture of other salary components from a player (for example, signing bonus, guaranteed money beyond base salary and performance

incentives) if the player: (1) Willfully fails to report, practice or play with the result that the player's ability to fully participate and contribute to the team is substantially undermined (for example, holding out or leaving the squad absent a showing of extreme personal hardship); (2) Is unavailable to the team due to conduct by him that results in his incarceration in jail; (3) Is unavailable to the team due to a non-football injury; or (4) Voluntarily retires from the game of football. *See* NFL CBA (2011), Article 4, Section 9(a). Brown and the NFLPA could argue that none of the above conditions were directly relevant, and therefore the Patriots owed Brown all of his $9 million signing bonus. In addition, the 2011 CBA provides that a team is permitted to fine a player in an amount equal to one week's salary and/or suspend a player without pay for a period not to exceed four weeks. *See* NFL CBA (2011), Article 42, Section 1(a)(xv). On the other hand, the Patriots could cite to several provisions within Brown's contract to support the position that the team did not owe Brown any money beyond compensation for playing in one game for the Patriots. The Patriots could also cite to provisions in his contract to support the position that the team had the right to terminate Brown's player contract. For example, the NFL standard player contract explains that each player agrees to give his best efforts and loyalty to the team, and to conduct himself on and off the field with appropriate recognition of the fact that the success of professional football depends largely on public respect for and approval of those associated with the game. All NFL players also agree to comply with and be bound by all reasonable team rules and regulations. A team is permitted to terminate a player's contract if the player has engaged in personal conduct reasonably judged by the team to adversely affect or reflect on the organization. *See* NFL CBA (2011), Appendix A, Sections 2, 11 and 14. In October 2019, Antonio Brown and the NFLPA also filed a similar grievance against the Oakland Raiders seeking approximately $30 million.

87 Transcript of Fan Forum with Commissioner Goodell (2011), *available at* www. panthers.com.

88 *See* Beaton, A. (2019). The Billion Dollar Question Hanging Over NFL Labor Talks, *Wall Street Journal* (explaining that, for the same reasons that an 18-game season would make both sides more money, the players believe it would also undercut several points they are focused on addressing in this round of collective bargaining. Those issues include improving conditions for middle-class players, who face short career spans, as well as addressing non-guaranteed contracts and post-career health concerns—concerns that might be undercut by playing more football games during the regular season).

89 Bogage, J. (2019). NFL Players' Union Rejects Latest Proposal for 18-Game Season, the *Washington Post*.

90 Kaplan, D. (2019). NFL Dropped 18-Game Proposal, Now Wants 17-Game Season (noting the lack of player and team owner support for the 18-game concept). In September 2019, NFL team owners suggested potentially expanding the number of playoff teams from 12 to 14, with two initial "play in" games similar to MLB's two "wild card" games. Players might also request that the league address additional concerns and opportunities. For example, players might decide to propose that the NFL increase the number of permitted active players each game from 46 to 53. *See* NFL CBA (2011), Article 25 (increasing the active list limit from 45 players to 46 players). In addition, players might push for expanding pension funds for retired players.

91 *See* Fainaru-Wada, M. and Fainaru, S. (2013). *League of Denial: The NFL, Concussions, and the Battle for the Truth.* Crown Publishing Group. *See also* Ellenbogen, R.G. *et al.* (2018). National Football League Head, Neck and Spine Committee's Concussion Diagnosis and Management Protocol: 2017–18 Season, *British Journal of Sports Medicine.*

92 *See* NFL Commitment to Player Health and Safety—A Letter from Commissioner Roger Goodell (2016), *available at* www.playsmartplaysafe.com.

93 Bonestell, M. (2017). NFL Players' Union Leader Says 2021 Labor War Is Almost a Virtual Certainty, the *Washington Post* (noting that DeMaurice Smith also mentioned that "the CBA evolves all the time").

94 *See* Draper, K. and Belson, K. (2019). NFL Begins Moves to Avoid Another Labor War, the *New York Times* (explaining that the NFL "has shifted away from its combative approach [during] the last round of bargaining. People involved in the current discussions expect the league to agree to a modest increase in the players share of league revenue, and for there to be few major changes to an agreement that has led to significant gains in league revenue and player compensation").

95 Official Release—Joint NFLPA-NFL Statement on Collective Bargaining Negotiations (2019), *available at* www.nflpa.com. In May 2019, John Mara (co-owner of the New York Giants and chairperson of the NFL's primary labor negotiating committee) acknowledged, "We've got a long way to go. There is a willingness on both sides to have continued conversation." Despite this sense of mutual optimism and willingness to engage in bargaining discussions, the NFLPA nonetheless informed NFL agents to prepare player clients for the possibility of another work stoppage. *See* Bell, J. (2019). List of Issues for NFL's Next Collective Bargaining Agreement Overshadowed by One Thing, *USA Today* (noting that one longtime NFL player agent believed that "the communication and spirit between NFLPA leadership and the agent community improved after being fractured, by some accounts, after the last labor deal" in 2011). In March 2019, a group of agents and NFL players met in conjunction with the overall annual NFLPA meeting. Some players felt that agents "came into the session grossly underestimating [players'] understanding of complex CBA [terms] and negotiating issues." *See* Letter from DeMaurice Smith (NFLPA executive director) to NFL Contract Advisors (2019), *available at* www.nflpa.com. Relatedly, according to a May 2019 letter from DeMaurice Smith to NFL player agents, the NFLPA advised agents to help player clients prepare for a work stoppage of at least a year in length in part by encouraging all players to save 50% of their salary and bonuses during the 2019 and 2020 NFL seasons. *See* Letter from DeMaurice Smith (NFLPA executive director) to NFL Contract Advisors (2019), *available at* www.nflpa.com. In August 2019, the NFLPA provided all players with a "Work Stoppage Guide," which included detailed practical advice and suggestions related to areas such as budgeting for housing costs and routine expenses, medical insurance coverage, continuing education opportunities, potential off-the-field entrepreneurial endeavors and best practice guidelines for media interviews.

96 Pelissero, T. (2019). Hope is Alive for New CBA as Talks Quietly Resume, *available at* www.nfl.com (explaining that one important issue within a complicated economic discussion is how to divide revenue from the new SoFi Stadium in Inglewood, California, which will be home to the Rams and the Chargers). The roughly $5 billion price tag for this new stadium project is much higher than all previously constructed NFL stadiums. Based on projections by the league, the stadium will generate much more revenue than other stadiums. As a result, team owners want the new CBA to reflect the substantial initial financial investment along with the significant forecasted return on investment, while players have pushed back at the idea of altering the revenue-sharing calculation and stadium credit threshold based on one new stadium construction project that players had no role in approving.

97 Jones, M. (2019). 'Stay Ready'—Inside DeMaurice Smith, NFLPA's Meeting with Chiefs Players on CBA Discussions, *USA Today*. Thomas Morstead, NFL player and NFLPA vice president, explained that the NFLPA "is at its strongest when we are prepared as a unit." Morstead also offered the following candid advice to all players in the league: "Don't rely on your agent, your team or anyone else. Get informed and get ready. Solidarity is our best weapon in fighting for what we deserve as players at the bargaining table." NFLPA Work Stoppage Guide (2019), *available at* www.nflpa.com.

98 Jessop, A. and Kaplan, D. (2019). NFLPA Brings Goldman Sachs Into Fold to Aid Players as Part of Work Stoppage Planning, *available at* www.theathletic.com (noting that the NFLPA registered two major financial firms—Goldman Sachs and Bessemer Trust—to manage players' money).

99 Draper, K. and Belson, K. (2019). NFL Begins Moves to Avoid Another Labor War, the *New York Times*. In September 2019, the NFL announced the league reached a new seven-year CBA with the NFL Referees Association (NFLRA). The referee CBA covers substantive areas such as training, compensation and benefits. Scott Green (NFLRA executive director) commented, "It was a mutual and cooperative effort that took over a year and a half, and the outcome is seven years of certainty for the league and our officials. We appreciate Troy Vincent and his staff for recognizing that working together to find solutions is the best course of action to reach a long-term agreement." Official Release—NFL, NFLRA Come to Seven-Year CBA Agreement (2019), *available at* www.nfl.com. This agreement between the league and its referees could be viewed as a positive indicator of anticipated future labor stability between the league and its players. Hopefully the NFL and the NFLPA will be in a position to announce a similar new agreement before expiration of the 2011 CBA.

6   The future of collective
       bargaining in professional sports

Overview of chapter contents

This chapter provides a concise recap of content included within the previous five chapters of this book. The primary goal of this chapter is to synthesize and reiterate some of the important themes and key takeaways related to collective bargaining within professional sports while also previewing future challenges and opportunities for professional sports leagues and players to address in the months and years ahead. The chapter concludes with several recommendations for future research on collective bargaining in professional sports.

Key book themes and takeaways

The collective bargaining process—revisited

The previous chapters within this book revealed that the overall legal framework and business operations of major professional sports leagues in the United States are direct byproducts of the collective bargaining process. For purposes of review, collective bargaining describes the process by which a players association negotiates with league management (team owners) to establish the working conditions, salaries, benefits and other important terms of employment for all players within the league. The resultant collective bargaining agreements contain provisions related to player salaries, free agency (player mobility), the distribution of revenue between team owners and players as well as the role and authority of league commissioners.[1] The primary purpose of a players association is to protect and advocate for the mutual interests of all athletes within a particular professional sports league concerning areas and issues such as player health/safety, player salaries/compensation and benefits for retired players (for example, continuing medical insurance coverage). A players association also functions as the exclusive collective bargaining representative for all athletes within the league.

The thorough analysis of collective bargaining within the NBA and NFL in previous chapters demonstrated that the overall collective bargaining process usually involves an inherent conflict between federal antitrust law and federal labor law with respect to either encouraging or prohibiting cooperation and collaboration among competitors. Labor disputes within professional sports leagues often result in formal legal proceedings, as both players and team owners attempt to gain negotiation leverage during the collective bargaining process. Unreasonable requests and an unwillingness to compromise during the negotiation process by both players and team owners—combined with strategic procedural posturing to gain negotiation leverage—regularly results in a players association and/or league representatives claiming that the other group refused to bargain in good faith. Professional sports leagues routinely challenge the merit and legality of decertifications or disclaimers of interest by players associations. Players routinely resort to the United States court system in order to increase negotiation leverage. The ultimate outcome of the collective bargaining process is oftentimes predictably unpredictable. Sporting contests inevitably carry on, albeit sometimes with a regular season cut short based on a league deciding to lock out its players. A variety of factors—including the general economic environment, the business metrics of a particular league and the leadership approach of league commissioners, team owners and players association executives—directly shape the bargaining process/timeline and impact negotiation leverage.[2]

The future of collective bargaining and league governance in the NBA and NFL

While certain negotiation elements of collective bargaining continue to remain central priorities for leagues and players—for example, agreeing to the revenue distribution between team owners and athletes—numerous emerging areas for potential future collective bargaining have surfaced in recent years.

The following list indicates some of the many areas and items that the NBA and NBPA might dedicate more time and energy to during future collective bargaining sessions:

- Monitoring the impact of changes to the initial eligibility requirements for the NBA draft
- Brainstorming potential expansion of the NBA draft beyond the current two rounds
- Refining the definition of Basketball Related Income (BRI) in order to increase or reduce the allowable deductions and credits for team owners and the league (for example, reducing the currently allowed expense deductions for league costs associated with international business development)
- Establishing guidelines regarding wearable biometric tracking devices/ systems and subsequent utilization of player data
- Implementing rules concerning the participation by prospective draft picks in the annual "NBA Draft Combine" along with the corresponding release of draft prospect medical reports/records
- Forming additional player health and wellness programs (including the allocation of additional resources to assist players with mental health

challenges as well as figuring out a way to improve player sleep patterns due to the arduous in-season travel schedule)

- Developing additional educational programming and career development initiatives for current and former players
- Revising substance abuse guidelines, policies and penalties (for example, addressing the evolving acceptance of recreational and medicinal use of marijuana and CBD oil)
- Revamping rules related to player participation in international basketball competitions such as the Olympic Games and the FIBA Basketball World Cup
- Implementing an overhauled playoff format and/or devising a potential in-season tournament along with a corresponding prospective reduction to the number of regular season games

The NBA might also decide to commit additional financial and human resources to some or all of the following league business and governance challenges/opportunities:

- Developing more punitive (and enforceable) rules related to contract tampering (having unauthorized conversations/communications) and circumvention of CBA rules (entering into unauthorized contracts, or taking steps to enter into unauthorized contracts)
- Expanding sports betting guidelines and protocols with respect to protecting league intellectual property rights and monetizing verified game and player data
- Updating the overall league revenue sharing plan formula in order to increase the total amount of shared revenue while simultaneously incentivizing every team to optimize local/team generated revenue (for example, ticket sales and team corporate sponsorships)
- Developing new rules governing permissible contact between NBA team scouts and players/families prior to the NBA draft
- Revamping the existing player dress code (originally established in 2005)
- Revising the percentage odds related to the NBA draft lottery in order to further discourage "tanking" by teams
- Developing protocols to address in-game player concussions and sudden cardiac arrest
- Revising the formula for determining how luxury tax payments are disbursed—based on the terms of the 2017 CBA, up to 50% of all luxury tax proceeds get distributed to teams that did not exceed the luxury tax threshold and the remaining funds are permitted to be utilized for one or more "league purposes" (in other words, the league could decide to be more precise in defining which specific league purposes will be supported by luxury tax payments)
- Implementing more definitive requirements for arena size and arena elements along with basketball court specifications (for example, standards to

regulate basketball arena temperature and to avoid slippery basketball court surfaces when hardwood is placed over an ice hockey rink within a multi-purpose venue)
- Instituting systematic training for league office executives and team personnel on media relations skill-sets and social media content best practices

The following list specifies some of the many areas and items that the NFL and NFLPA might commit more time and energy to during future collective bargaining sessions:

- Transforming the power/authority of the league commissioner concerning player misconduct—especially during the discipline appeals process for off-the-field player conduct
- Increasing salary guarantee criteria and scope within all player contracts
- Reducing the initial length of certain categories of rookie contracts (for example, contracts for first and second round draft picks), allowing rookies to renegotiate contract terms earlier in their careers and/or potentially eliminating the current fifth-year team option on contracts of former first round draft picks
- Modifying the current franchise and transition player designation system
- Changing the number of preseason and regular season games (that is, potentially reducing the number of preseason games in order to add one or more regular season games)
- Providing team owners with additional stadium credits in order to help fund future stadium renovations and new stadium construction (as a reminder, stadium credits allow team owners to take money off the top of the total revenue pile before sharing revenue with players; as of December 2019, team owners had essentially depleted the allotted stadium credit amounts permitted by the 2011 NFL collective bargaining agreement)
- Eliminating the requirement that teams deposit cash related to specific categories of deferred and guaranteed player future compensation into an escrow account—the general purpose behind this CBA provision is to ensure that all teams have adequate cash to meet deferred and guaranteed payment obligations (for example, in March 2018, Kirk Cousins became the first NFL player to sign a fully guaranteed multi-year contract when he agreed to a three-year $84 million deal with the Minnesota Vikings)
- Expanding benefits for retired players (for example, pension contributions and health insurance)
- Altering current rules and leaguewide policies related to performance enhancing substances and substances of abuse
- Creating additional opportunities for current players to intern/work at the league office and with league partners or other companies during the offseason, and likewise creating additional opportunities for former players to work as coaches and administrators for NFL teams—for example, in 2019, 66 NFL players enrolled across 27 organizations as part of the NFLPA's offseason externship program that provided players with practical workplace experience

- Amplifying the current tuition assistance plan for current and former players (along with an overall expansion in efforts to inform players about the variety of available continuing education and career-related programs and resources)
- Increasing the size of practice squads, and raising the salary of practice squad players
- Developing additional programs to promote and protect the health of players[3]

The NFL might also decide to designate additional financial and human resources to some or all of the following league business and governance challenges/opportunities:

- Modifying the current maximum debt threshold for NFL teams (current debt limit is $350 million per team)
- Adjusting team ownership requirements in order to attract a larger pool of prospective future buyers (current NFL guidelines require that the principal investor own at least 30% of the equity in a team)
- Clarifying league rules related to players wearing headbands or wristbands with customized images and/or words, watches and other uniform accessories not provided by a team or the league—during the 2017 season, the league launched an initiative granting players permission to wear custom cleats to promote charitable causes
- Preparing for potential eventual decreases in annual leaguewide media rights revenues as cable companies such as ESPN become less willing to pay inflated amounts for sports programming and streaming platforms such as Twitch and Twitter likewise express reluctance to pay premiums for sports programming
- Adopting timely, relevant and sensible policies and best practices that support player social activism (for example, establishing clearer leaguewide guidance on player protests during games and player-created content on social media)[4]

Next steps for further research on collective bargaining in professional sports

Sports business industry scholars and practitioners are encouraged to continue the discussion and analysis of contemporary collective bargaining in professional sports. Future books—perhaps including potential future editions of this book—should explore current collective bargaining themes and trends within Major League Baseball (MLB), the National Hockey League (NHL), Major League Soccer (MLS) and the Women's National Basketball Association (WNBA). Future research could also explore the viability and potential impact of collective bargaining in emerging sports and entertainment areas such as eSports (competitive video gaming). Finally, future research might also analyze how best practices from collective bargaining within professional sports leagues in the United States might impact rules and regulations of professional sports leagues in other countries.

Notes

1 *See* International Labour Organization—Labour Relations and Collective Bargaining (2017), *available at* www.ilo.org (explaining that the collective bargaining process affords labor protection to workers, creates the legitimacy of rules and provides stability to employers). As explained by the International Labour Organization, the stability or increase in bargaining coverage depends on the strategies of the social partners and on government policies that support collective bargaining, which includes an enabling legal framework that ensures respect for organizational rights and facilitates the effective recognition of unions and employers for the purposes of collective bargaining. Stable or increased bargaining coverage also requires the adoption by governments of appropriate measures and policies to encourage and promote collective bargaining.

2 The NBA and NFL lockouts in 2011 underscored the tension between federal labor law and federal antitrust law. It is likely only a matter of time before this inherent conflict between these two areas of law arises again, and players respond to a lockout by dissolving the players association and subsequently filing an antitrust lawsuit in federal court. *See* Feldman, G. (2018). Collective Bargaining in Professional Sports, in *The Oxford Handbook of American Sports Law*.

3 *See* Deubert, C.R., Cohen, I.G., and Lynch, H.F. (2016). Protecting and Promoting the Health of NFL Players: Legal and Ethical Analysis and Recommendations, *available at* www.footballplayershealth.harvard.edu (explaining that, as an ethical matter, players should not be expected to make concessions in other domains in order to achieve gains in the health domain; rather, player health should be a joint priority and not be up for negotiation—collective bargaining over player health issues should not be an adversarial process). In 2009, DeMaurice Smith emphatically pronounced that, "The players will not bargain for medical care; we will not bargain for health and safety; and we will not bargain for basic provisions of the law as patients. We will continue to work with the league but medical care is not and will never be a collective bargaining issue." Football Players Head Injuries Before the House Committee on the Judiciary, 111th Congress (2009) (Statement of DeMaurice Smith), *available at* https://judiciary.house.gov/.

4 *See* Giorgio, P. (2019). Deloitte's Sports Industry Starting Lineup, *available at* www.deloitte.com (explaining that, "Player activism has continued to persist across leagues, with players banding together to advocate for causes that transcend the sports landscape and enter the realm of social and political actions").

Index

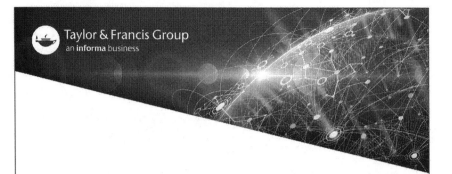